CHICAGO ORGANIZED WORKERS LEAGUE
C O W L
est. 1949
EQUITAS VENERATIO POTENTIA

IMAGE COMICS, INC.

Robert Kirkman – Chief Operating Officer
Erik Larsen – Chief Financial Officer
Todd McFarlane – President
Marc Silvestri – Chief Executive Officer
Jim Valentino – Vice-President

Eric Stephenson – Publisher
Ron Richards – Director of Business Development
Jennifer de Guzman – Director of Trade Book Sales
Kat Salazar – Director of PR & Marketing
Corey Murphy – Director of Retail Sales
Jeremy Sullivan – Director of Digital Sales
Emilio Bautista – Sales Assistant
Branwyn Bigglestone – Senior Accounts Manager
Emily Miller – Accounts Manager
Jessica Ambriz – Administrative Assistant
Tyler Shainline – Events Coordinator
David Brothers – Content Manager
Jonathan Chan – Production Manager
Drew Gill – Art Director
Meredith Wallace – Print Manager
Monica Garcia – Senior Production Artist
Jenna Savage – Production Artist
Addison Duke – Production Artist
Tricia Ramos – Production Assistant
IMAGECOMICS.COM

Principles of
Power

KYLE HIGGINS   ALEC SIEGEL
STORY

ROD REIS
ART

STÉPHANE PERGER
ADDITIONAL ART ISSUE 4

TROY PETERI
LETTERS

ANDY SCHMIDT
EDITS

TREVOR MCCARTHY
COVERS

RICH BLOOM
DESIGN

LOGO BY ERIC WIGHT

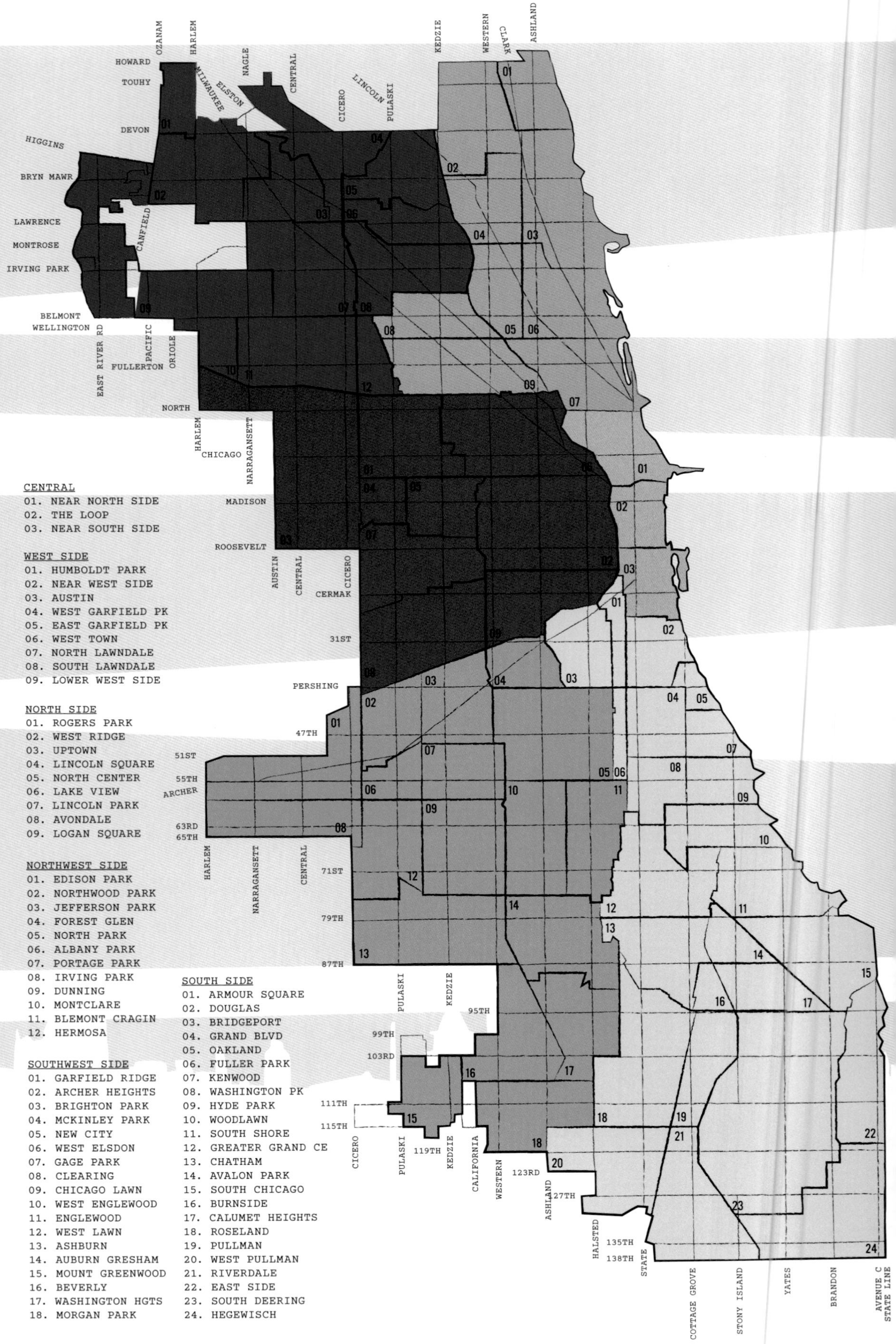
CENTRAL
01. NEAR NORTH SIDE
02. THE LOOP
03. NEAR SOUTH SIDE

WEST SIDE
01. HUMBOLDT PARK
02. NEAR WEST SIDE
03. AUSTIN
04. WEST GARFIELD PK
05. EAST GARFIELD PK
06. WEST TOWN
07. NORTH LAWNDALE
08. SOUTH LAWNDALE
09. LOWER WEST SIDE

NORTH SIDE
01. ROGERS PARK
02. WEST RIDGE
03. UPTOWN
04. LINCOLN SQUARE
05. NORTH CENTER
06. LAKE VIEW
07. LINCOLN PARK
08. AVONDALE
09. LOGAN SQUARE

NORTHWEST SIDE
01. EDISON PARK
02. NORTHWOOD PARK
03. JEFFERSON PARK
04. FOREST GLEN
05. NORTH PARK
06. ALBANY PARK
07. PORTAGE PARK
08. IRVING PARK
09. DUNNING
10. MONTCLARE
11. BLEMONT CRAGIN
12. HERMOSA

SOUTHWEST SIDE
01. GARFIELD RIDGE
02. ARCHER HEIGHTS
03. BRIGHTON PARK
04. MCKINLEY PARK
05. NEW CITY
06. WEST ELSDON
07. GAGE PARK
08. CLEARING
09. CHICAGO LAWN
10. WEST ENGLEWOOD
11. ENGLEWOOD
12. WEST LAWN
13. ASHBURN
14. AUBURN GRESHAM
15. MOUNT GREENWOOD
16. BEVERLY
17. WASHINGTON HGTS
18. MORGAN PARK

SOUTH SIDE
01. ARMOUR SQUARE
02. DOUGLAS
03. BRIDGEPORT
04. GRAND BLVD
05. OAKLAND
06. FULLER PARK
07. KENWOOD
08. WASHINGTON PK
09. HYDE PARK
10. WOODLAWN
11. SOUTH SHORE
12. GREATER GRAND CE
13. CHATHAM
14. AVALON PARK
15. SOUTH CHICAGO
16. BURNSIDE
17. CALUMET HEIGHTS
18. ROSELAND
19. PULLMAN
20. WEST PULLMAN
21. RIVERDALE
22. EAST SIDE
23. SOUTH DEERING
24. HEGEWISCH

OZANAM
HARLEM
HOWARD
TOUHY
MILWAUKEE
ELSTON
NAGLE
CENTRAL
CICERO
LINCOLN
PULASKI
KEDZIE
WESTERN
CLARK
ASHLAND
DEVON
HIGGINS
BRYN MAWR
LAWRENCE
MONTROSE
IRVING PARK
CANFIELD
BELMONT
WELLINGTON
EAST RIVER RD
PACIFIC
ORIOLE
FULLERTON
NORTH
HARLEM
NARRAGANSETT
CHICAGO
MADISON
ROOSEVELT
AUSTIN
CENTRAL
CICERO
CERMAK
31ST
PERSHING
47TH
51ST
55TH
ARCHER
63RD
65TH
HARLEM
NARRAGANSETT
CENTRAL
71ST
79TH
87TH
PULASKI
KEDZIE
95TH
99TH
103RD
111TH
115TH
CICERO
PULASKI
119TH
KEDZIE
CALIFORNIA
WESTERN
123RD
ASHLAND
127TH
HALSTED
135TH
138TH
STATE
COTTAGE GROVE
STONY ISLAND
YATES
BRANDON
AVENUE C
STATE LINE

Geoffrey Warner (The Grey Raven)
C.O.W.L. Chief
Sharpshooter, Master Strategist, Unpowered

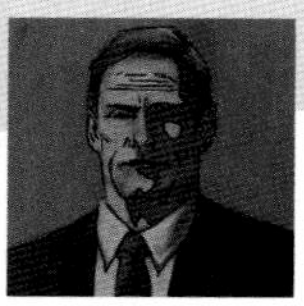

Reginald Davis (Blaze)
Deputy C.O.W.L. Chief/Head of Tactical
Zero–Point Energy Gauntlet

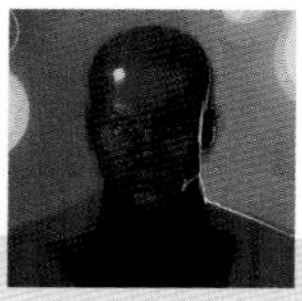

Kathryn Mitchell (Radia)
Tactical Division
Telekinesis

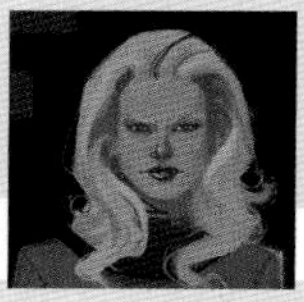

Tom Haydn (Arclight)
Tactical Division
Flight, Focused Energy Bursts

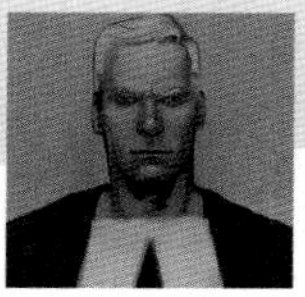

John Pierce
Investigations
Detective, Unpowered

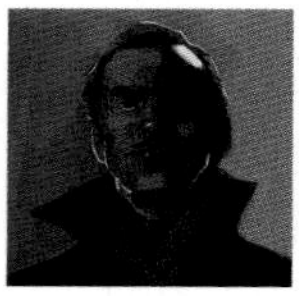

Grant Marlow
Patrol Division – West Side
Sharpshooter, Unpowered

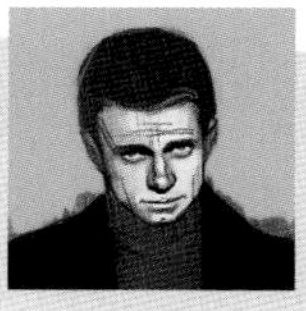

Karl Samoski (Eclipse)
Patrol Division – West Side
Anti–Kinetics, Power Disruption

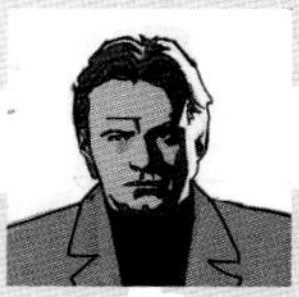

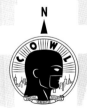

PATROL DISTRICTS

CENTRAL
NORTH
NORTHWEST
SOUTH
SOUTHWEST
WEST SIDE

CHICAGO, 1962

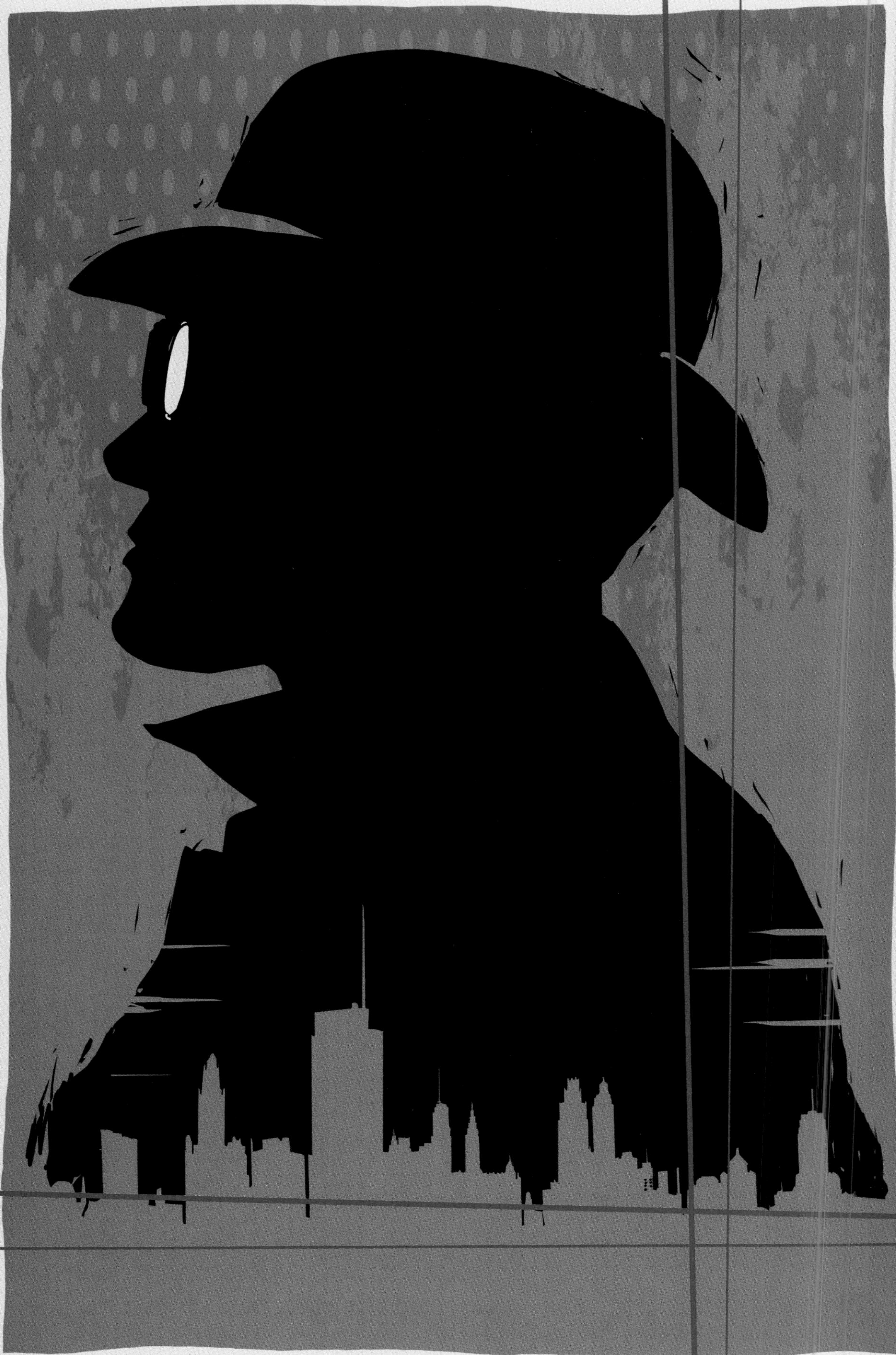

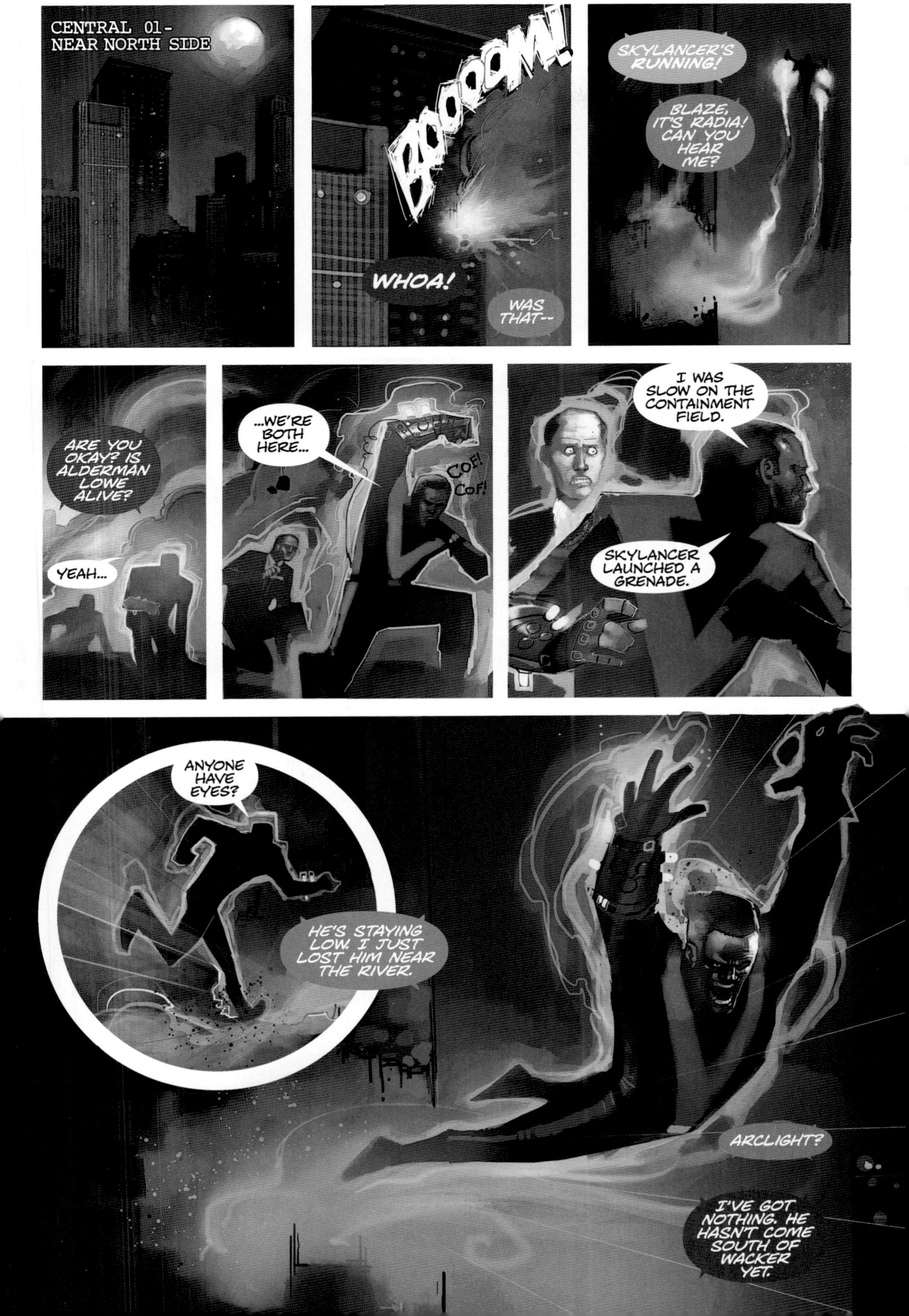

CENTRAL 01-
NEAR NORTH SIDE
BOOOOM!
WHOA!
WAS THAT--
SKYLANCER'S RUNNING!
BLAZE, IT'S RADIA! CAN YOU HEAR ME?
ARE YOU OKAY? IS ALDERMAN LOWE ALIVE?
YEAH...
...WE'RE BOTH HERE...
COF! COF!
I WAS SLOW ON THE CONTAINMENT FIELD.
SKYLANCER LAUNCHED A GRENADE.
ANYONE HAVE EYES?
HE'S STAYING LOW. I JUST LOST HIM NEAR THE RIVER.
ARCLIGHT?
I'VE GOT NOTHING. HE HASN'T COME SOUTH OF WACKER YET.

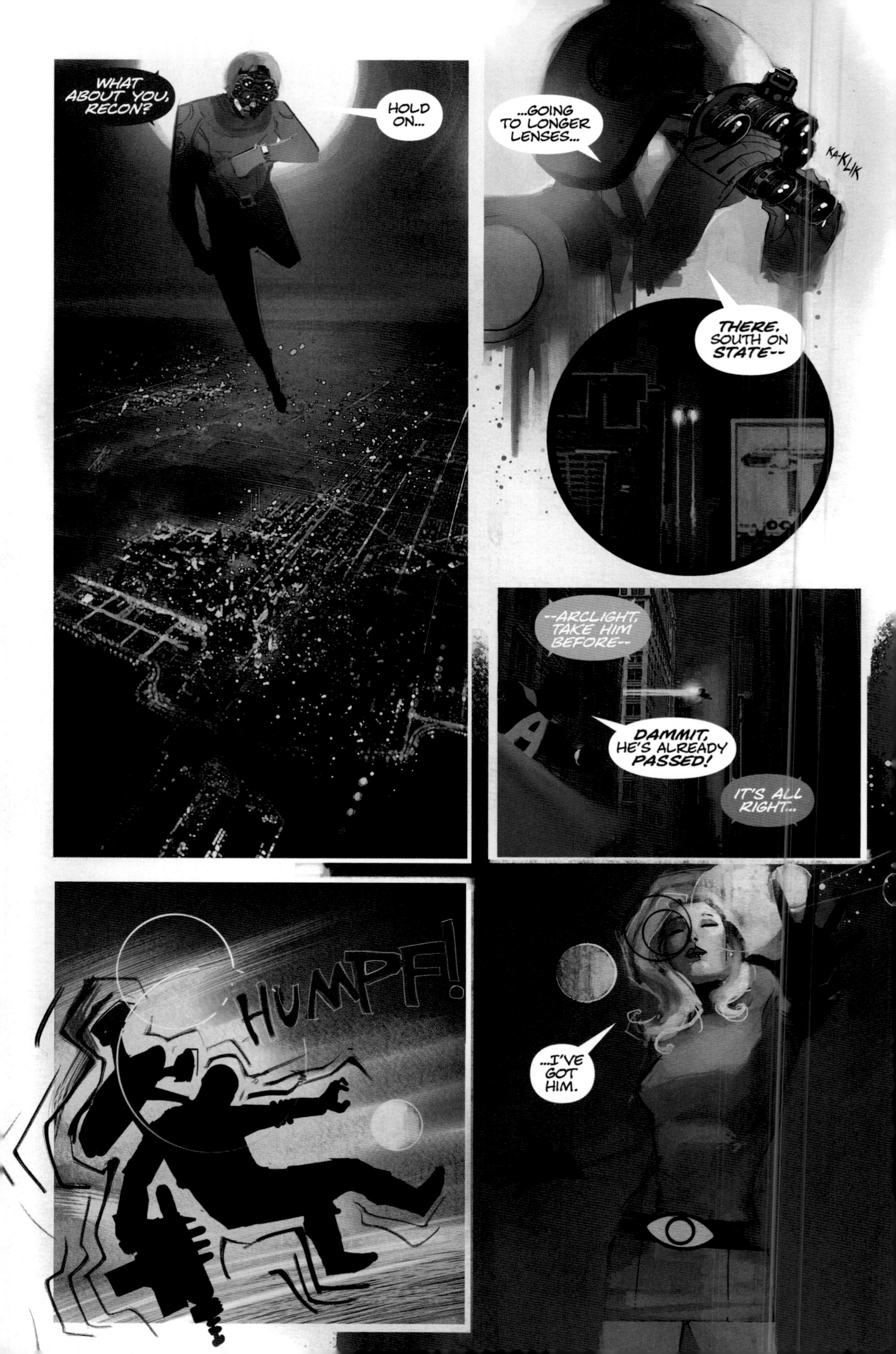
WHAT ABOUT YOU, RECON?
HOLD ON...
...GOING TO LONGER LENSES...
KA-KLIK
THERE. SOUTH ON STATE--
--ARCLIGHT, TAKE HIM BEFORE--
DAMMIT, HE'S ALREADY PASSED!
IT'S ALL RIGHT...
HUMPF!
...I'VE GOT HIM.

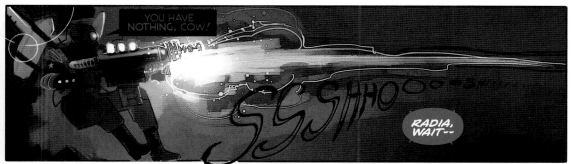

YOU HAVE NOTHING, COW!

SSSHHOOOOSHH

RADIA, WAIT--

--IT'S A FLASH--

SKOOOOM

UHN!

HOLD ON--

UUUHHHH...

--I'VE GOT YOU! YOU'RE OKAY!

I-I CAN'T SEE... M-MY EYES...

HEY, IVAN!

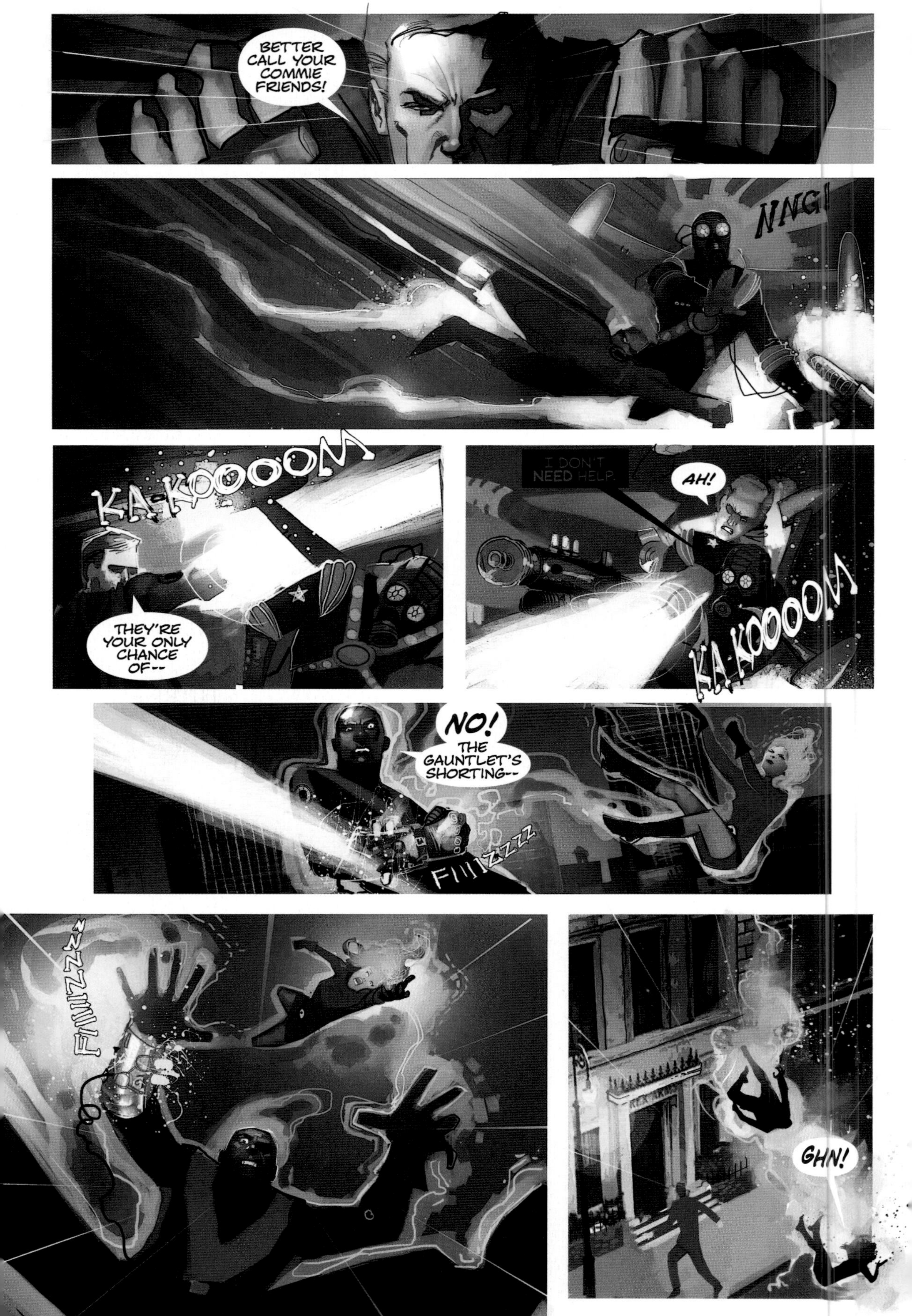
BETTER CALL YOUR COMMIE FRIENDS!
NNG!
KA-KOOOOM
THEY'RE YOUR ONLY CHANCE OF--
I DON'T NEED HELP.
AH!
KA-KOOOOM
NO! THE GAUNTLET'S SHORTING--
FIIIIZZZZ
FIIIIIZZZZ
GHN!

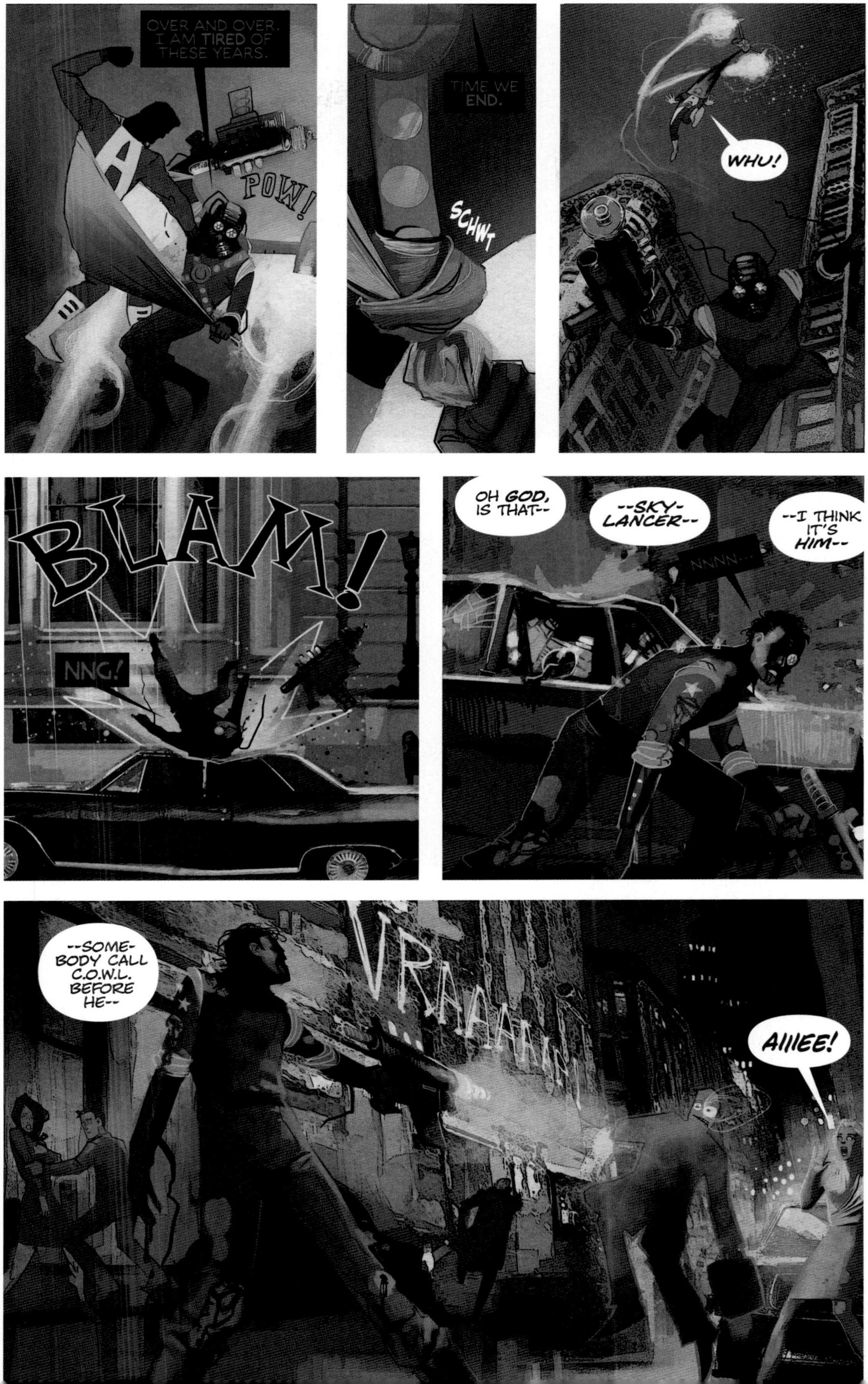
OVER AND OVER. I AM TIRED OF THESE YEARS.
POW!
TIME WE END.
SCHWT
WHU!
BLAM!
NNG!
OH GOD, IS THAT--
--SKY-LANCER--
--I THINK IT'S HIM--
NNNN...
--SOME-BODY CALL C.O.W.L. BEFORE HE--
AIIIEE!

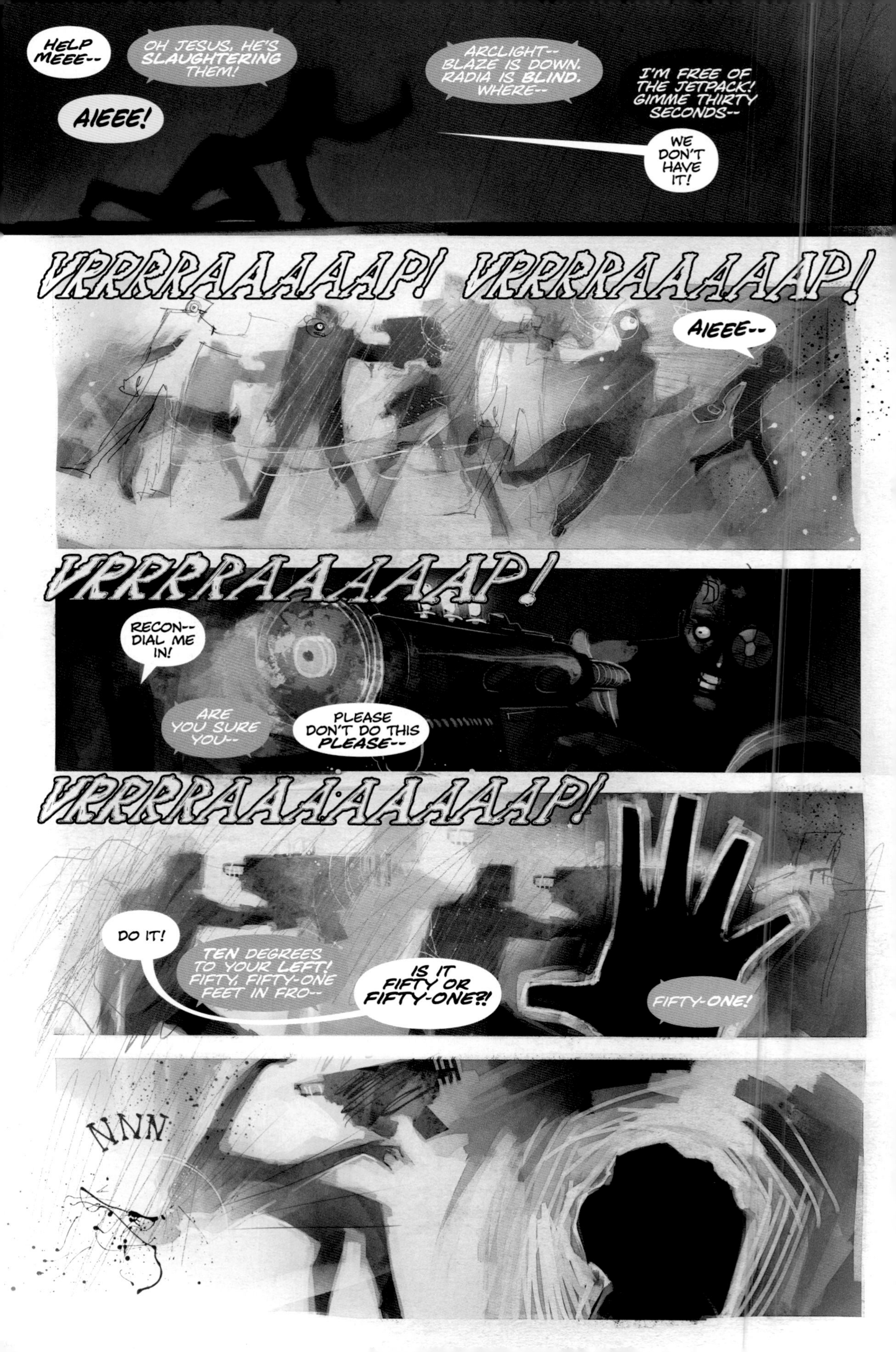
HELP MEEE--
OH JESUS, HE'S SLAUGHTERING THEM!
AIEEE!
ARCLIGHT-- BLAZE IS DOWN. RADIA IS BLIND. WHERE--
I'M FREE OF THE JETPACK! GIMME THIRTY SECONDS--
WE DON'T HAVE IT!
VRRRRAAAAAP! VRRRRAAAAAP!
AIEEE--
VRRRRAAAAAP!
RECON-- DIAL ME IN!
ARE YOU SURE YOU--
PLEASE DON'T DO THIS PLEASE--
VRRRRAAAAAAAAP!
DO IT!
TEN DEGREES TO YOUR LEFT! FIFTY, FIFTY-ONE FEET IN FRO--
IS IT FIFTY OR FIFTY-ONE?!
FIFTY-ONE!
NNN

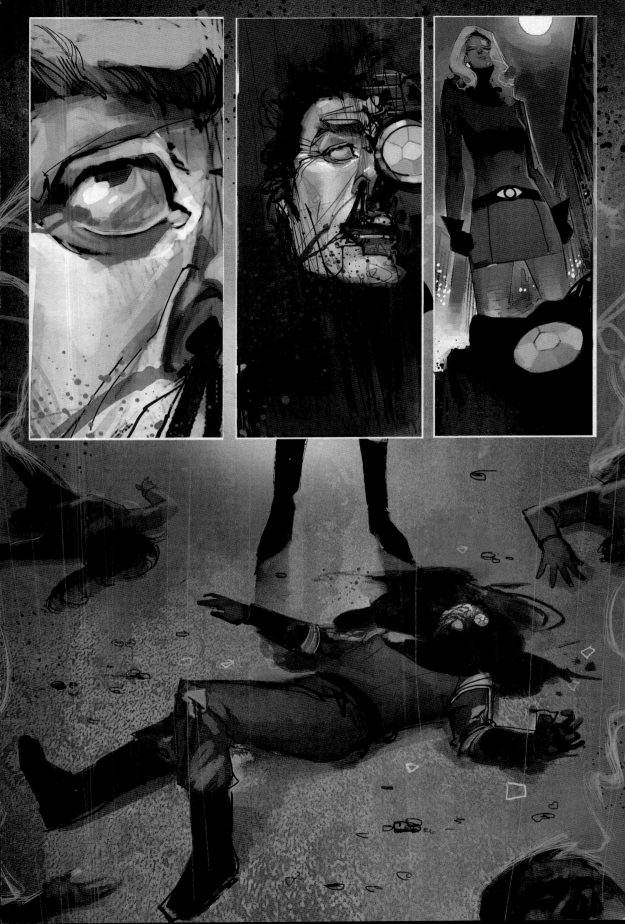

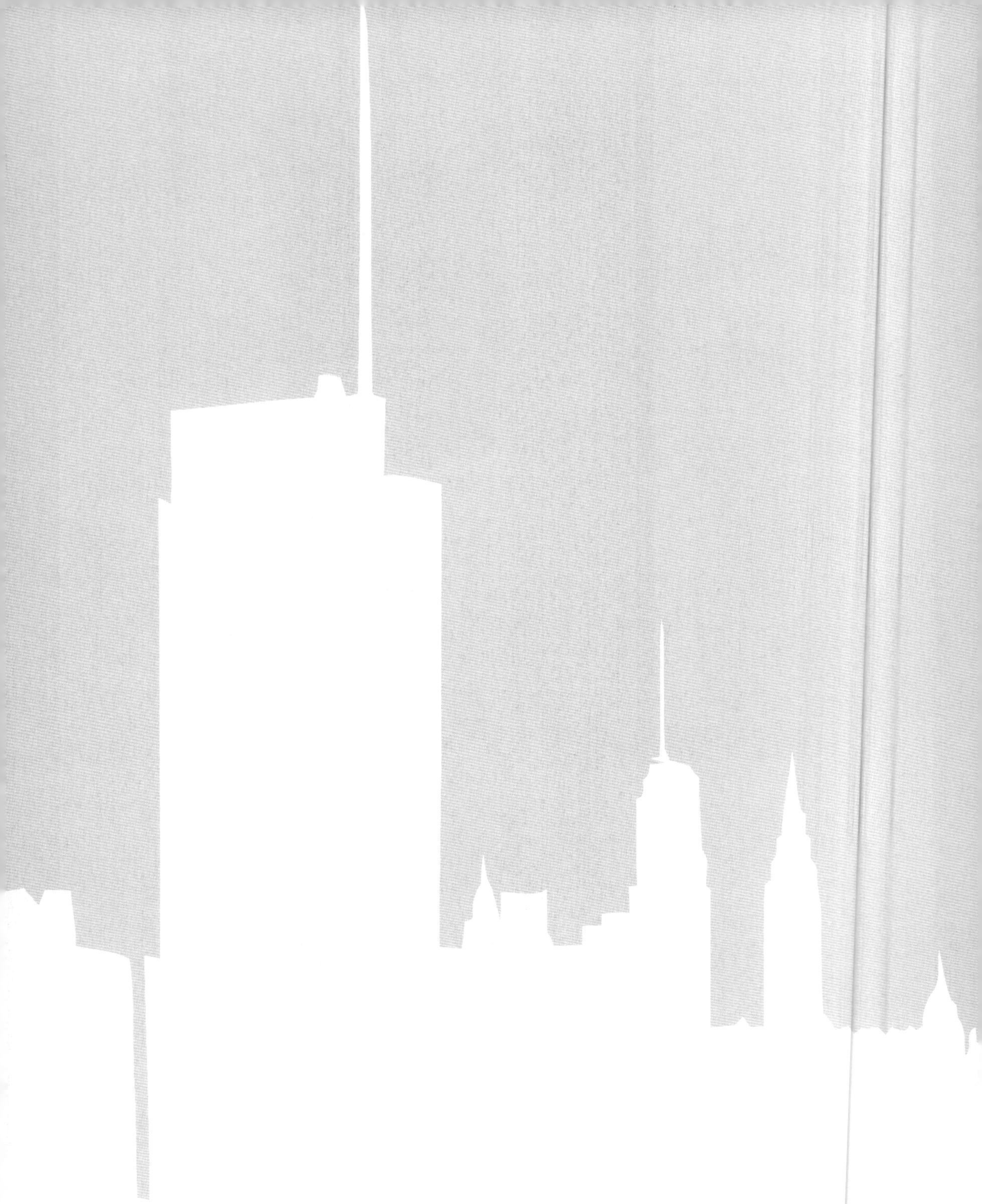

CHAPTER 1
Motivation

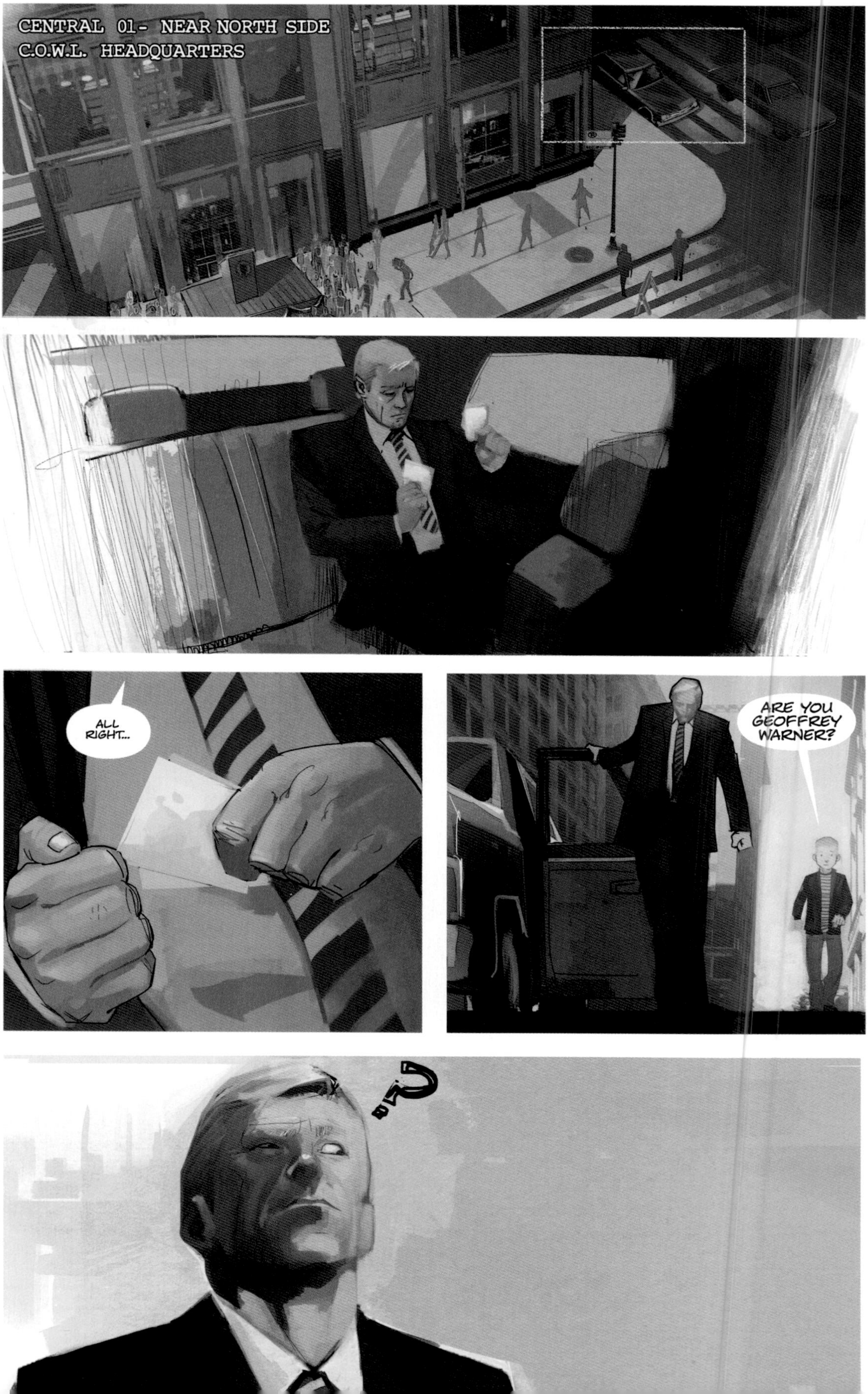
CENTRAL 01- NEAR NORTH SIDE
C.O.W.L. HEADQUARTERS
ALL RIGHT...
ARE YOU GEOFFREY WARNER?

THE GREY RAVEN?

YES, I AM.

WOULD YOU LIKE AN AUTOGRAPH?

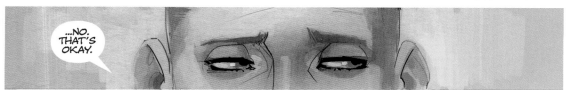

...NO. THAT'S OKAY.

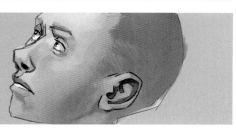

ARE YOU SURE?

YEAH. MY DAD SAYS YOU'RE A SELF-CENTERED ASSHOLE.

AND WHAT WOULD HE SAY ABOUT YOU TALKING LIKE THAT?

MR. WARNER? THEY'RE ALL *WAITING* FOR YOU...

GEOFFREY! OVER HERE!

GREY RAVEN!

KSSH

POP

KSSH

WHILE IT'S STILL UNCLEAR WHAT PRECIPITATED THE ATTACK--

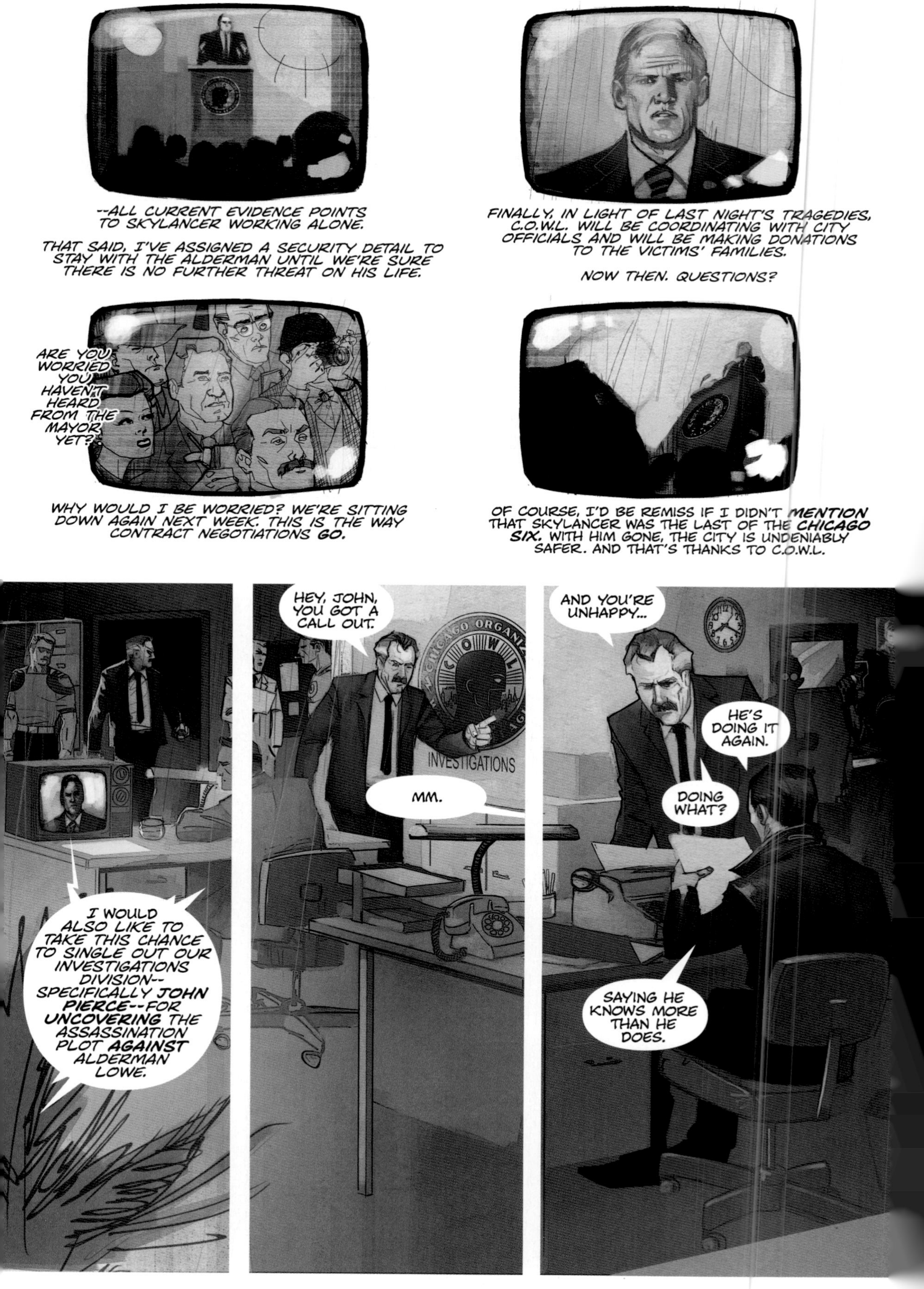
--ALL CURRENT EVIDENCE POINTS TO SKYLANCER WORKING ALONE.
THAT SAID, I'VE ASSIGNED A SECURITY DETAIL TO STAY WITH THE ALDERMAN UNTIL WE'RE SURE THERE IS NO FURTHER THREAT ON HIS LIFE.
FINALLY, IN LIGHT OF LAST NIGHT'S TRAGEDIES, C.O.W.L. WILL BE COORDINATING WITH CITY OFFICIALS AND WILL BE MAKING DONATIONS TO THE VICTIMS' FAMILIES.
NOW THEN. QUESTIONS?
ARE YOU WORRIED YOU HAVEN'T HEARD FROM THE MAYOR YET?
WHY WOULD I BE WORRIED? WE'RE SITTING DOWN AGAIN NEXT WEEK. THIS IS THE WAY CONTRACT NEGOTIATIONS GO.
OF COURSE, I'D BE REMISS IF I DIDN'T MENTION THAT SKYLANCER WAS THE LAST OF THE CHICAGO SIX. WITH HIM GONE, THE CITY IS UNDENIABLY SAFER. AND THAT'S THANKS TO C.O.W.L.
I WOULD ALSO LIKE TO TAKE THIS CHANCE TO SINGLE OUT OUR INVESTIGATIONS DIVISION--SPECIFICALLY JOHN PIERCE--FOR UNCOVERING THE ASSASSINATION PLOT AGAINST ALDERMAN LOWE.
HEY, JOHN, YOU GOT A CALL OUT.
INVESTIGATIONS
MM.
AND YOU'RE UNHAPPY...
HE'S DOING IT AGAIN.
DOING WHAT?
SAYING HE KNOWS MORE THAN HE DOES.

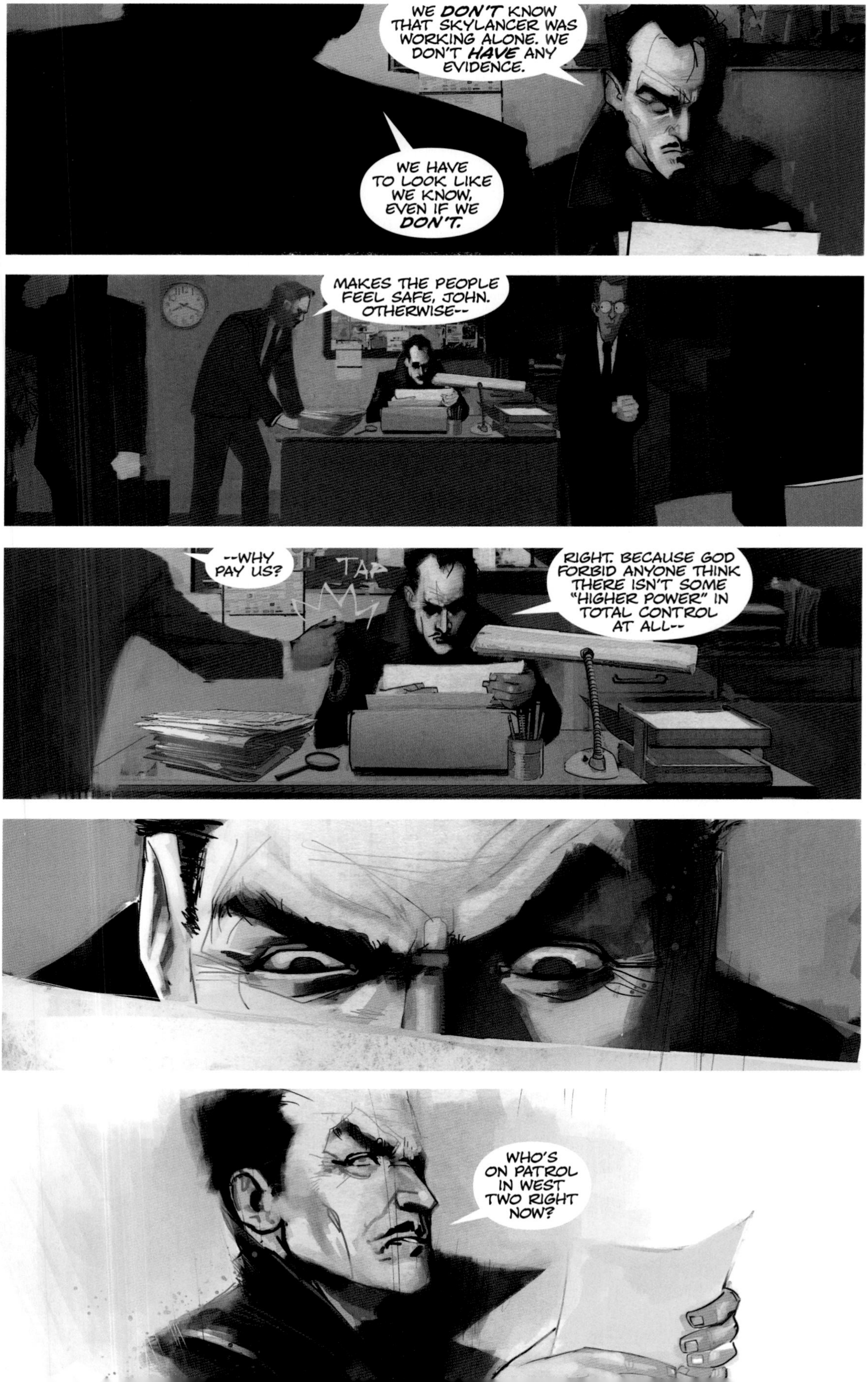
WE DON'T KNOW THAT SKYLANCER WAS WORKING ALONE. WE DON'T HAVE ANY EVIDENCE.
WE HAVE TO LOOK LIKE WE KNOW, EVEN IF WE DON'T.
MAKES THE PEOPLE FEEL SAFE, JOHN. OTHERWISE--
--WHY PAY US?
TAP
RIGHT. BECAUSE GOD FORBID ANYONE THINK THERE ISN'T SOME "HIGHER POWER" IN TOTAL CONTROL AT ALL--
WHO'S ON PATROL IN WEST TWO RIGHT NOW?

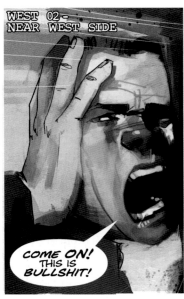

COME ON! THIS IS BULLSHIT!

BULLSHIT IS YOU NOT LISTENING TO ME, KEN! I SPECIFICALLY WARNED YOU TO CUT OUT THIS PEEPING TOM SHIT!

IT ≡EHN≡ WASN'T ME, ECLIPSE!

YEAH? CLAUDIA WORKS FOR C.O.W.L. ARE YOU REALLY THIS STUPID?

UNGH!

YOU KNOW WHAT? FUCK IT. YOU WANNA WATCH PEOPLE GET NAKED? FINE.

LET'S GET NAKED.

JESUS!

SHI.....

DISPATCH TO UNIT FOUR.

GO AHEAD.

SHI...

KARL, I'VE GOT GRANT'S WIFE. SHE SAYS IT'S REALLY IMPORTANT.

ARE YOU TWO NEAR A BOX?

PHONE SEVENTEEN.

SENDING IT OVER.

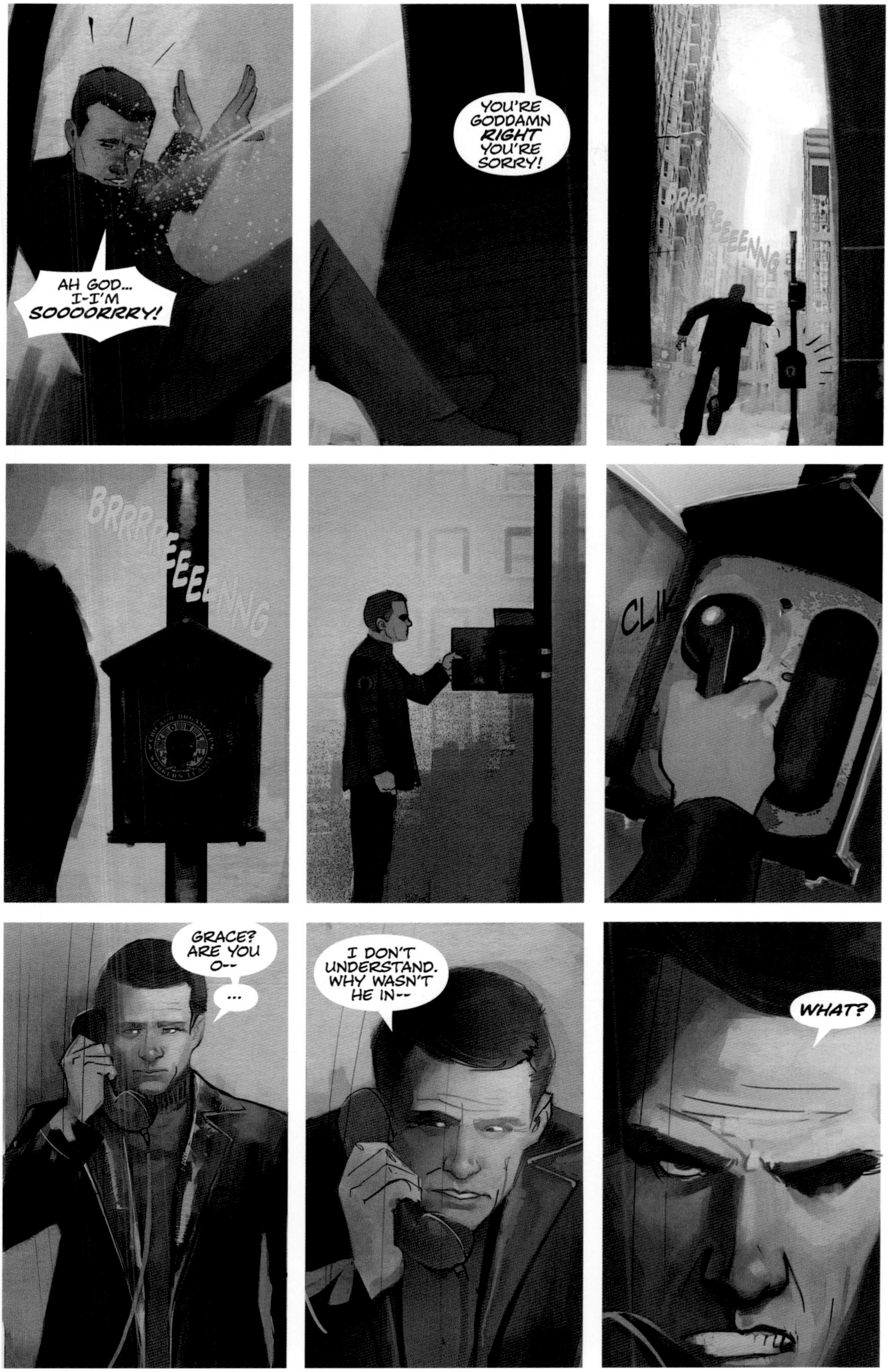

AH GOD... I-I'M SOOOORRRY!
YOU'RE GODDAMN RIGHT YOU'RE SORRY!
BRRRREEEENNG
BRRRREEEENNG
CLIK
GRACE? ARE YOU O--
...
I DON'T UNDERSTAND. WHY WASN'T HE IN--
WHAT?

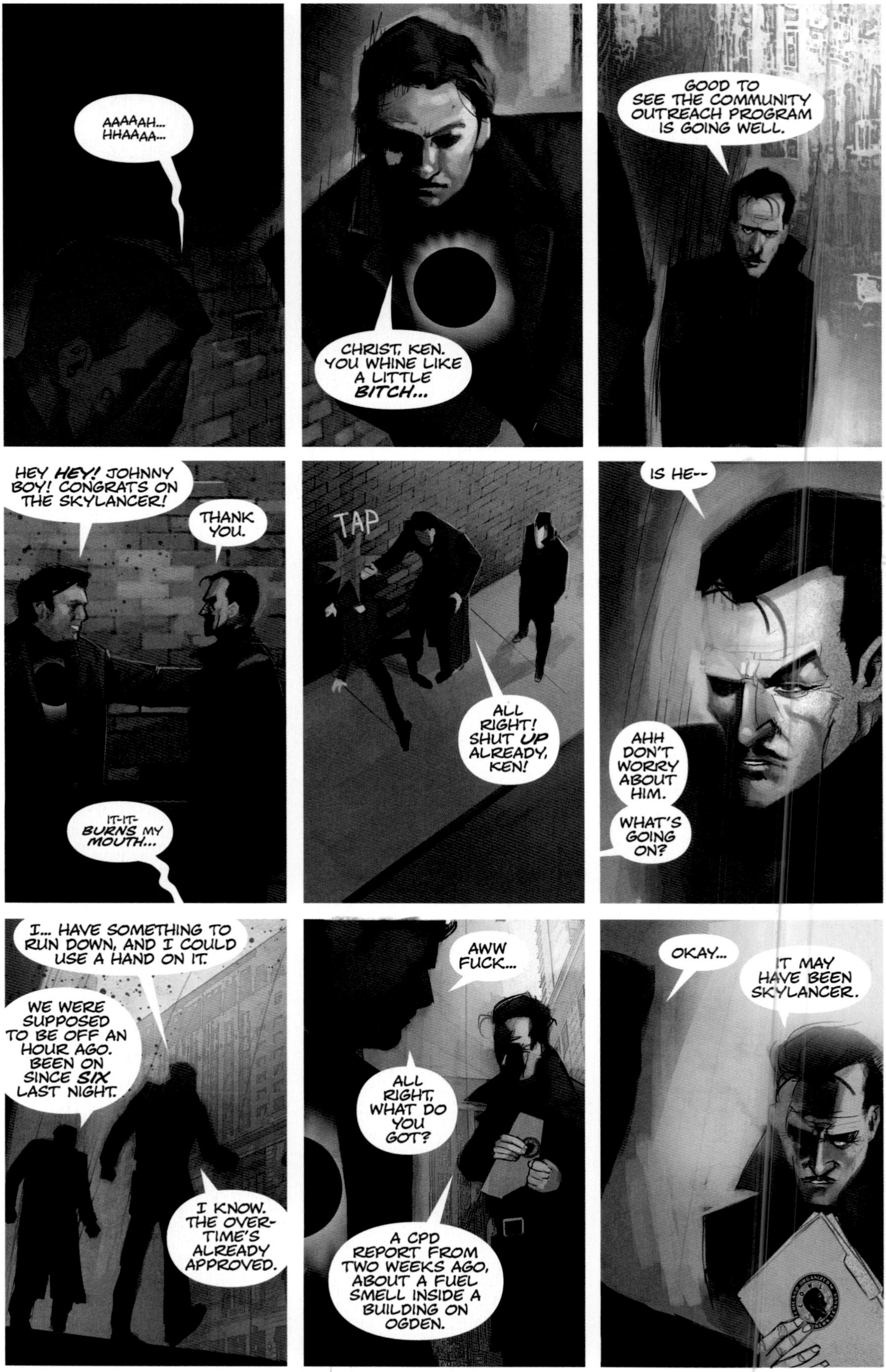
AAAAAH... HHAAAAA...
CHRIST, KEN. YOU WHINE LIKE A LITTLE BITCH...
GOOD TO SEE THE COMMUNITY OUTREACH PROGRAM IS GOING WELL.
HEY HEY! JOHNNY BOY! CONGRATS ON THE SKYLANCER!
THANK YOU.
IT-IT-BURNS MY MOUTH...
TAP
ALL RIGHT! SHUT UP ALREADY, KEN!
IS HE--
AHH DON'T WORRY ABOUT HIM.
WHAT'S GOING ON?
I... HAVE SOMETHING TO RUN DOWN, AND I COULD USE A HAND ON IT.
WE WERE SUPPOSED TO BE OFF AN HOUR AGO. BEEN ON SINCE SIX LAST NIGHT.
I KNOW. THE OVER-TIME'S ALREADY APPROVED.
AWW FUCK...
ALL RIGHT, WHAT DO YOU GOT?
A CPD REPORT FROM TWO WEEKS AGO, ABOUT A FUEL SMELL INSIDE A BUILDING ON OGDEN.
OKAY...
IT MAY HAVE BEEN SKYLANCER.

PLEASE...

IF SKYLANCER **WAS** OPERATING OUT OF THAT BUILDING, HIS CACHE COULD STILL BE THERE.

DO YOU REALLY WANT TO RISK LETTING THOSE WEAPONS GET OUT IN THE OPEN?

THAT'S LIKE, FORTY DOORS TO KNOCK ON. JUST ON A **HUNCH.** A **WEAK** HUNCH.

I KNOW. CALL IT BEING THOROUGH.

I'LL CALL IT A **SHIT-LOAD** OF DOUBLE TIME.

HEY, JOHN.

GRANT.

CONGRATS ON SKYLANCER.

THANK YOU.

HEY. SO WHAT'S UP WITH GRACE? EVERYTHING OKAY?

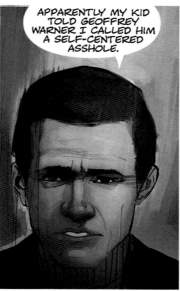

APPARENTLY MY KID TOLD GEOFFREY WARNER I CALLED HIM A SELF-CENTERED ASSHOLE.

HOW WOULD **YOU** HAVE HANDLED IT?

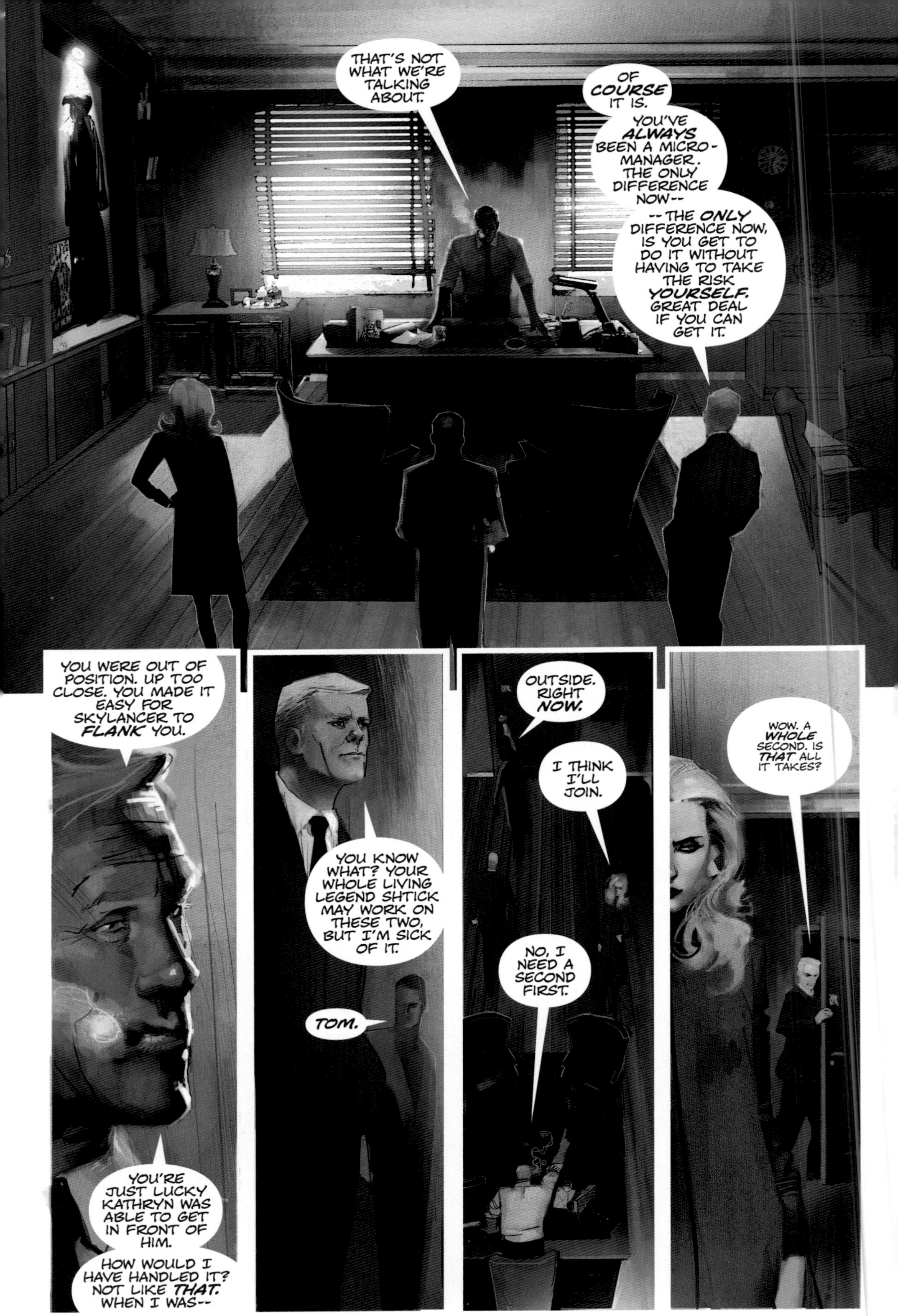
THAT'S NOT WHAT WE'RE TALKING ABOUT.
OF COURSE IT IS.
YOU'VE ALWAYS BEEN A MICRO-MANAGER. THE ONLY DIFFERENCE NOW--
--THE ONLY DIFFERENCE NOW, IS YOU GET TO DO IT WITHOUT HAVING TO TAKE THE RISK YOURSELF. GREAT DEAL IF YOU CAN GET IT.
YOU WERE OUT OF POSITION. UP TOO CLOSE. YOU MADE IT EASY FOR SKYLANCER TO FLANK YOU.
YOU'RE JUST LUCKY KATHRYN WAS ABLE TO GET IN FRONT OF HIM.
HOW WOULD I HAVE HANDLED IT? NOT LIKE THAT. WHEN I WAS--
YOU KNOW WHAT? YOUR WHOLE LIVING LEGEND SHTICK MAY WORK ON THESE TWO, BUT I'M SICK OF IT.
TOM.
OUTSIDE. RIGHT NOW.
I THINK I'LL JOIN.
NO, I NEED A SECOND FIRST.
WOW. A WHOLE SECOND. IS THAT ALL IT TAKES?

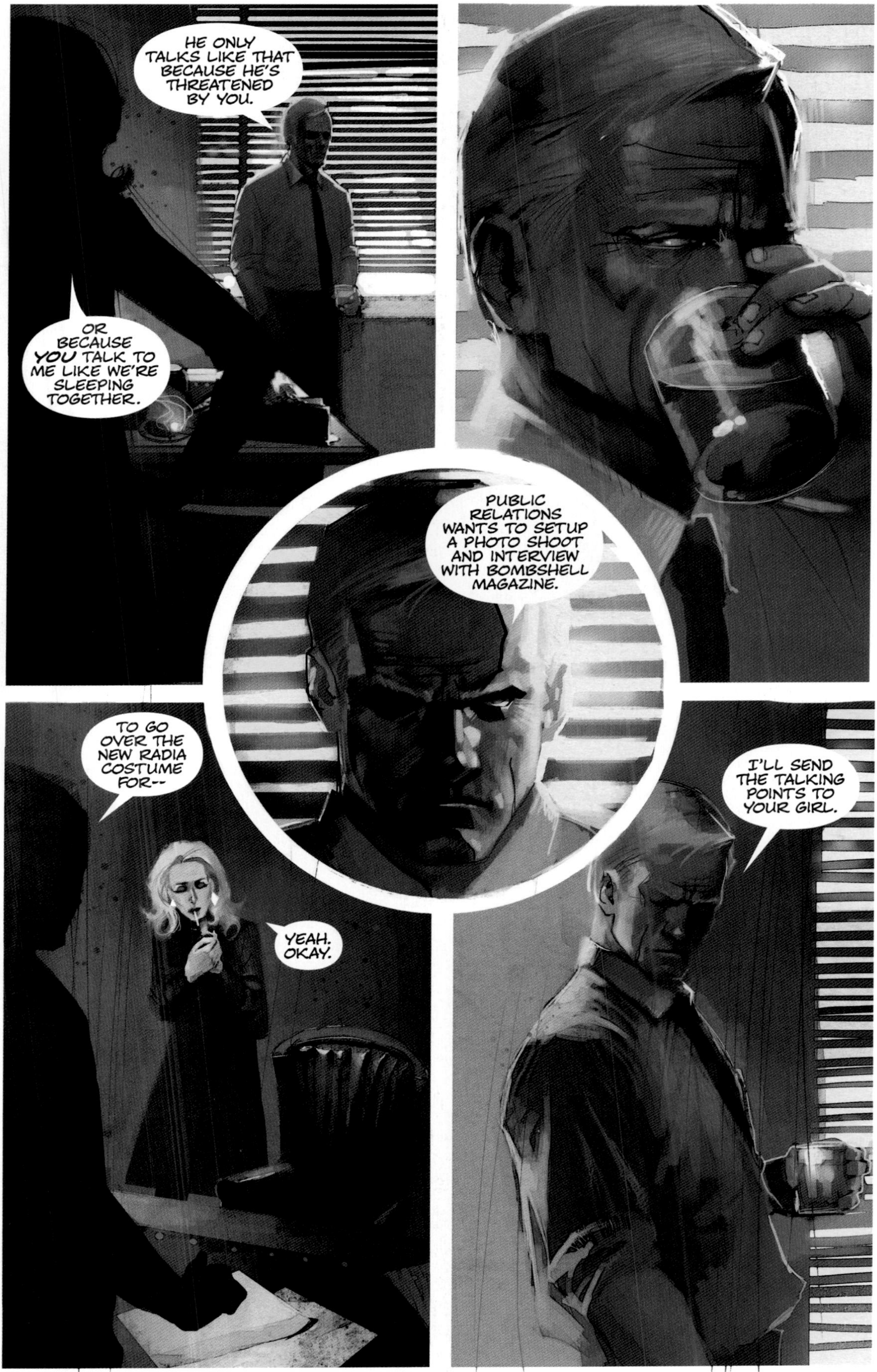
HE ONLY TALKS LIKE THAT BECAUSE HE'S THREATENED BY YOU.
OR BECAUSE YOU TALK TO ME LIKE WE'RE SLEEPING TOGETHER.
PUBLIC RELATIONS WANTS TO SETUP A PHOTO SHOOT AND INTERVIEW WITH BOMBSHELL MAGAZINE.
TO GO OVER THE NEW RADIA COSTUME FOR--
YEAH. OKAY.
I'LL SEND THE TALKING POINTS TO YOUR GIRL.

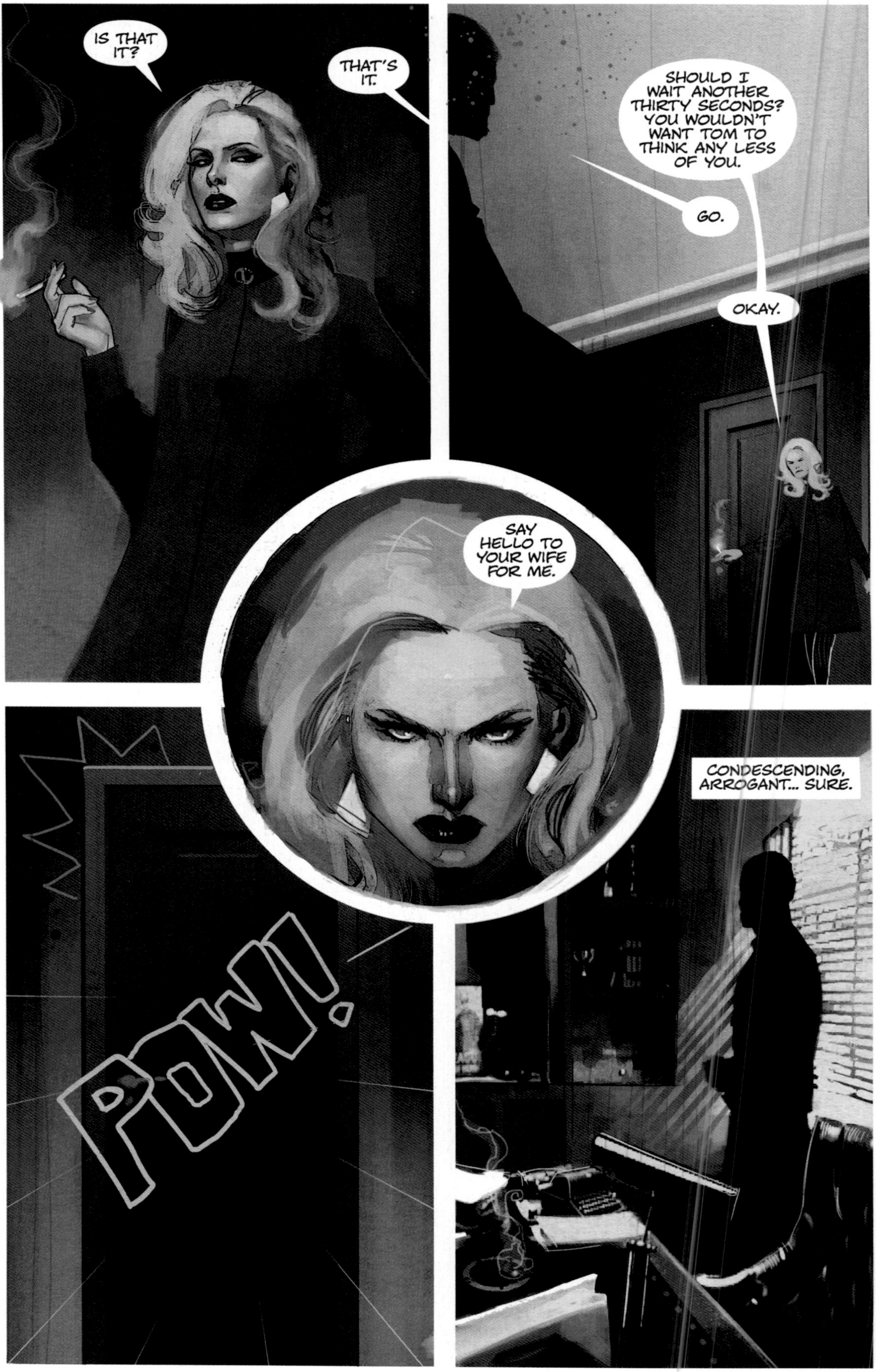
IS THAT IT?
THAT'S IT.
SHOULD I WAIT ANOTHER THIRTY SECONDS? YOU WOULDN'T WANT TOM TO THINK ANY LESS OF YOU.
GO.
OKAY.
SAY HELLO TO YOUR WIFE FOR ME.
POW!
CONDESCENDING, ARROGANT... SURE.

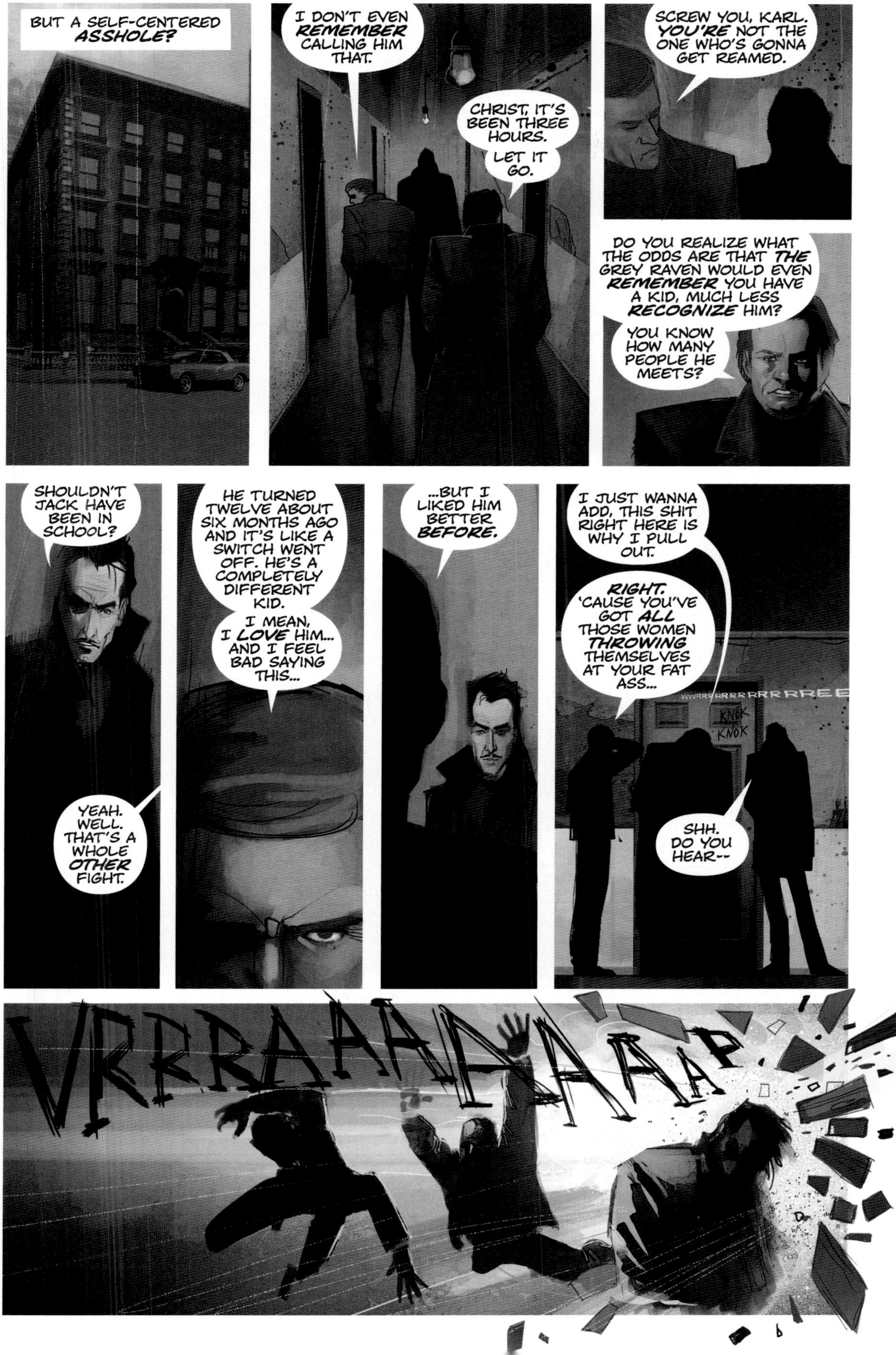

BUT A SELF-CENTERED ASSHOLE?
I DON'T EVEN REMEMBER CALLING HIM THAT.
CHRIST, IT'S BEEN THREE HOURS.
LET IT GO.
SCREW YOU, KARL. YOU'RE NOT THE ONE WHO'S GONNA GET REAMED.
DO YOU REALIZE WHAT THE ODDS ARE THAT THE GREY RAVEN WOULD EVEN REMEMBER YOU HAVE A KID, MUCH LESS RECOGNIZE HIM?
YOU KNOW HOW MANY PEOPLE HE MEETS?
SHOULDN'T JACK HAVE BEEN IN SCHOOL?
YEAH. WELL. THAT'S A WHOLE OTHER FIGHT.
HE TURNED TWELVE ABOUT SIX MONTHS AGO AND IT'S LIKE A SWITCH WENT OFF. HE'S A COMPLETELY DIFFERENT KID.
I MEAN, I LOVE HIM... AND I FEEL BAD SAYING THIS...
...BUT I LIKED HIM BETTER BEFORE.
I JUST WANNA ADD, THIS SHIT RIGHT HERE IS WHY I PULL OUT.
RIGHT. 'CAUSE YOU'VE GOT ALL THOSE WOMEN THROWING THEMSELVES AT YOUR FAT ASS...
WVVRRRRRRRRRRRREE
KNOK KNOK
SHH. DO YOU HEAR--
VRRRAAADAAAP

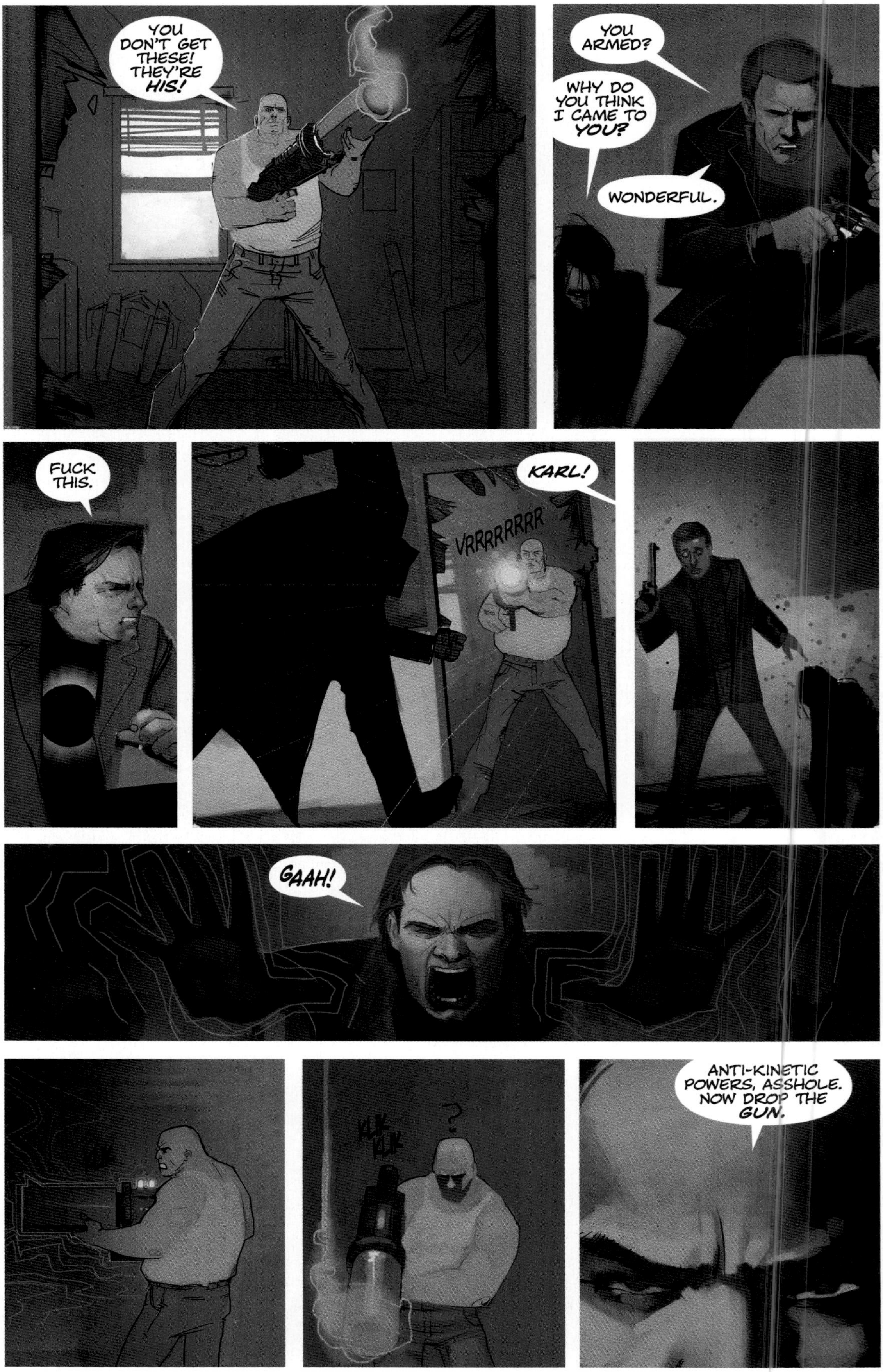
YOU DON'T GET THESE! THEY'RE HIS!
YOU ARMED?
WHY DO YOU THINK I CAME TO YOU?
WONDERFUL.
FUCK THIS.
KARL!
VRRRRRRRR
GAAH!
KLIK KLIK
?
ANTI-KINETIC POWERS, ASSHOLE. NOW DROP THE GUN.

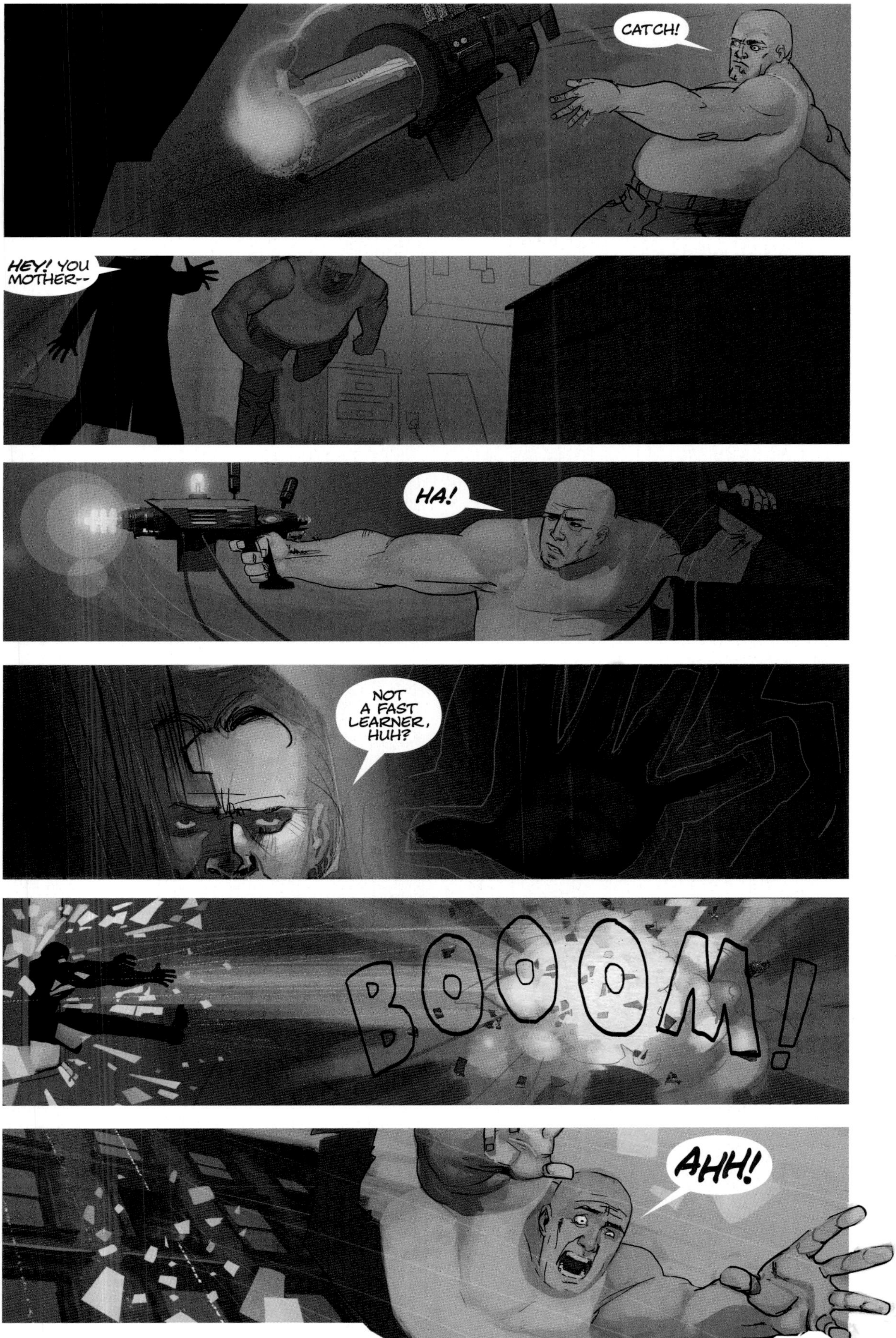
CATCH!
HEY! YOU MOTHER--
HA!
NOT A FAST LEARNER, HUH?
BOOOM!
AHH!

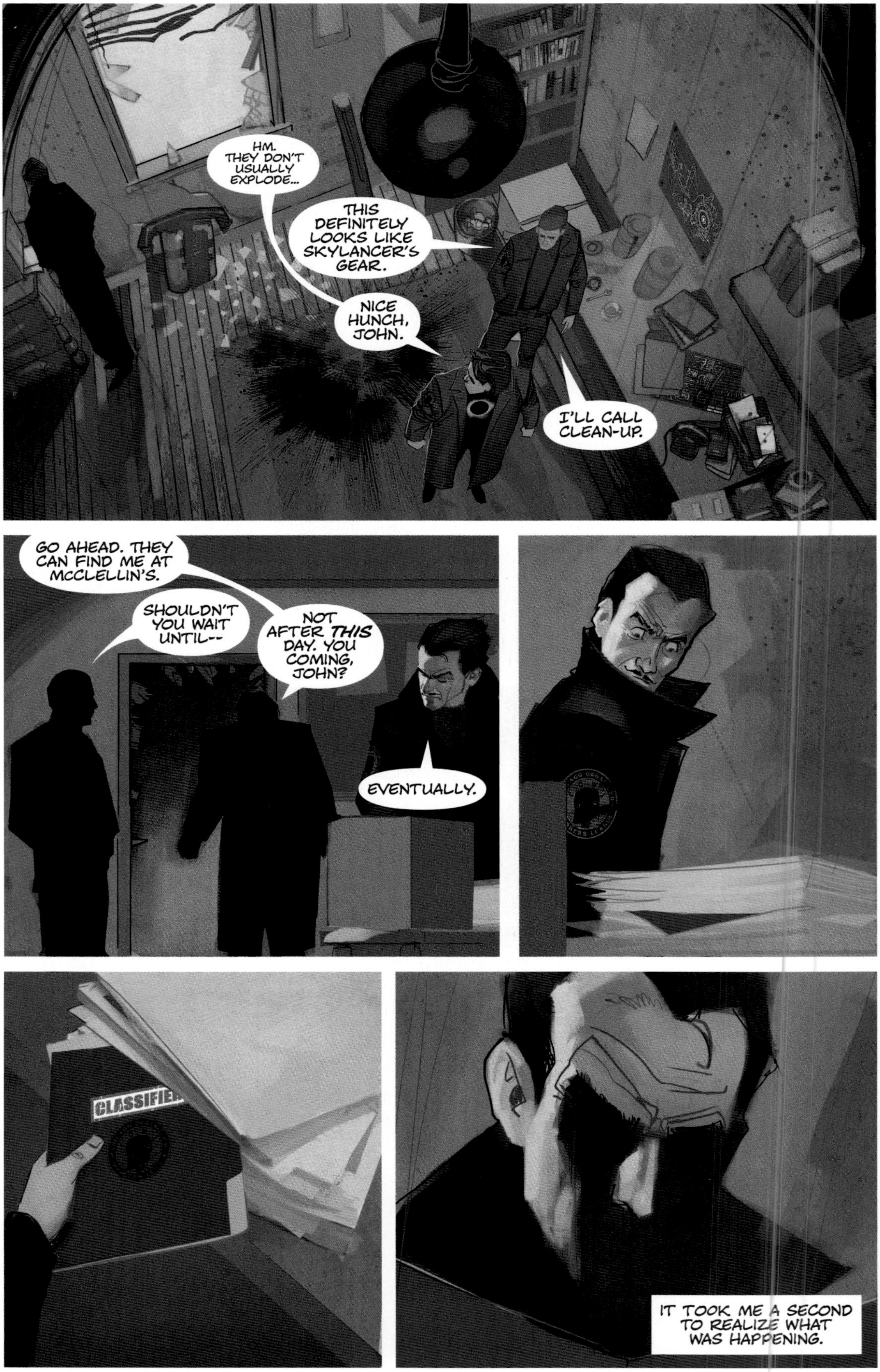
HM. THEY DON'T USUALLY EXPLODE...
THIS DEFINITELY LOOKS LIKE SKYLANCER'S GEAR.
NICE HUNCH, JOHN.
I'LL CALL CLEAN-UP.
GO AHEAD. THEY CAN FIND ME AT McCLELLIN'S.
SHOULDN'T YOU WAIT UNTIL--
NOT AFTER THIS DAY. YOU COMING, JOHN?
EVENTUALLY.
CLASSIFIE
IT TOOK ME A SECOND TO REALIZE WHAT WAS HAPPENING.

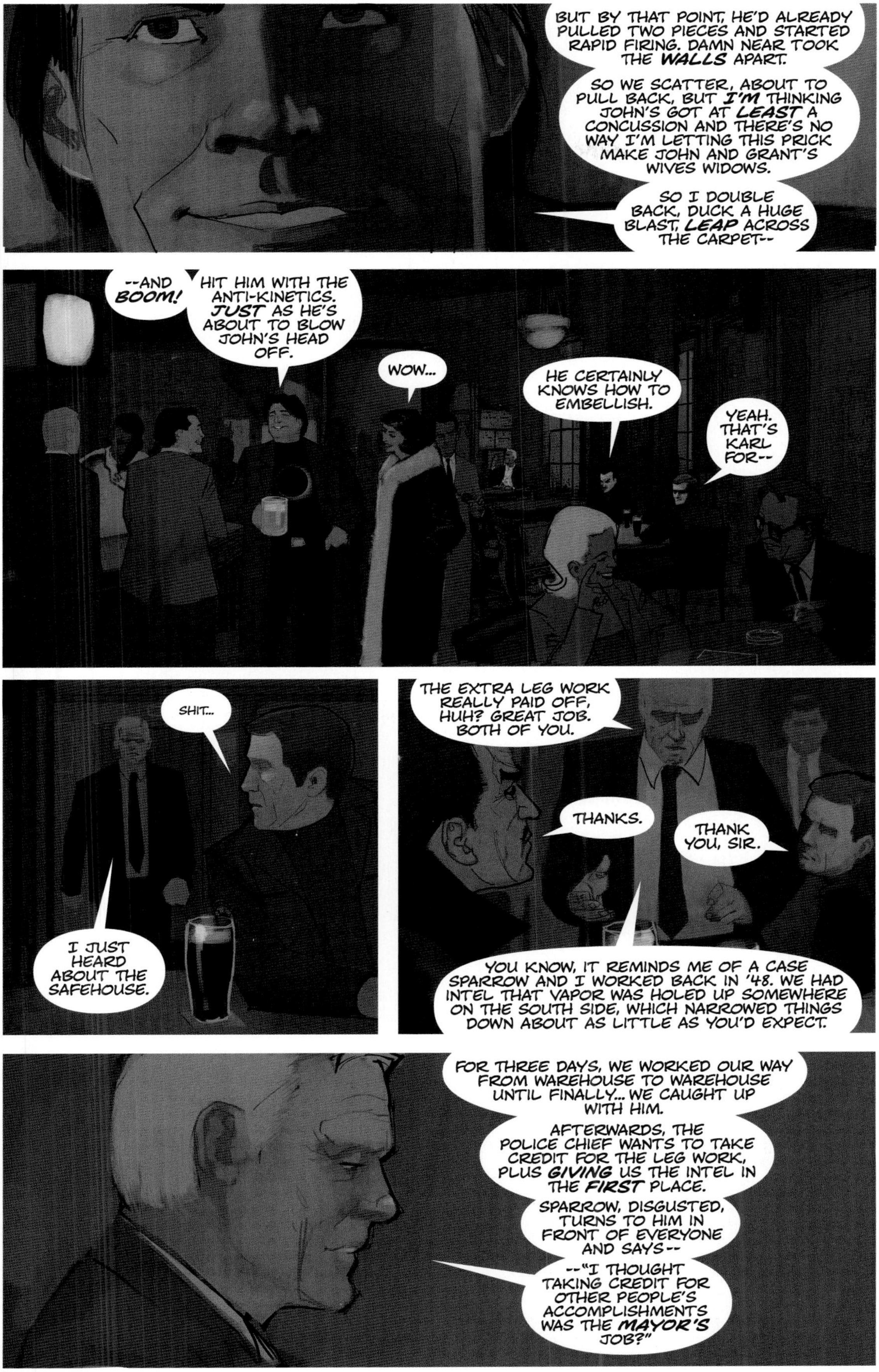
BUT BY THAT POINT, HE'D ALREADY PULLED TWO PIECES AND STARTED RAPID FIRING. DAMN NEAR TOOK THE WALLS APART.
SO WE SCATTER, ABOUT TO PULL BACK, BUT I'M THINKING JOHN'S GOT AT LEAST A CONCUSSION AND THERE'S NO WAY I'M LETTING THIS PRICK MAKE JOHN AND GRANT'S WIVES WIDOWS.
SO I DOUBLE BACK, DUCK A HUGE BLAST, LEAP ACROSS THE CARPET--
--AND BOOM!
HIT HIM WITH THE ANTI-KINETICS. JUST AS HE'S ABOUT TO BLOW JOHN'S HEAD OFF.
WOW...
HE CERTAINLY KNOWS HOW TO EMBELLISH.
YEAH. THAT'S KARL FOR--
SHIT...
I JUST HEARD ABOUT THE SAFEHOUSE.
THE EXTRA LEG WORK REALLY PAID OFF, HUH? GREAT JOB. BOTH OF YOU.
THANKS.
THANK YOU, SIR.
YOU KNOW, IT REMINDS ME OF A CASE SPARROW AND I WORKED BACK IN '48. WE HAD INTEL THAT VAPOR WAS HOLED UP SOMEWHERE ON THE SOUTH SIDE, WHICH NARROWED THINGS DOWN ABOUT AS LITTLE AS YOU'D EXPECT.
FOR THREE DAYS, WE WORKED OUR WAY FROM WAREHOUSE TO WAREHOUSE UNTIL FINALLY... WE CAUGHT UP WITH HIM.
AFTERWARDS, THE POLICE CHIEF WANTS TO TAKE CREDIT FOR THE LEG WORK, PLUS GIVING US THE INTEL IN THE FIRST PLACE.
SPARROW, DISGUSTED, TURNS TO HIM IN FRONT OF EVERYONE AND SAYS--
--"I THOUGHT TAKING CREDIT FOR OTHER PEOPLE'S ACCOMPLISHMENTS WAS THE MAYOR'S JOB?"

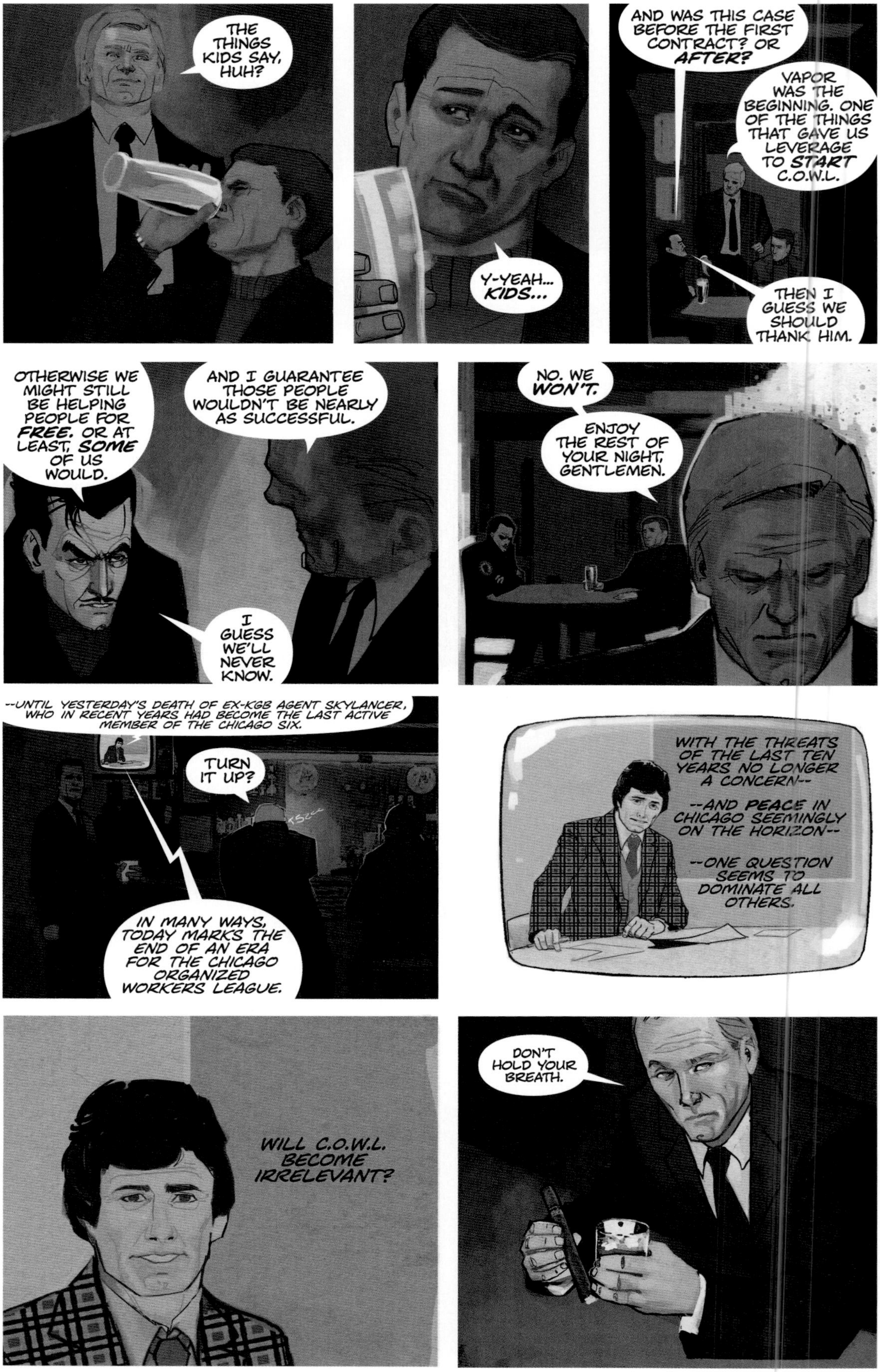
THE THINGS KIDS SAY, HUH?
Y-YEAH... KIDS...
AND WAS THIS CASE BEFORE THE FIRST CONTRACT? OR AFTER?
VAPOR WAS THE BEGINNING. ONE OF THE THINGS THAT GAVE US LEVERAGE TO START C.O.W.L.
THEN I GUESS WE SHOULD THANK HIM.
OTHERWISE WE MIGHT STILL BE HELPING PEOPLE FOR FREE. OR AT LEAST, SOME OF US WOULD.
AND I GUARANTEE THOSE PEOPLE WOULDN'T BE NEARLY AS SUCCESSFUL.
I GUESS WE'LL NEVER KNOW.
NO. WE WON'T.
ENJOY THE REST OF YOUR NIGHT, GENTLEMEN.
--UNTIL YESTERDAY'S DEATH OF EX-KGB AGENT SKYLANCER, WHO IN RECENT YEARS HAD BECOME THE LAST ACTIVE MEMBER OF THE CHICAGO SIX.
TURN IT UP?
TSCCC
IN MANY WAYS, TODAY MARKS THE END OF AN ERA FOR THE CHICAGO ORGANIZED WORKERS LEAGUE.
WITH THE THREATS OF THE LAST TEN YEARS NO LONGER A CONCERN--
--AND PEACE IN CHICAGO SEEMINGLY ON THE HORIZON--
--ONE QUESTION SEEMS TO DOMINATE ALL OTHERS.
WILL C.O.W.L. BECOME IRRELEVANT?
DON'T HOLD YOUR BREATH.

CHICAGO ORGANIZED WORKERS LEAGUE

C O W L

EQUITAS VENERATIO POTENTIA

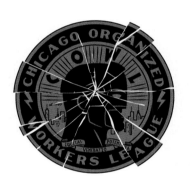

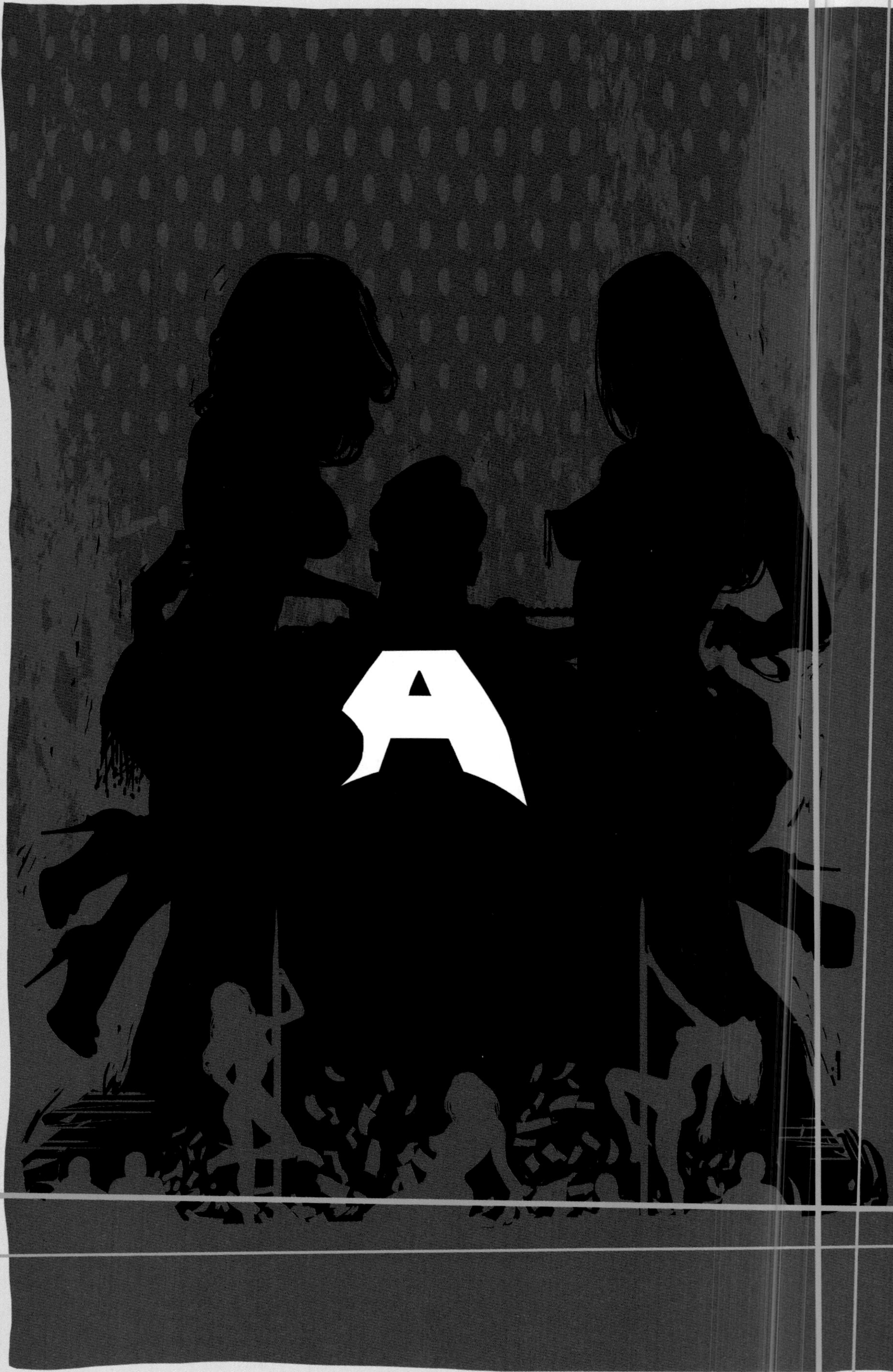
A

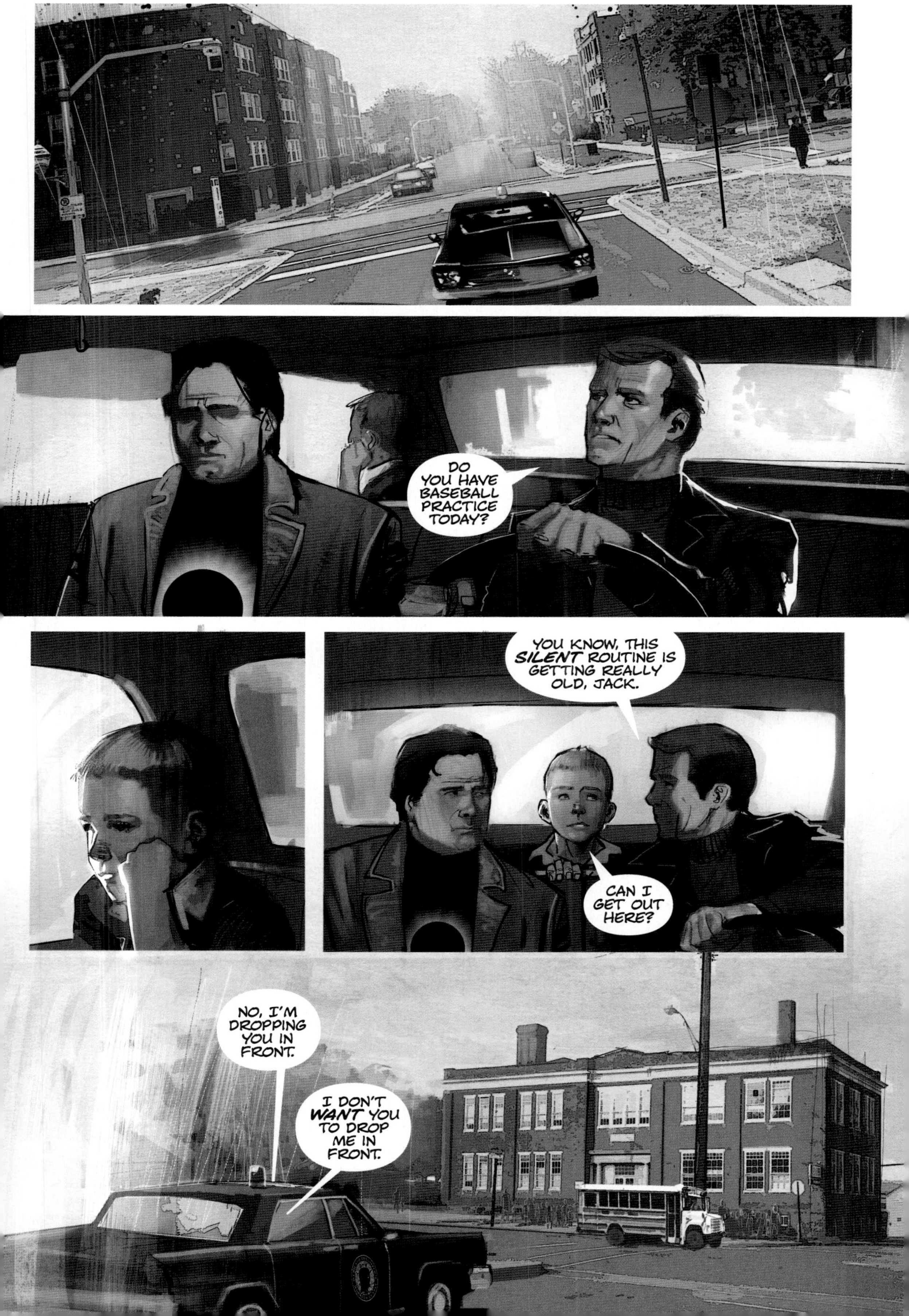
DO YOU HAVE BASEBALL PRACTICE TODAY?
YOU KNOW, THIS SILENT ROUTINE IS GETTING REALLY OLD, JACK.
CAN I GET OUT HERE?
NO, I'M DROPPING YOU IN FRONT.
I DON'T WANT YOU TO DROP ME IN FRONT.

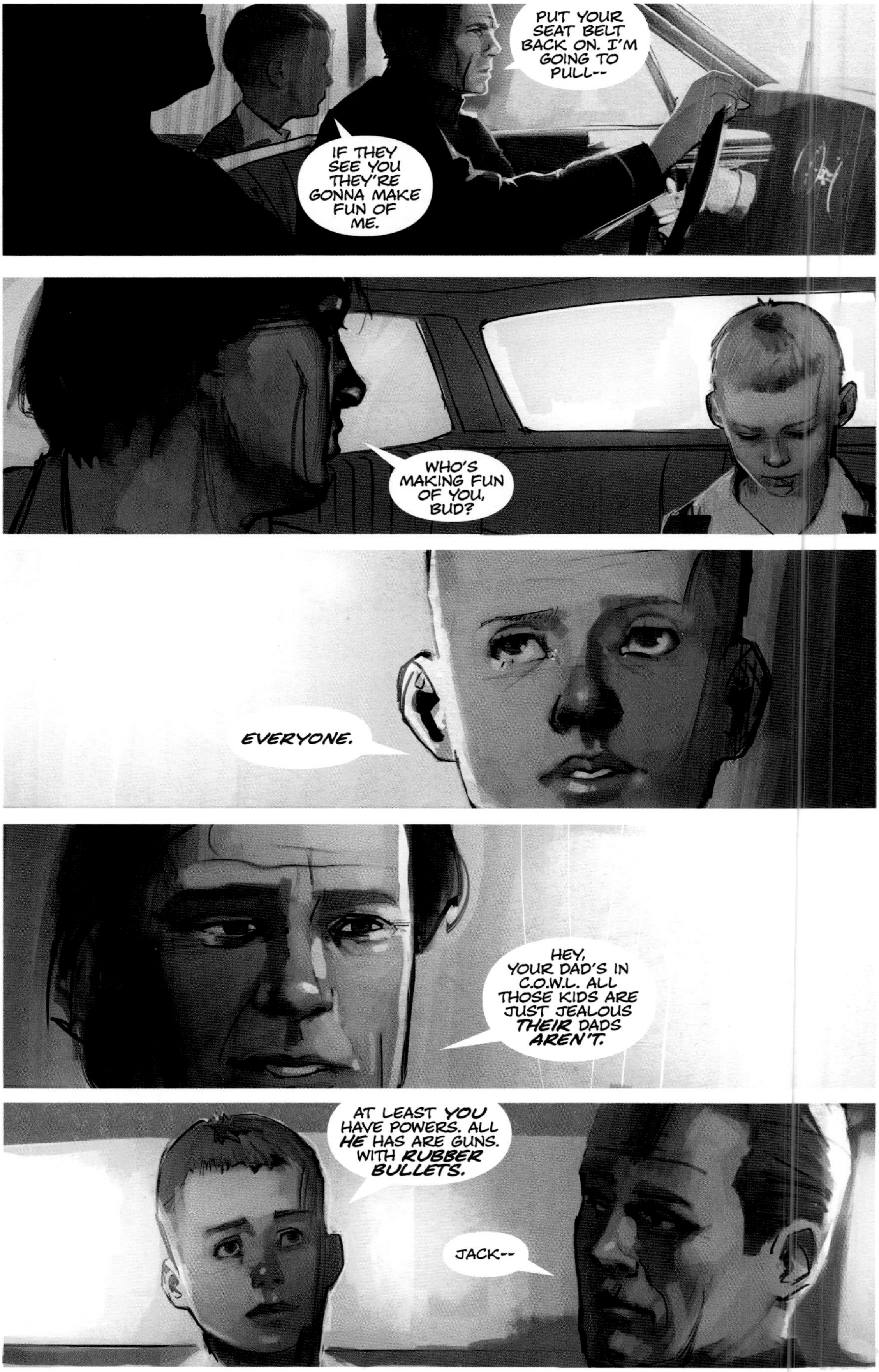
PUT YOUR SEAT BELT BACK ON. I'M GOING TO PULL--
IF THEY SEE YOU THEY'RE GONNA MAKE FUN OF ME.
WHO'S MAKING FUN OF YOU, BUD?
EVERYONE.
HEY, YOUR DAD'S IN C.O.W.L. ALL THOSE KIDS ARE JUST JEALOUS ***THEIR*** DADS ***AREN'T.***
AT LEAST ***YOU*** HAVE POWERS. ALL ***HE*** HAS ARE GUNS. WITH ***RUBBER BULLETS.***
JACK--

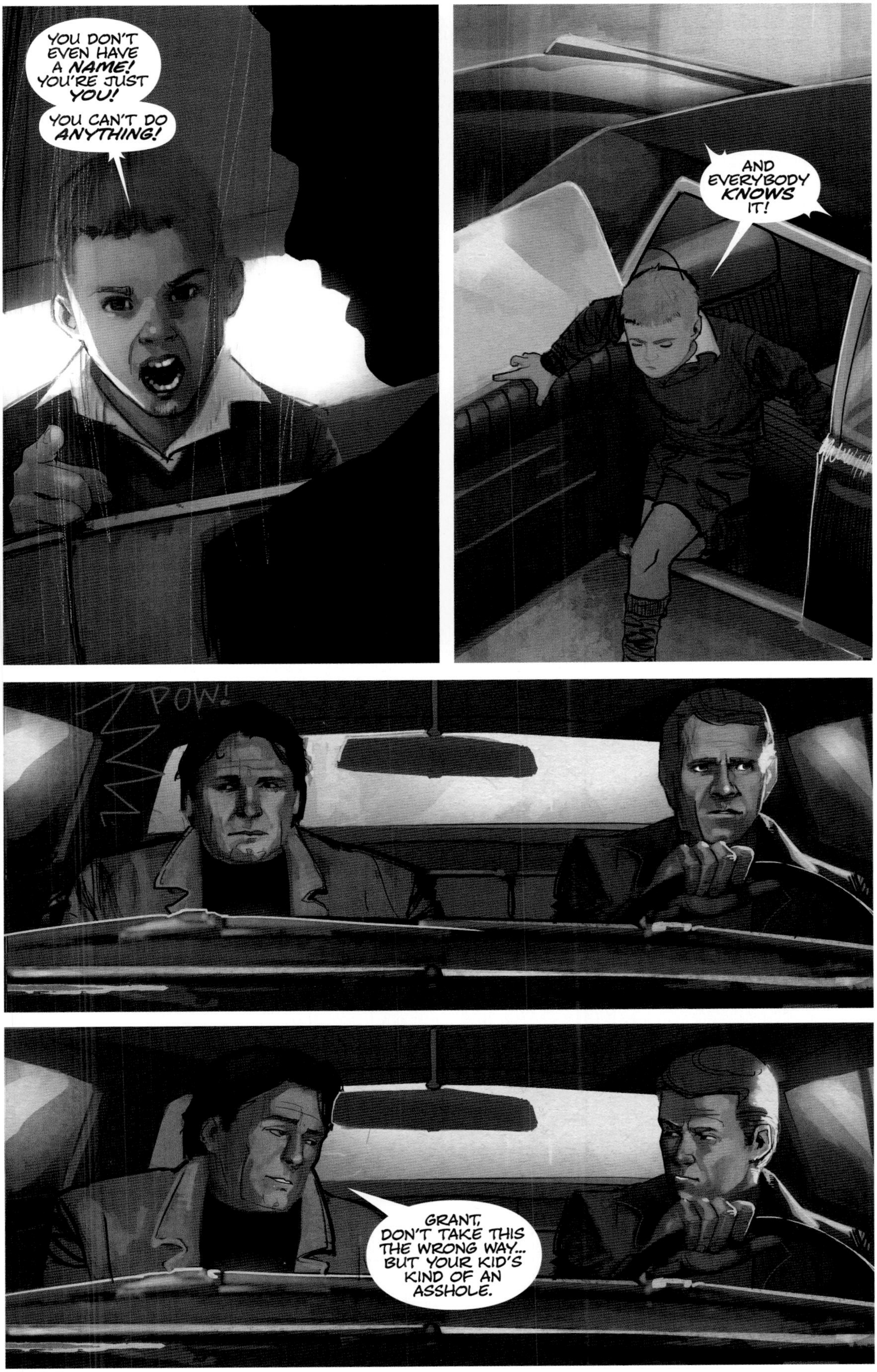
YOU DON'T EVEN HAVE A NAME! YOU'RE JUST YOU!
YOU CAN'T DO ANYTHING!
AND EVERYBODY KNOWS IT!
POW!
GRANT, DON'T TAKE THIS THE WRONG WAY... BUT YOUR KID'S KIND OF AN ASSHOLE.

CHAPTER 2
Self-Deception

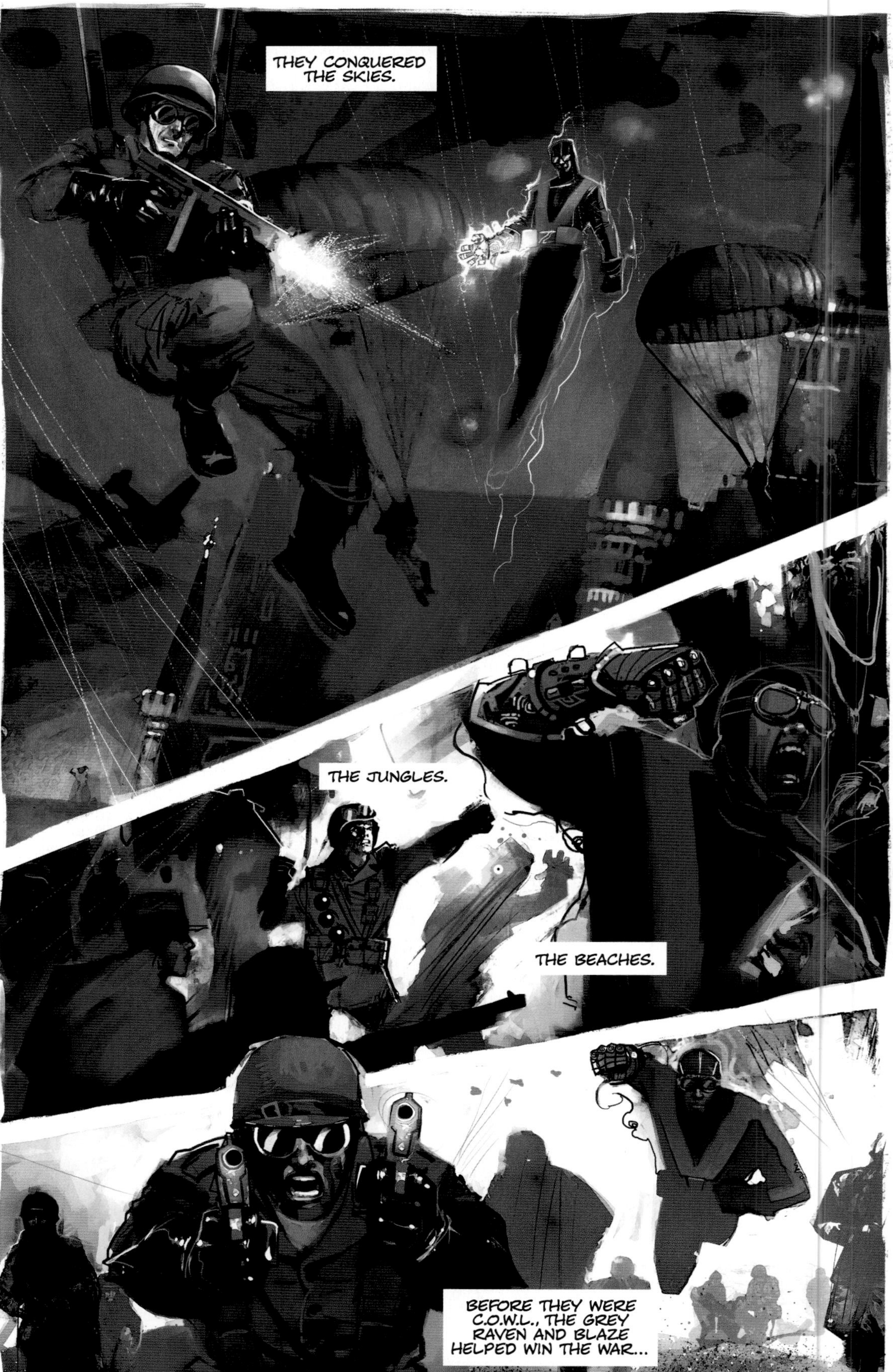
THEY CONQUERED THE SKIES.
THE JUNGLES.
THE BEACHES.
BEFORE THEY WERE C.O.W.L., THE GREY RAVEN AND BLAZE HELPED WIN THE WAR...

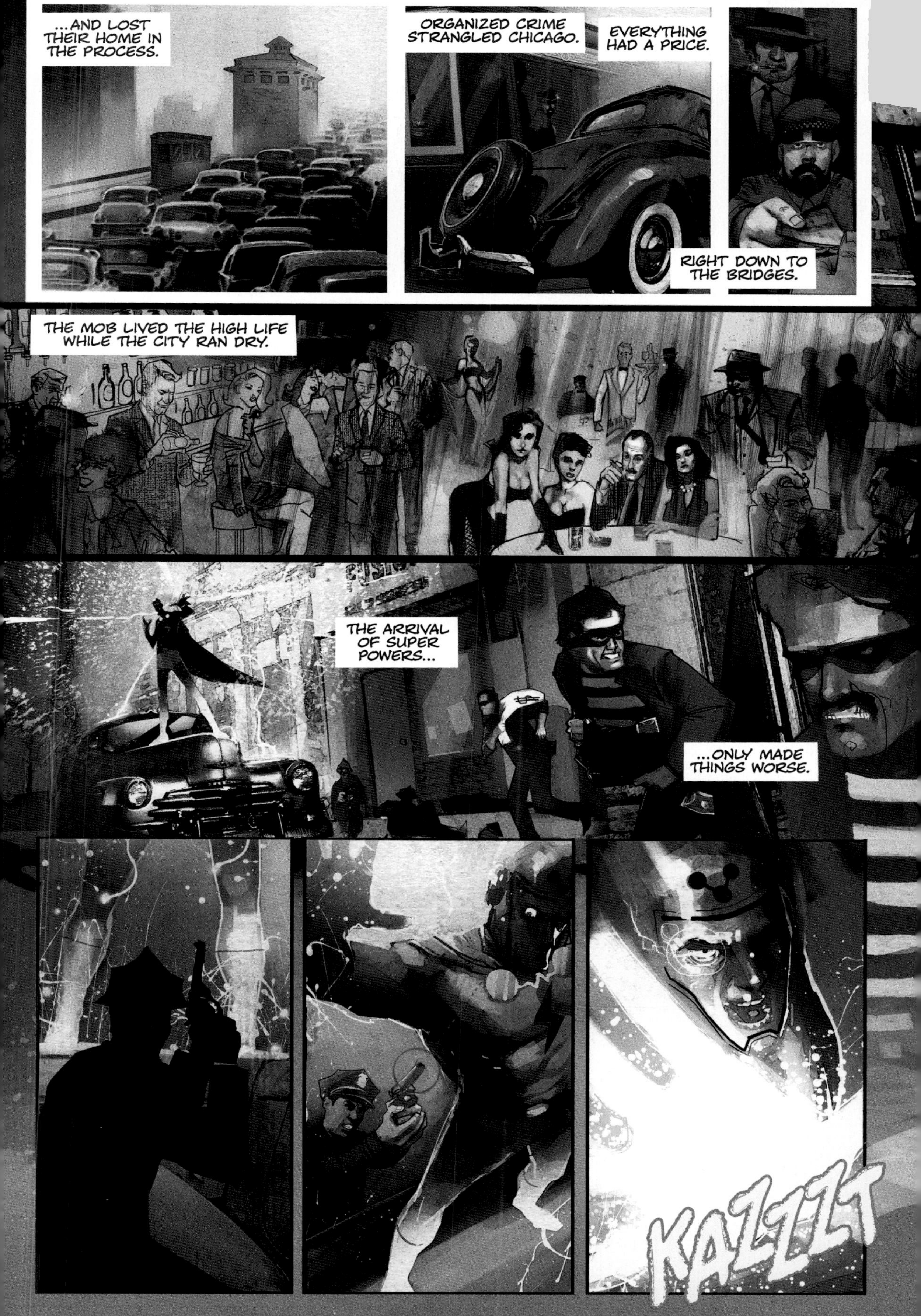
...AND LOST THEIR HOME IN THE PROCESS.
ORGANIZED CRIME STRANGLED CHICAGO.
EVERYTHING HAD A PRICE.
RIGHT DOWN TO THE BRIDGES.
THE MOB LIVED THE HIGH LIFE WHILE THE CITY RAN DRY.
THE ARRIVAL OF SUPER POWERS...
...ONLY MADE THINGS WORSE.
KAZZZT

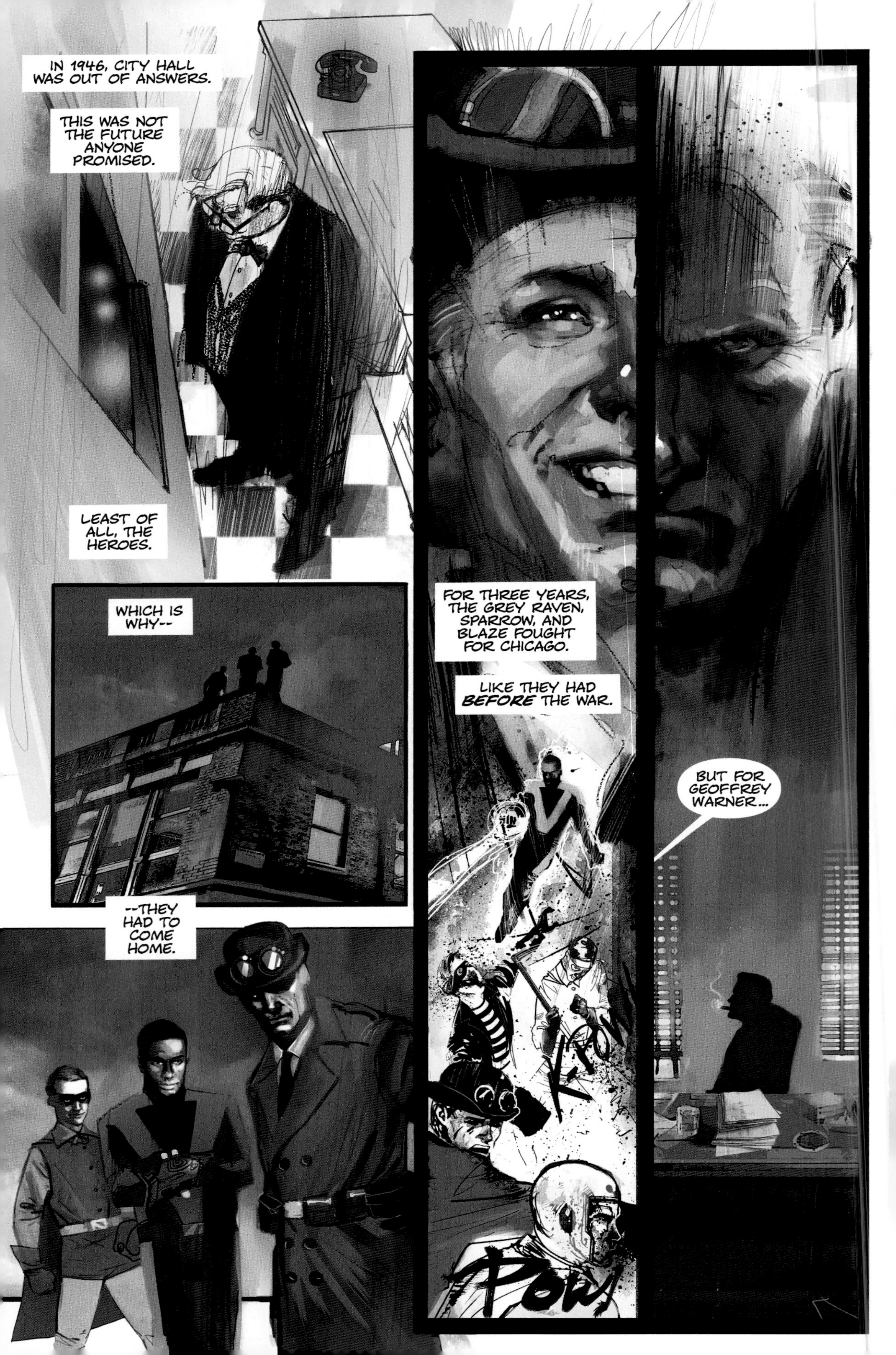

IN 1946, CITY HALL WAS OUT OF ANSWERS.
THIS WAS NOT THE FUTURE ANYONE PROMISED.
LEAST OF ALL, THE HEROES.
WHICH IS WHY--
--THEY HAD TO COME HOME.
FOR THREE YEARS, THE GREY RAVEN, SPARROW, AND BLAZE FOUGHT FOR CHICAGO.
LIKE THEY HAD *BEFORE* THE WAR.
POW
BUT FOR GEOFFREY WARNER...

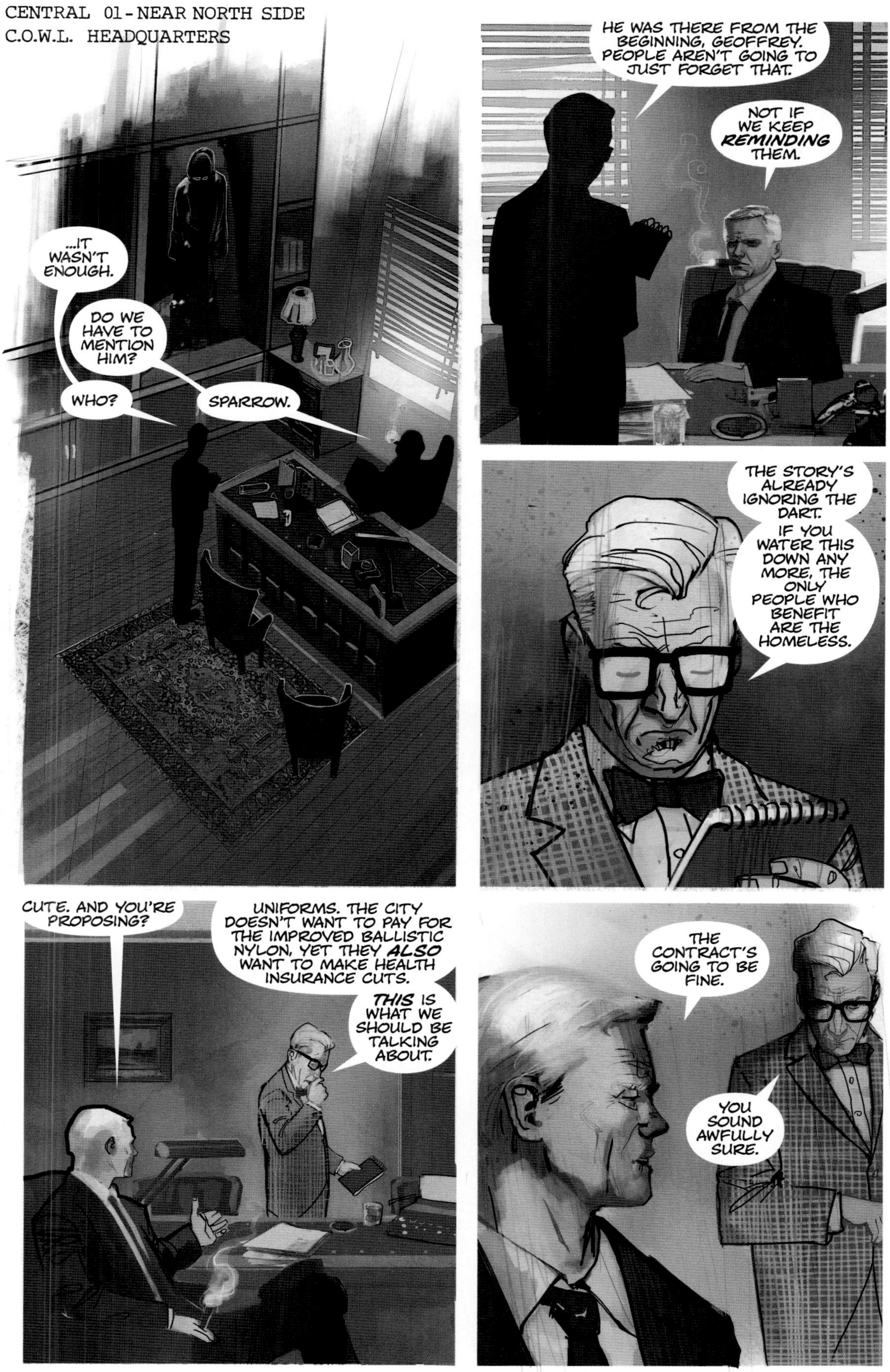
CENTRAL 01 - NEAR NORTH SIDE
C.O.W.L. HEADQUARTERS
...IT WASN'T ENOUGH.
DO WE HAVE TO MENTION HIM?
WHO?
SPARROW.
HE WAS THERE FROM THE BEGINNING, GEOFFREY. PEOPLE AREN'T GOING TO JUST FORGET THAT.
NOT IF WE KEEP *REMINDING* THEM.
THE STORY'S ALREADY IGNORING THE DART.
IF YOU WATER THIS DOWN ANY MORE, THE ONLY PEOPLE WHO BENEFIT ARE THE HOMELESS.
CUTE. AND YOU'RE PROPOSING?
UNIFORMS. THE CITY DOESN'T WANT TO PAY FOR THE IMPROVED BALLISTIC NYLON, YET THEY *ALSO* WANT TO MAKE HEALTH INSURANCE CUTS.
THIS IS WHAT WE SHOULD BE TALKING ABOUT.
THE CONTRACT'S GOING TO BE FINE.
YOU SOUND AWFULLY SURE.

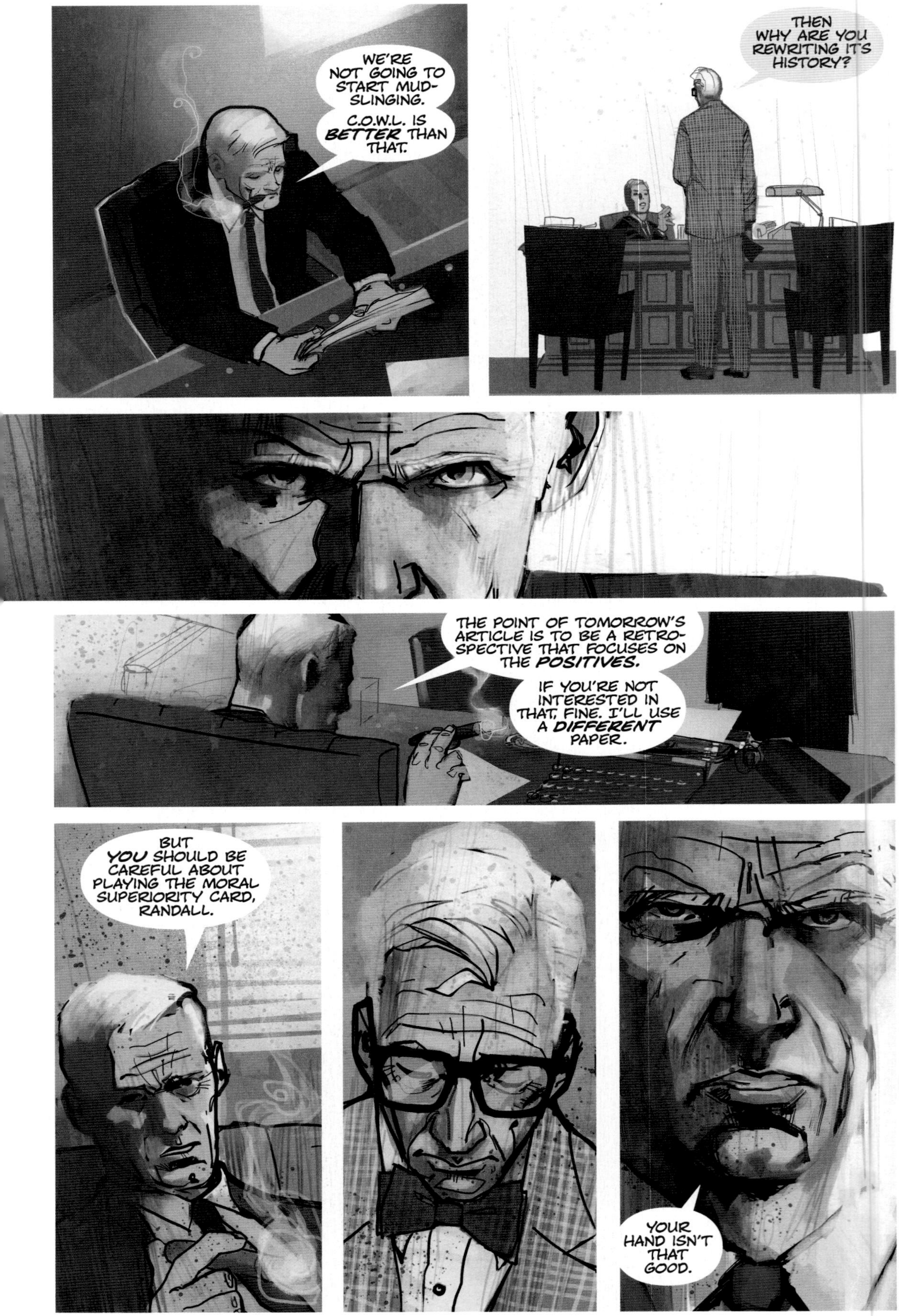
WE'RE NOT GOING TO START MUD-SLINGING.
C.O.W.L. IS BETTER THAN THAT.
THEN WHY ARE YOU REWRITING ITS HISTORY?
THE POINT OF TOMORROW'S ARTICLE IS TO BE A RETRO-SPECTIVE THAT FOCUSES ON THE POSITIVES.
IF YOU'RE NOT INTERESTED IN THAT, FINE. I'LL USE A DIFFERENT PAPER.
BUT YOU SHOULD BE CAREFUL ABOUT PLAYING THE MORAL SUPERIORITY CARD, RANDALL.
YOUR HAND ISN'T THAT GOOD.

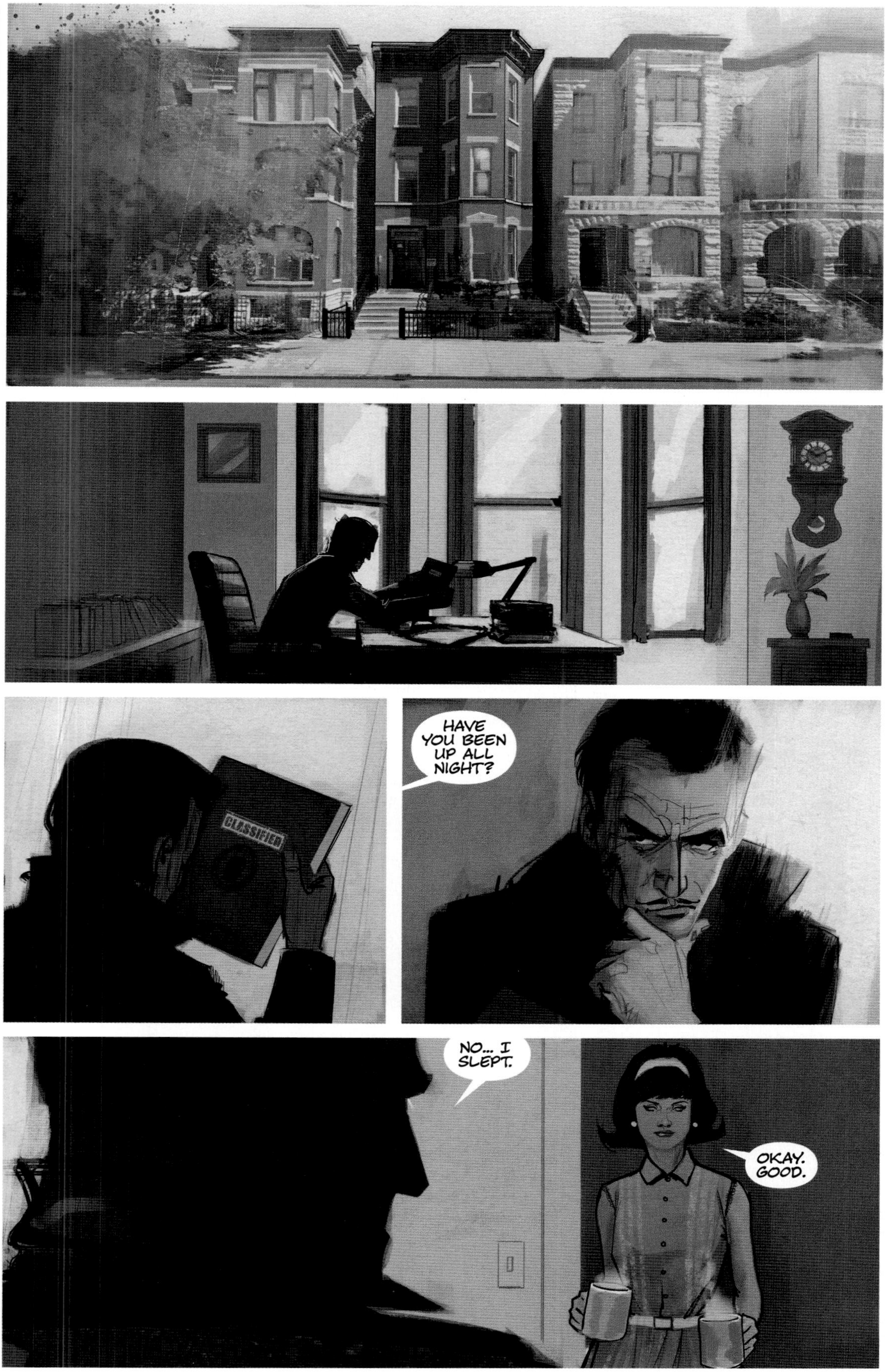
CLASSIFIED
HAVE YOU BEEN UP ALL NIGHT?
NO... I SLEPT.
OKAY. GOOD.

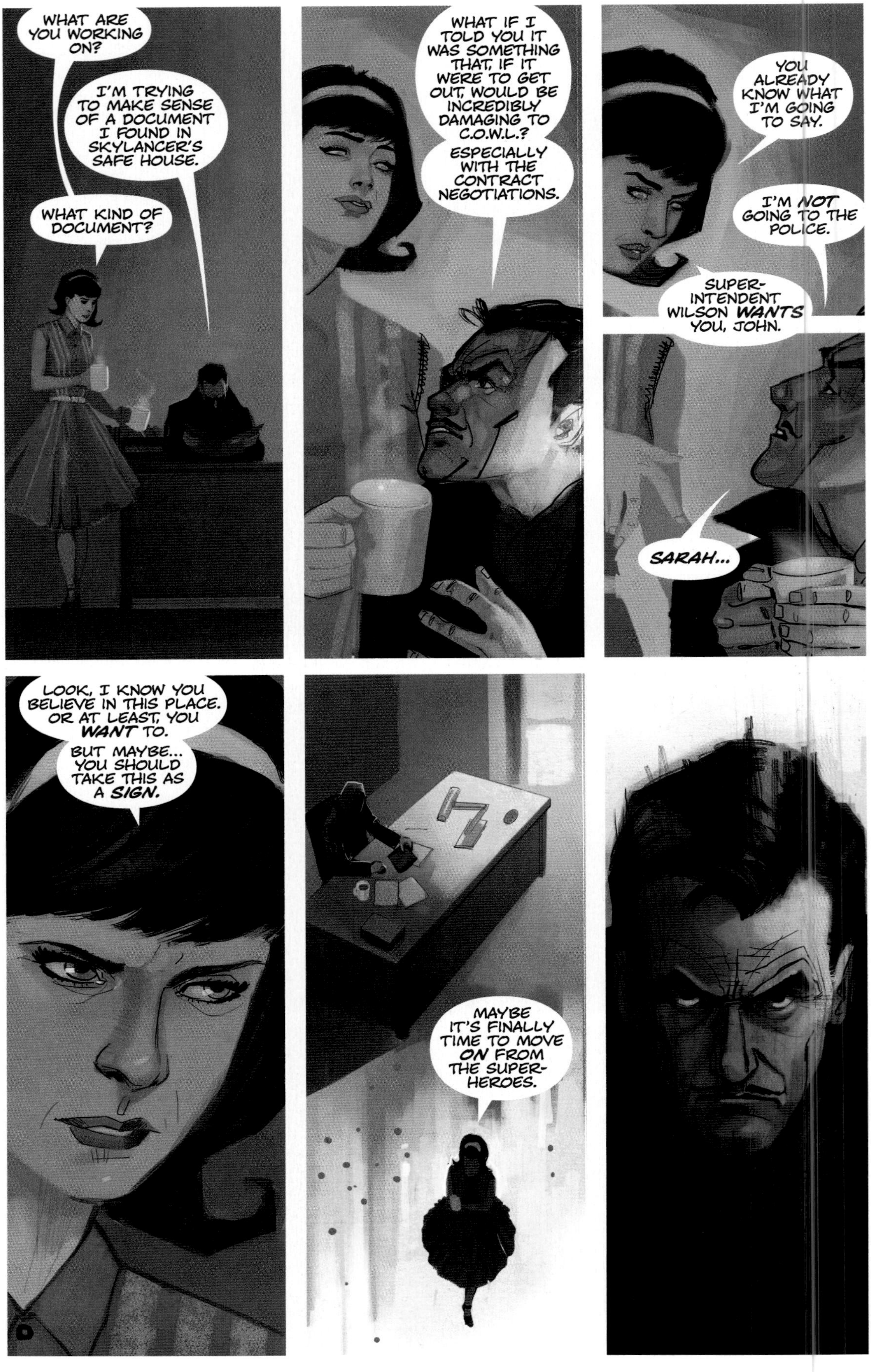
WHAT ARE YOU WORKING ON?
I'M TRYING TO MAKE SENSE OF A DOCUMENT I FOUND IN SKYLANCER'S SAFE HOUSE.
WHAT KIND OF DOCUMENT?
WHAT IF I TOLD YOU IT WAS SOMETHING THAT, IF IT WERE TO GET OUT, WOULD BE INCREDIBLY DAMAGING TO C.O.W.L.?
ESPECIALLY WITH THE CONTRACT NEGOTIATIONS.
YOU ALREADY KNOW WHAT I'M GOING TO SAY.
I'M NOT GOING TO THE POLICE.
SUPER-INTENDENT WILSON WANTS YOU, JOHN.
SARAH...
LOOK, I KNOW YOU BELIEVE IN THIS PLACE. OR AT LEAST, YOU WANT TO.
BUT MAYBE... YOU SHOULD TAKE THIS AS A SIGN.
MAYBE IT'S FINALLY TIME TO MOVE ON FROM THE SUPER-HEROES.

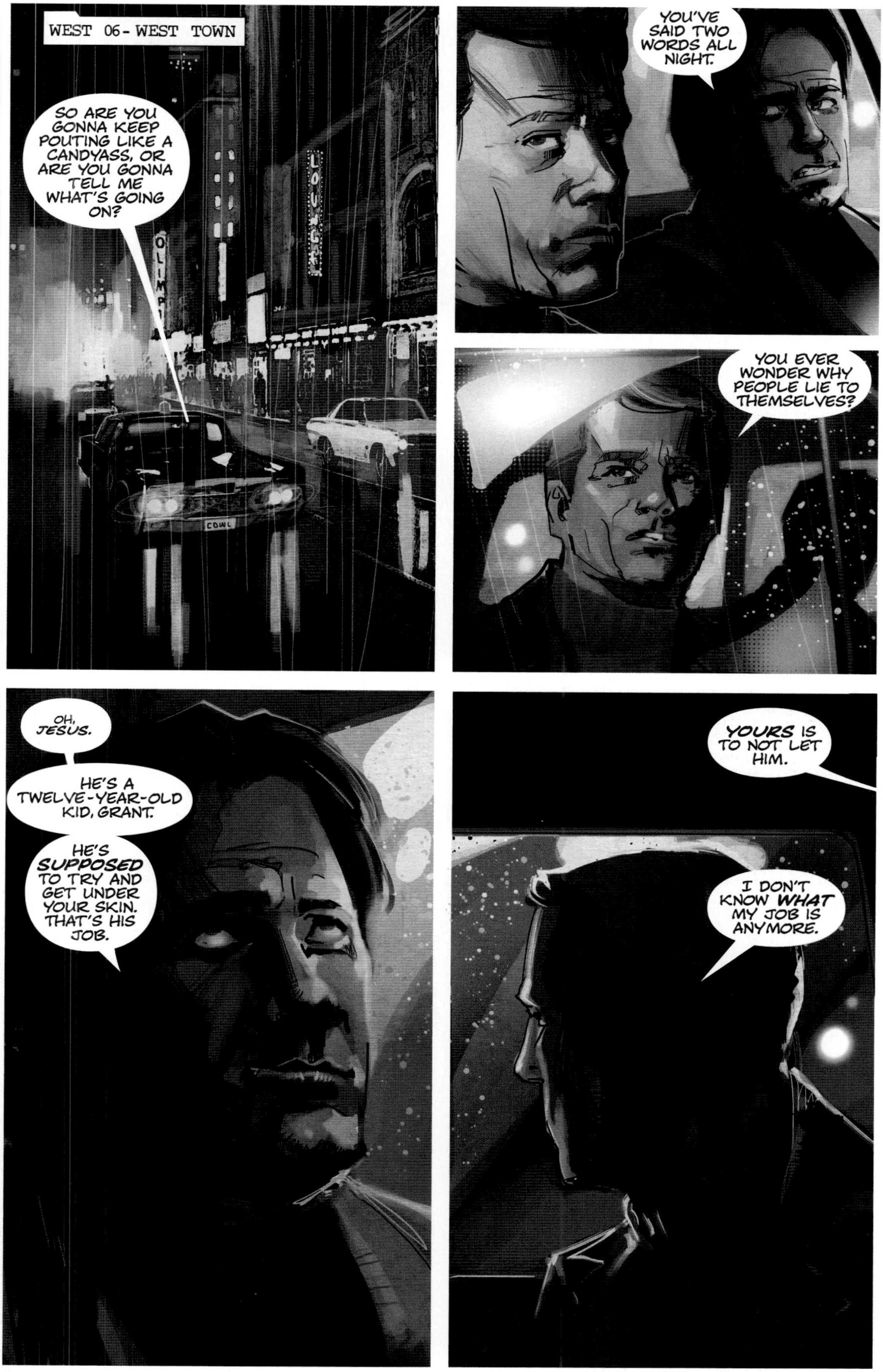
WEST 06- WEST TOWN
SO ARE YOU GONNA KEEP POUTING LIKE A CANDYASS, OR ARE YOU GONNA TELL ME WHAT'S GOING ON?
COWL
YOU'VE SAID TWO WORDS ALL NIGHT.
YOU EVER WONDER WHY PEOPLE LIE TO THEMSELVES?
OH, JESUS.
HE'S A TWELVE-YEAR-OLD KID, GRANT.
HE'S SUPPOSED TO TRY AND GET UNDER YOUR SKIN. THAT'S HIS JOB.
YOURS IS TO NOT LET HIM.
I DON'T KNOW WHAT MY JOB IS ANYMORE.

IT WAS MY **CHOICE** NOT TO TAKE A NAME, KARL.

I'M A GUY WITH A GOOD SHOT. THAT'S ABOUT AS HIGH AS MY CEILING GOES.

THE SECOND I TAKE A COSTUME AND START TRYING TO BE **MORE** THAN THAT...

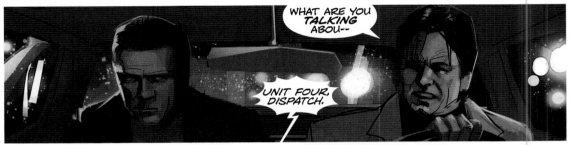

WHAT ARE YOU **TALKING** ABOU--

UNIT FOUR, DISPATCH.

UNIT FOUR. GO.

POSSIBLE EIGHT-OH-ONE ON THE SEVENTEEN HUNDRED BLOCK OF WEST ERIE. SINGLE ATTACKER.

CALLER THINKS THE PERPETRATOR HAS INCREASED STRENGTH.

COPY. WE'RE TWO BLOCKS OUT.

GET YOUR FUCKING HEAD RIGHT, GRANT.

WROOOOOO

YOU THINK YOU'RE **SPECIAL?**

C.O.W.L.

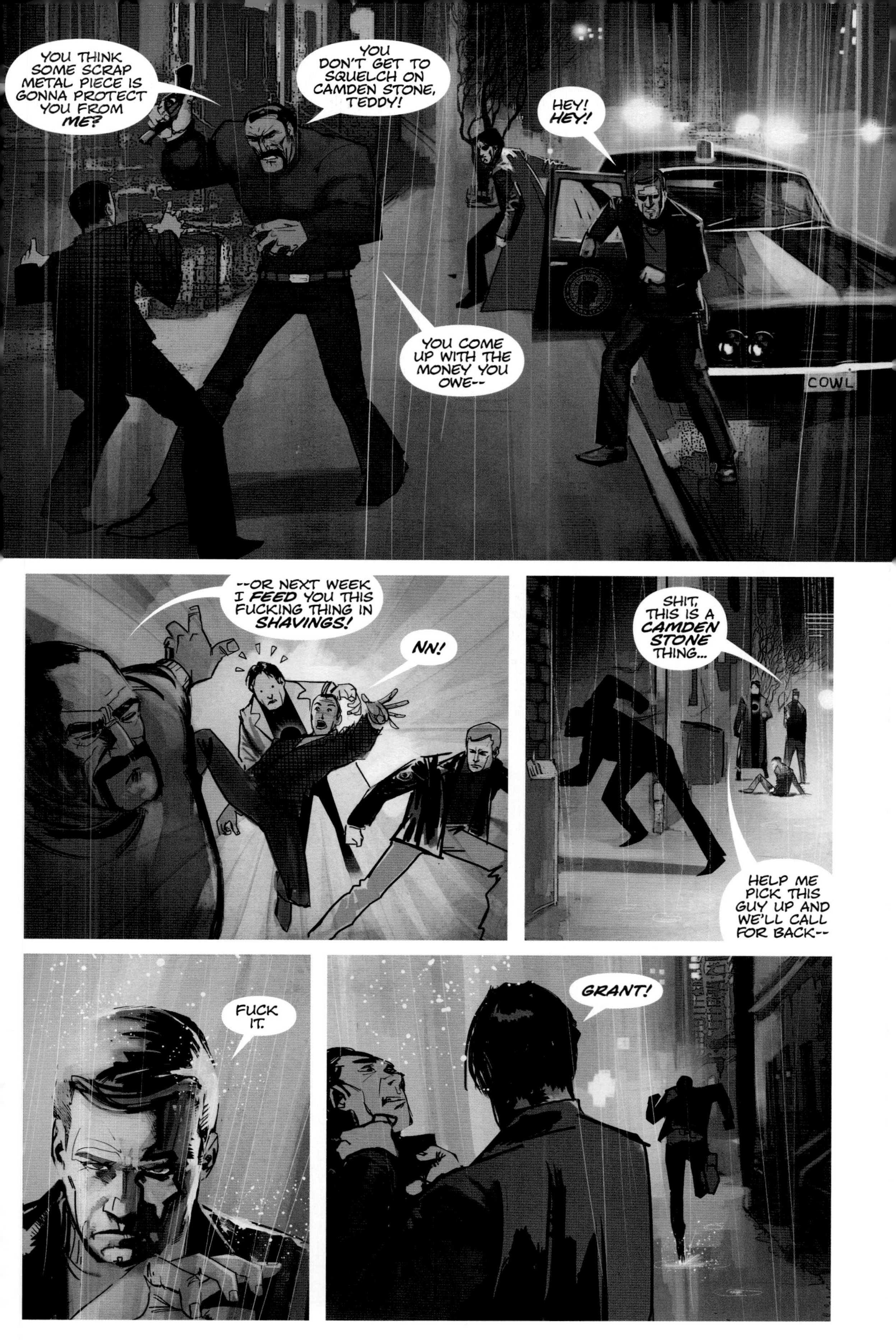
YOU THINK SOME SCRAP METAL PIECE IS GONNA PROTECT YOU FROM ME?
YOU DON'T GET TO SQUELCH ON CAMDEN STONE, TEDDY!
HEY! HEY!
YOU COME UP WITH THE MONEY YOU OWE--
COWL
--OR NEXT WEEK I FEED YOU THIS FUCKING THING IN SHAVINGS!
NN!
SHIT, THIS IS A CAMDEN STONE THING...
HELP ME PICK THIS GUY UP AND WE'LL CALL FOR BACK--
FUCK IT.
GRANT!

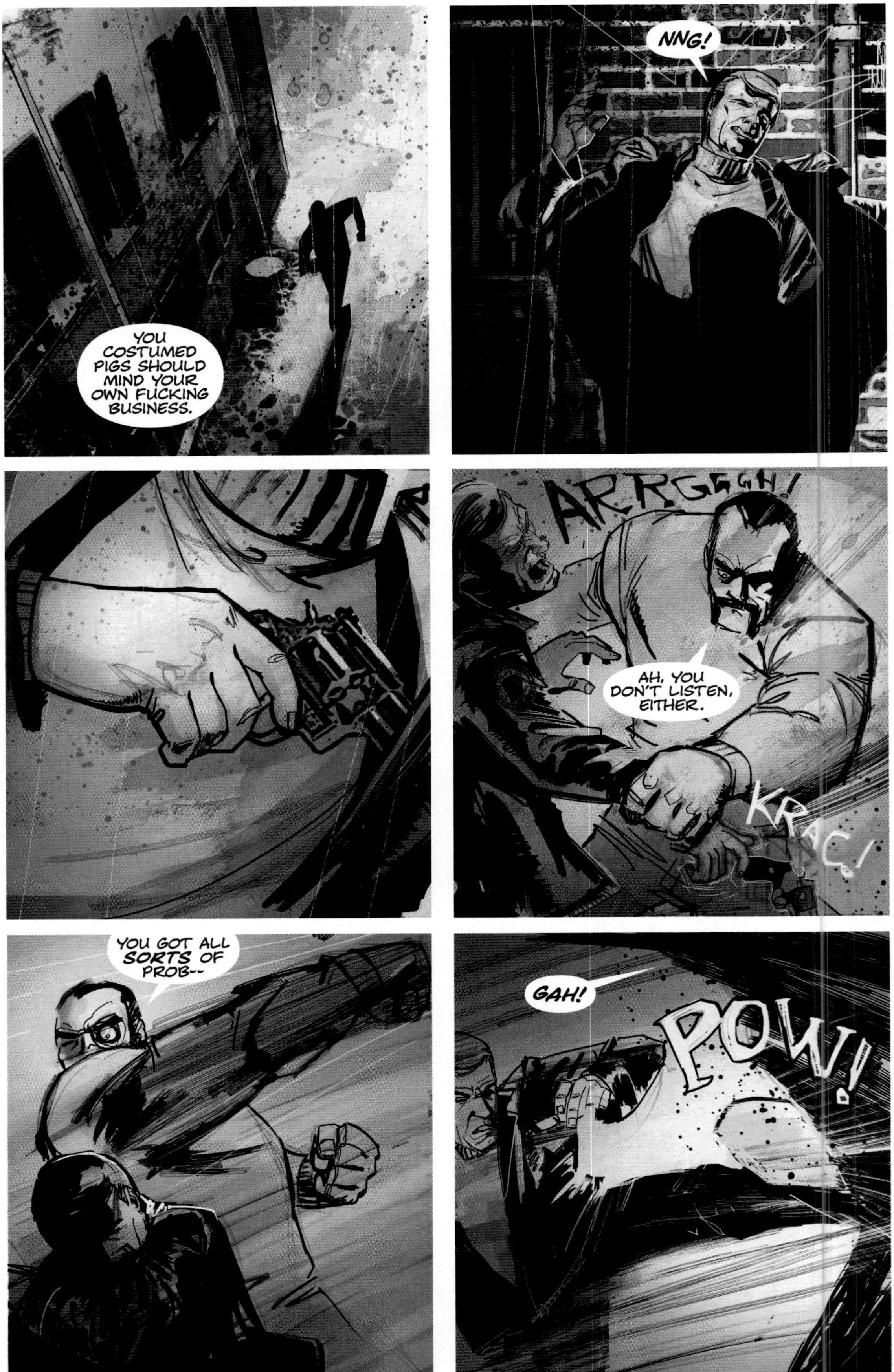
YOU COSTUMED PIGS SHOULD MIND YOUR OWN FUCKING BUSINESS.
NNG!
ARRGGGH!
AH, YOU DON'T LISTEN, EITHER.
KRAC!
YOU GOT ALL SORTS OF PROB--
GAH!
POW!

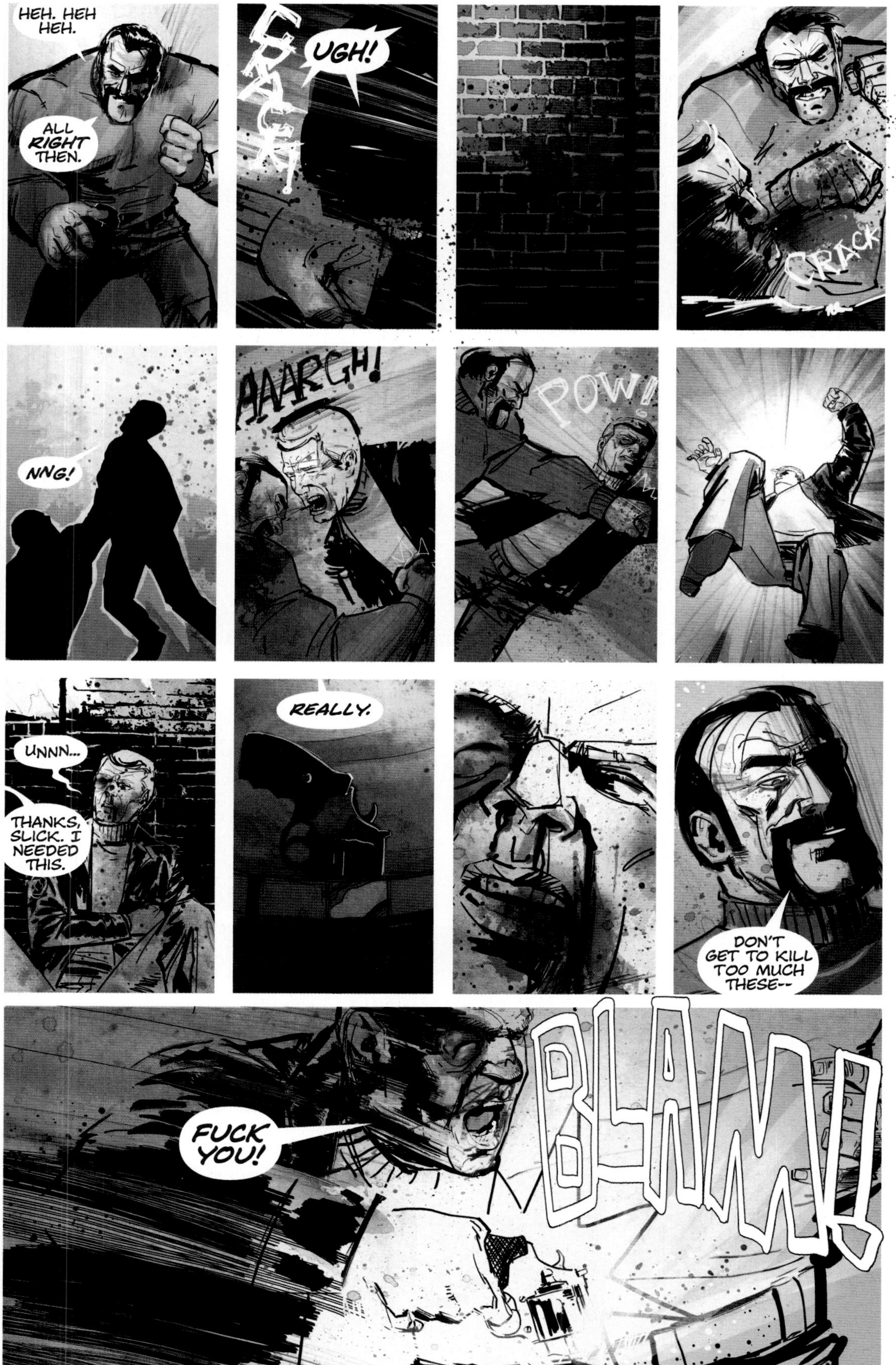
HEH. HEH HEH.
ALL RIGHT THEN.
CRACK!
UGH!
CRACK
NNG!
AAARGH!
POW!
UNNN...
THANKS, SLICK. I NEEDED THIS.
REALLY.
DON'T GET TO KILL TOO MUCH THESE--
FUCK YOU!
BLAM!

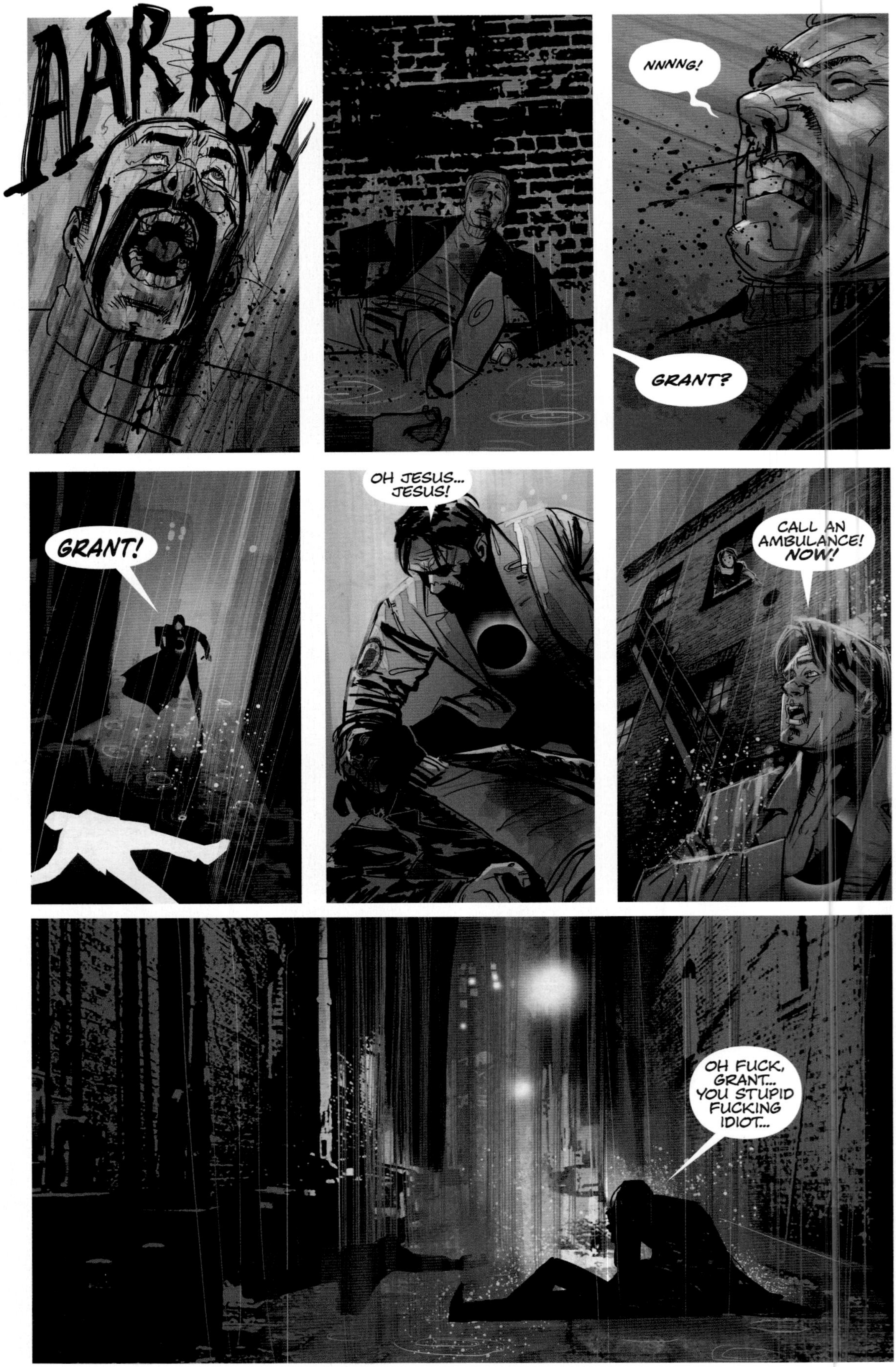
AARRGH
NNNNG!
GRANT?
GRANT!
OH JESUS... JESUS!
CALL AN AMBULANCE! NOW!
OH FUCK, GRANT... YOU STUPID FUCKING IDIOT...

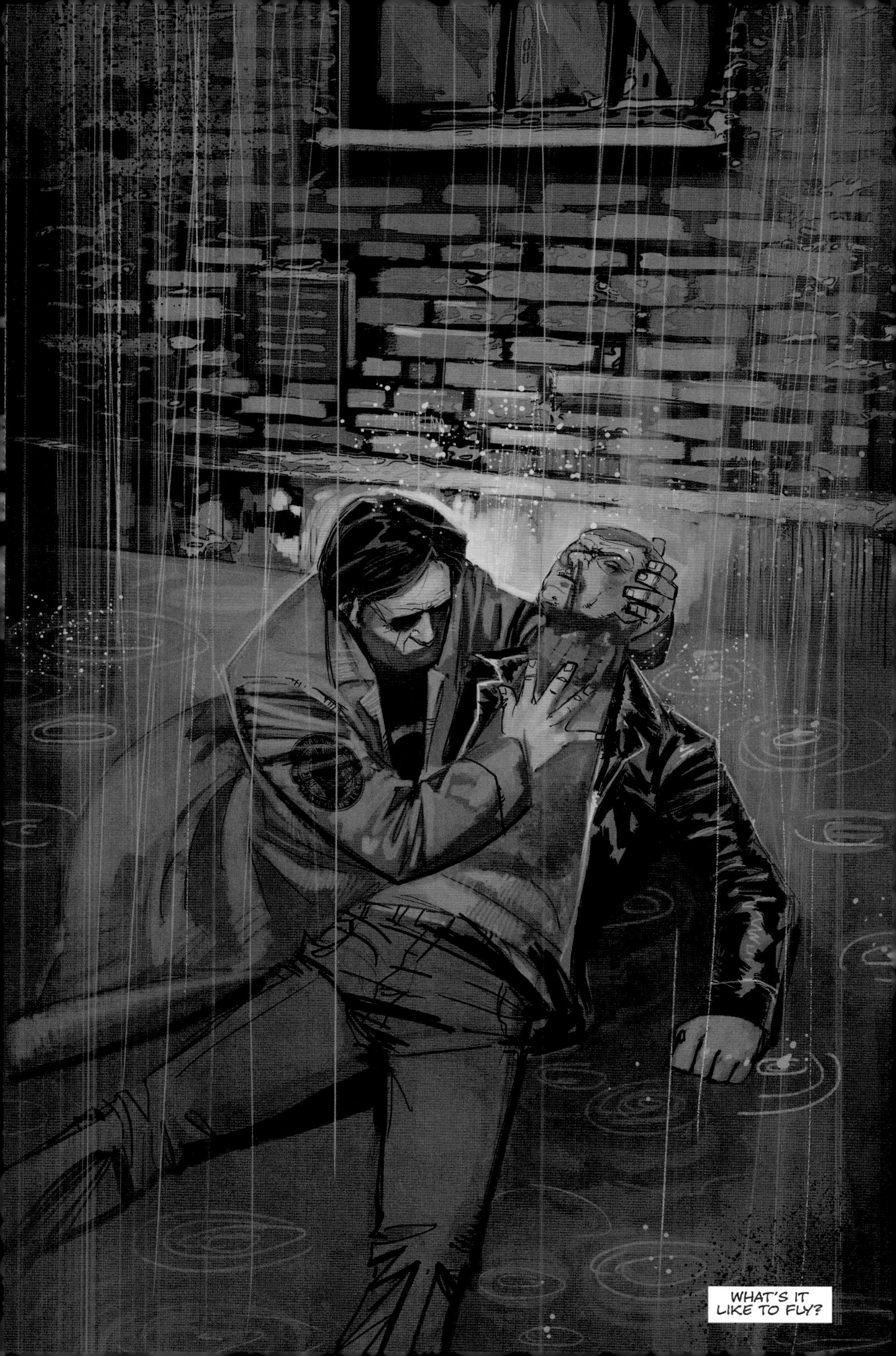
WHAT'S IT LIKE TO FLY?

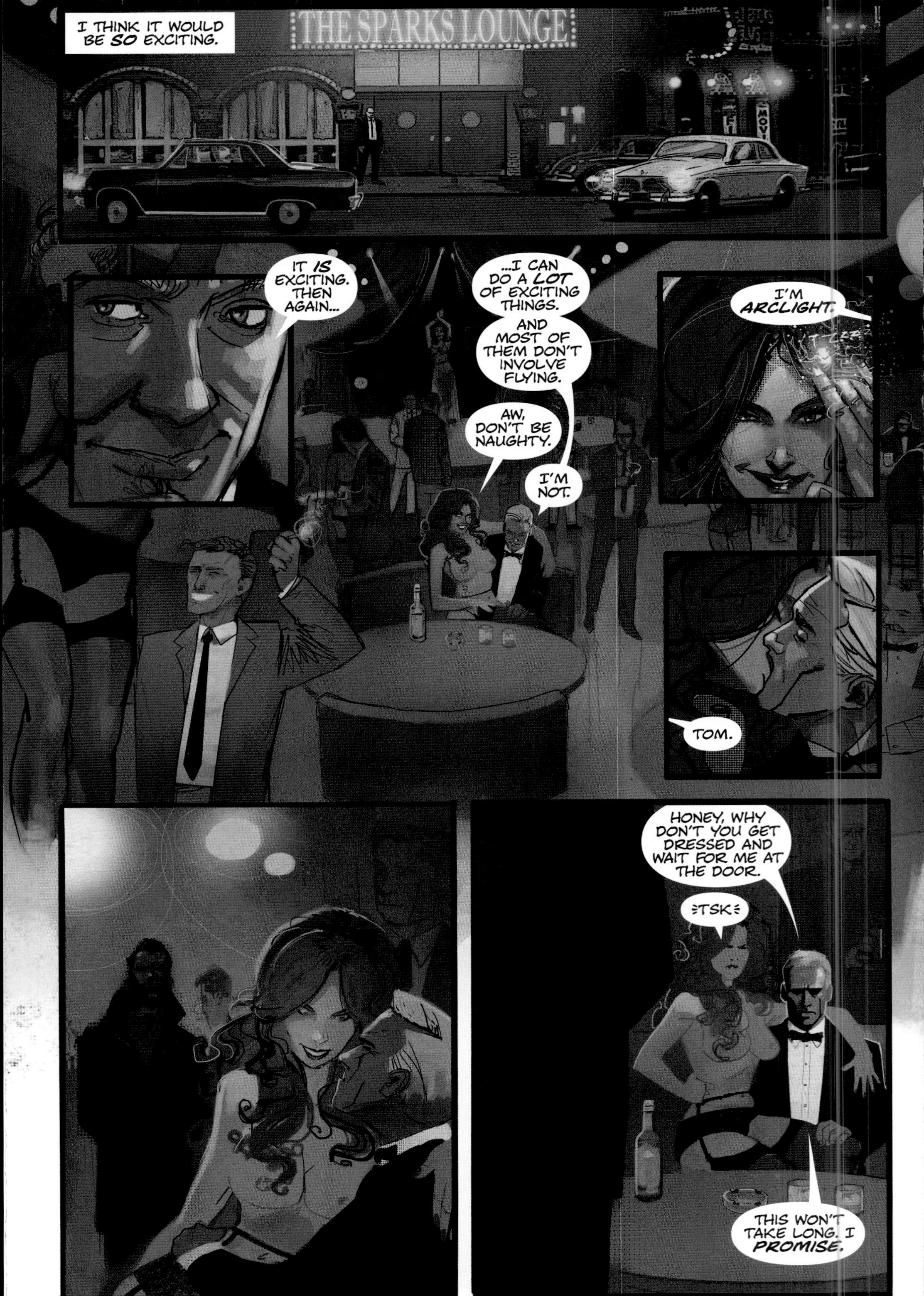
I THINK IT WOULD BE SO EXCITING.
THE SPARKS LOUNGE
IT IS EXCITING. THEN AGAIN...
...I CAN DO A LOT OF EXCITING THINGS.
AND MOST OF THEM DON'T INVOLVE FLYING.
AW, DON'T BE NAUGHTY.
I'M NOT.
I'M ARCLIGHT.
TOM.
HONEY, WHY DON'T YOU GET DRESSED AND WAIT FOR ME AT THE DOOR.
TSK
THIS WON'T TAKE LONG. I PROMISE.

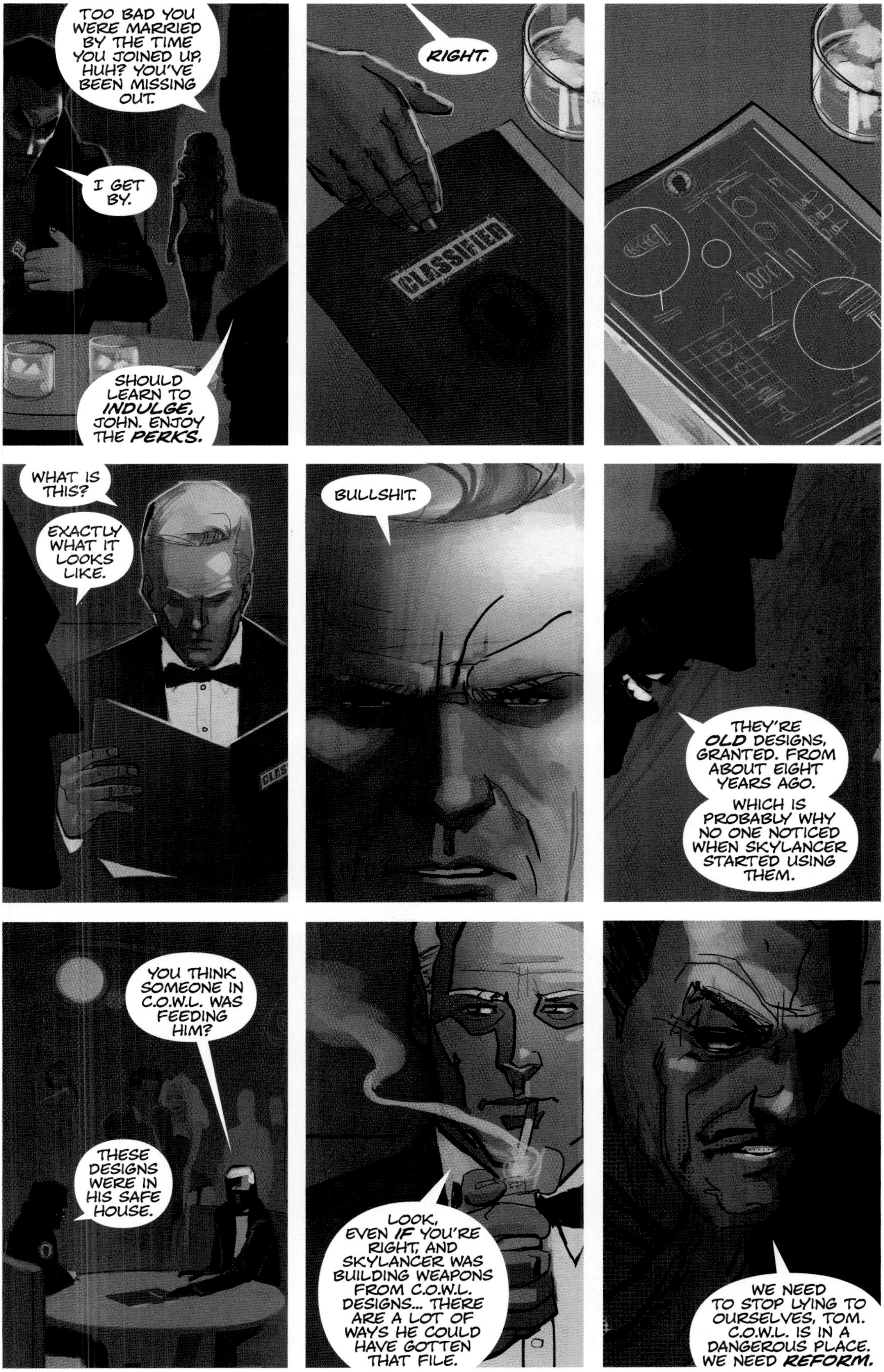

TOO BAD YOU WERE MARRIED BY THE TIME YOU JOINED UP, HUH? YOU'VE BEEN MISSING OUT.
I GET BY.
SHOULD LEARN TO *INDULGE*, JOHN. ENJOY THE *PERKS*.
RIGHT.
CLASSIFIED
WHAT IS THIS?
EXACTLY WHAT IT LOOKS LIKE.
BULLSHIT.
THEY'RE *OLD* DESIGNS, GRANTED. FROM ABOUT EIGHT YEARS AGO.
WHICH IS PROBABLY WHY NO ONE NOTICED WHEN SKYLANCER STARTED USING THEM.
YOU THINK SOMEONE IN C.O.W.L. WAS FEEDING HIM?
THESE DESIGNS WERE IN HIS SAFE HOUSE.
LOOK, EVEN *IF* YOU'RE RIGHT, AND SKYLANCER WAS BUILDING WEAPONS FROM C.O.W.L. DESIGNS... THERE ARE A LOT OF WAYS HE COULD HAVE GOTTEN THAT FILE.
WE NEED TO STOP LYING TO OURSELVES, TOM. C.O.W.L. IS IN A DANGEROUS PLACE. WE NEED *REFORM*.

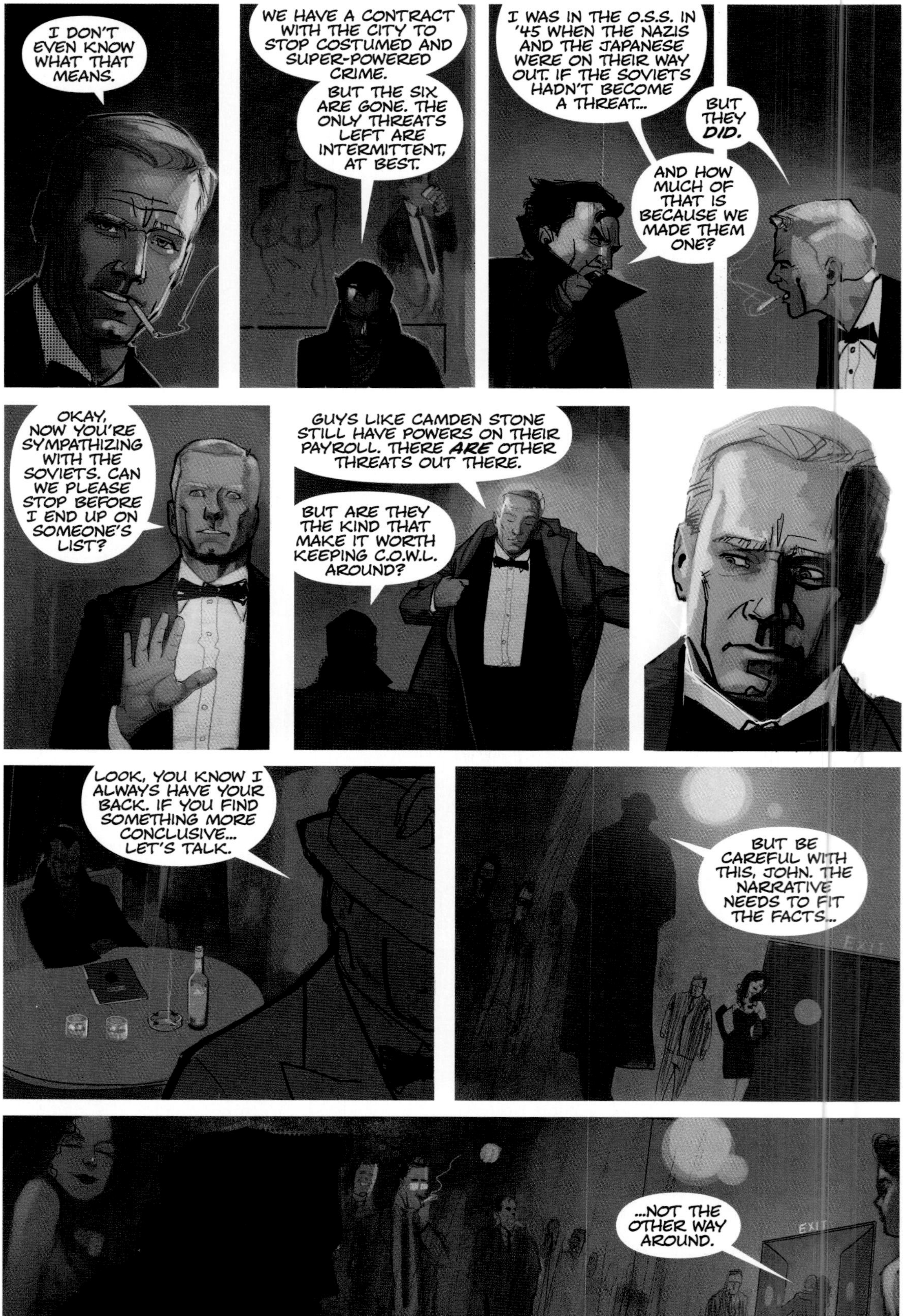
I DON'T EVEN KNOW WHAT THAT MEANS.
WE HAVE A CONTRACT WITH THE CITY TO STOP COSTUMED AND SUPER-POWERED CRIME.
BUT THE SIX ARE GONE. THE ONLY THREATS LEFT ARE INTERMITTENT, AT BEST.
I WAS IN THE O.S.S. IN '45 WHEN THE NAZIS AND THE JAPANESE WERE ON THEIR WAY OUT. IF THE SOVIETS HADN'T BECOME A THREAT...
BUT THEY *DID.*
AND HOW MUCH OF THAT IS BECAUSE WE MADE THEM ONE?
OKAY, NOW YOU'RE SYMPATHIZING WITH THE SOVIETS. CAN WE PLEASE STOP BEFORE I END UP ON SOMEONE'S LIST?
GUYS LIKE CAMDEN STONE STILL HAVE POWERS ON THEIR PAYROLL. THERE *ARE* OTHER THREATS OUT THERE.
BUT ARE THEY THE KIND THAT MAKE IT WORTH KEEPING C.O.W.L. AROUND?
LOOK, YOU KNOW I ALWAYS HAVE YOUR BACK. IF YOU FIND SOMETHING MORE CONCLUSIVE... LET'S TALK.
BUT BE CAREFUL WITH THIS, JOHN. THE NARRATIVE NEEDS TO FIT THE FACTS...
EXIT
...NOT THE OTHER WAY AROUND.
EXIT

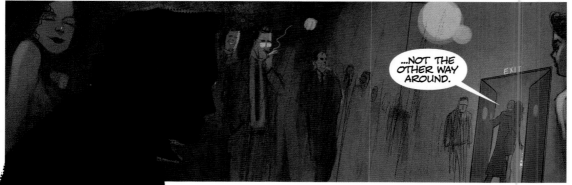

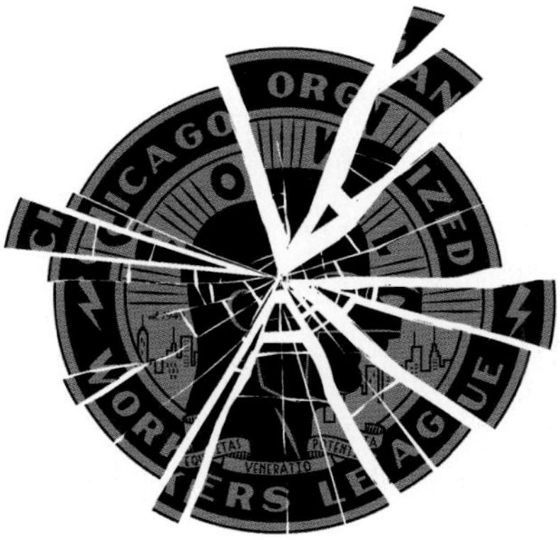
CHICAGO ORGANIZED WORKERS LEAGUE

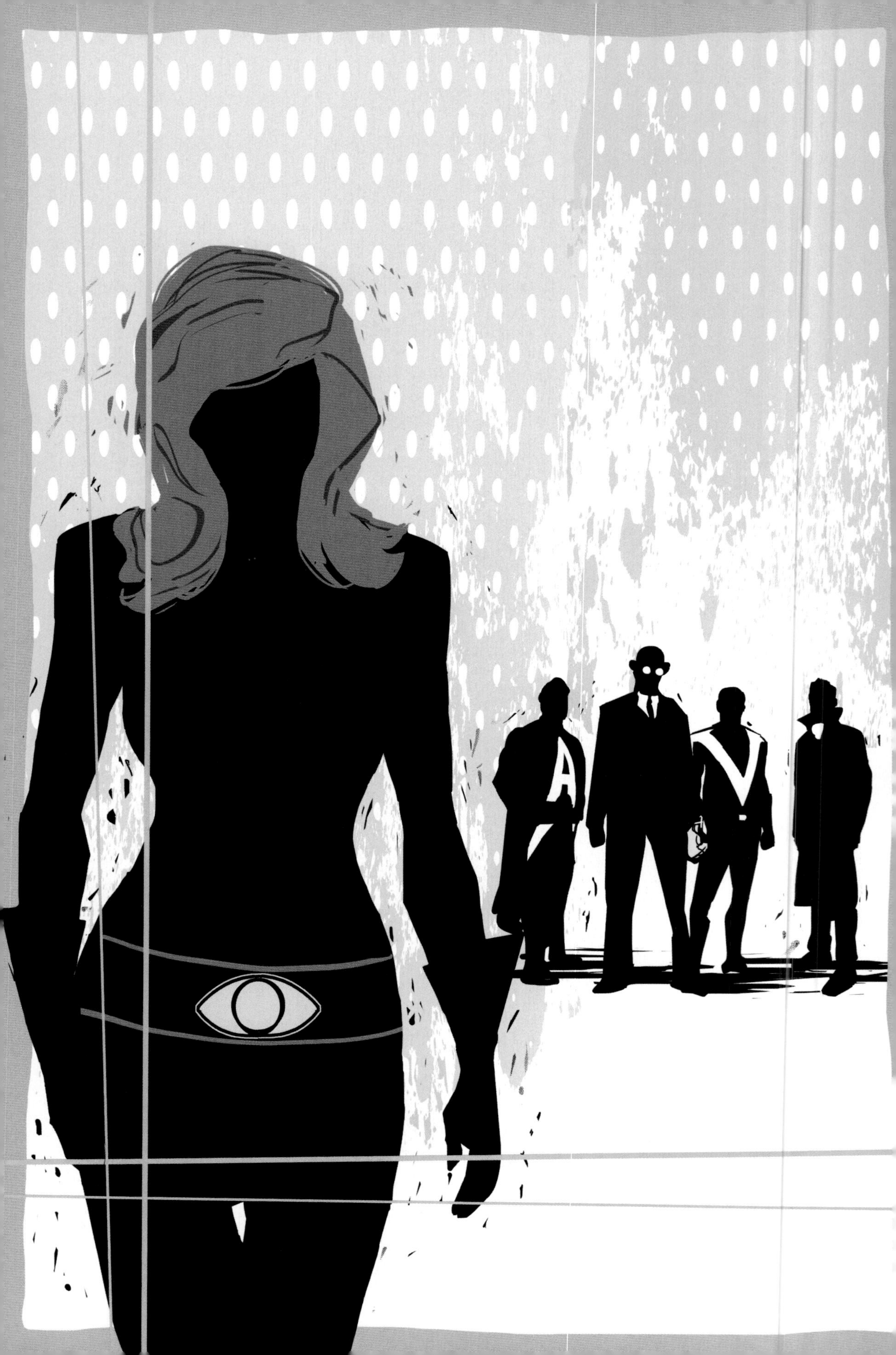

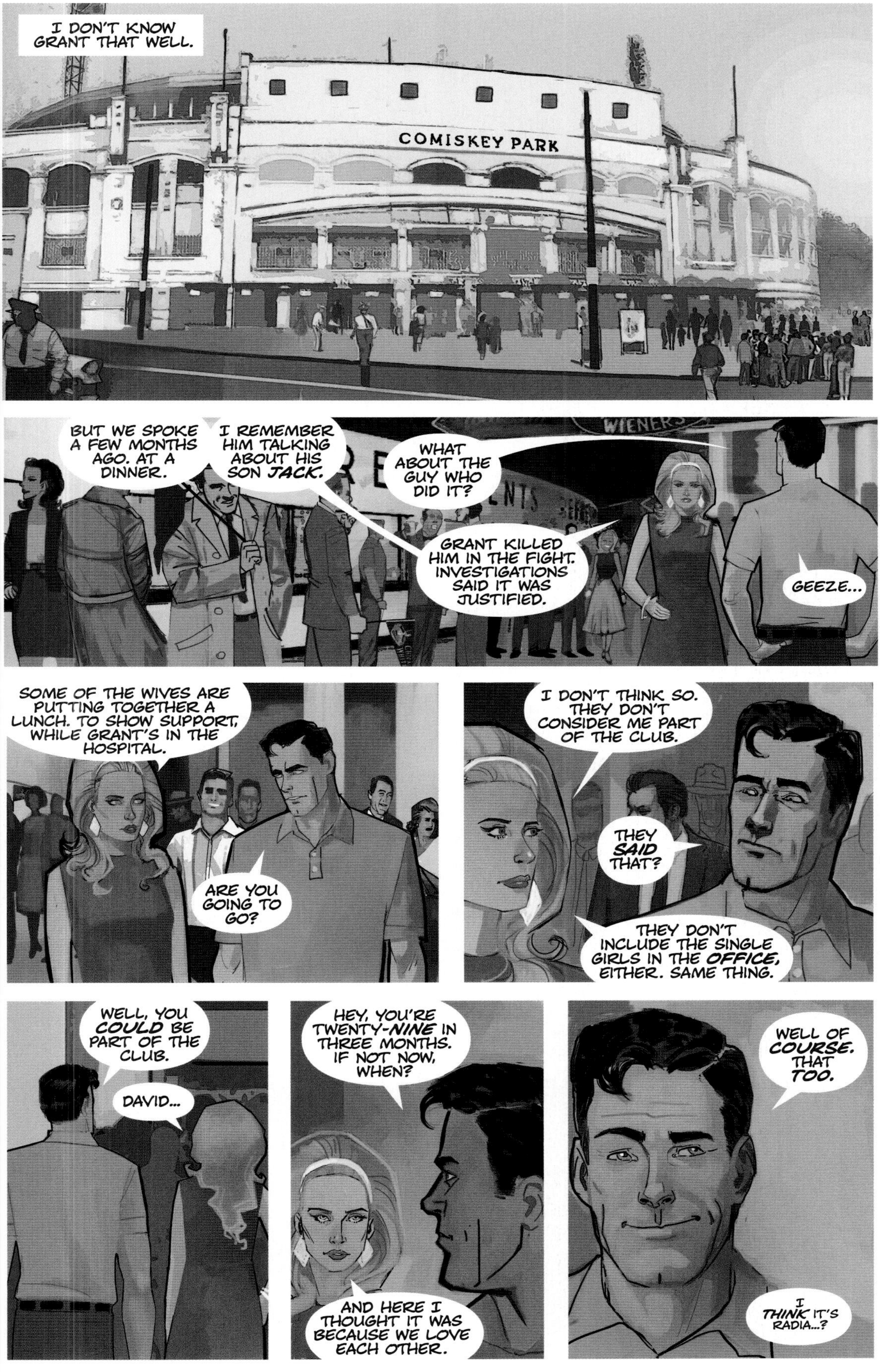
I DON'T KNOW GRANT THAT WELL.
COMISKEY PARK
BUT WE SPOKE A FEW MONTHS AGO. AT A DINNER.
I REMEMBER HIM TALKING ABOUT HIS SON *JACK.*
WHAT ABOUT THE GUY WHO DID IT?
GRANT KILLED HIM IN THE FIGHT. INVESTIGATIONS SAID IT WAS JUSTIFIED.
GEEZE...
SOME OF THE WIVES ARE PUTTING TOGETHER A LUNCH. TO SHOW SUPPORT, WHILE GRANT'S IN THE HOSPITAL.
ARE YOU GOING TO GO?
I DON'T THINK SO. THEY DON'T CONSIDER ME PART OF THE CLUB.
THEY *SAID* THAT?
THEY DON'T INCLUDE THE SINGLE GIRLS IN THE *OFFICE,* EITHER. SAME THING.
WELL, YOU *COULD* BE PART OF THE CLUB.
DAVID...
HEY, YOU'RE TWENTY-*NINE* IN THREE MONTHS. IF NOT NOW, WHEN?
AND HERE I THOUGHT IT WAS BECAUSE WE LOVE EACH OTHER.
WELL OF *COURSE.* THAT *TOO.*
I *THINK* IT'S RADIA...?

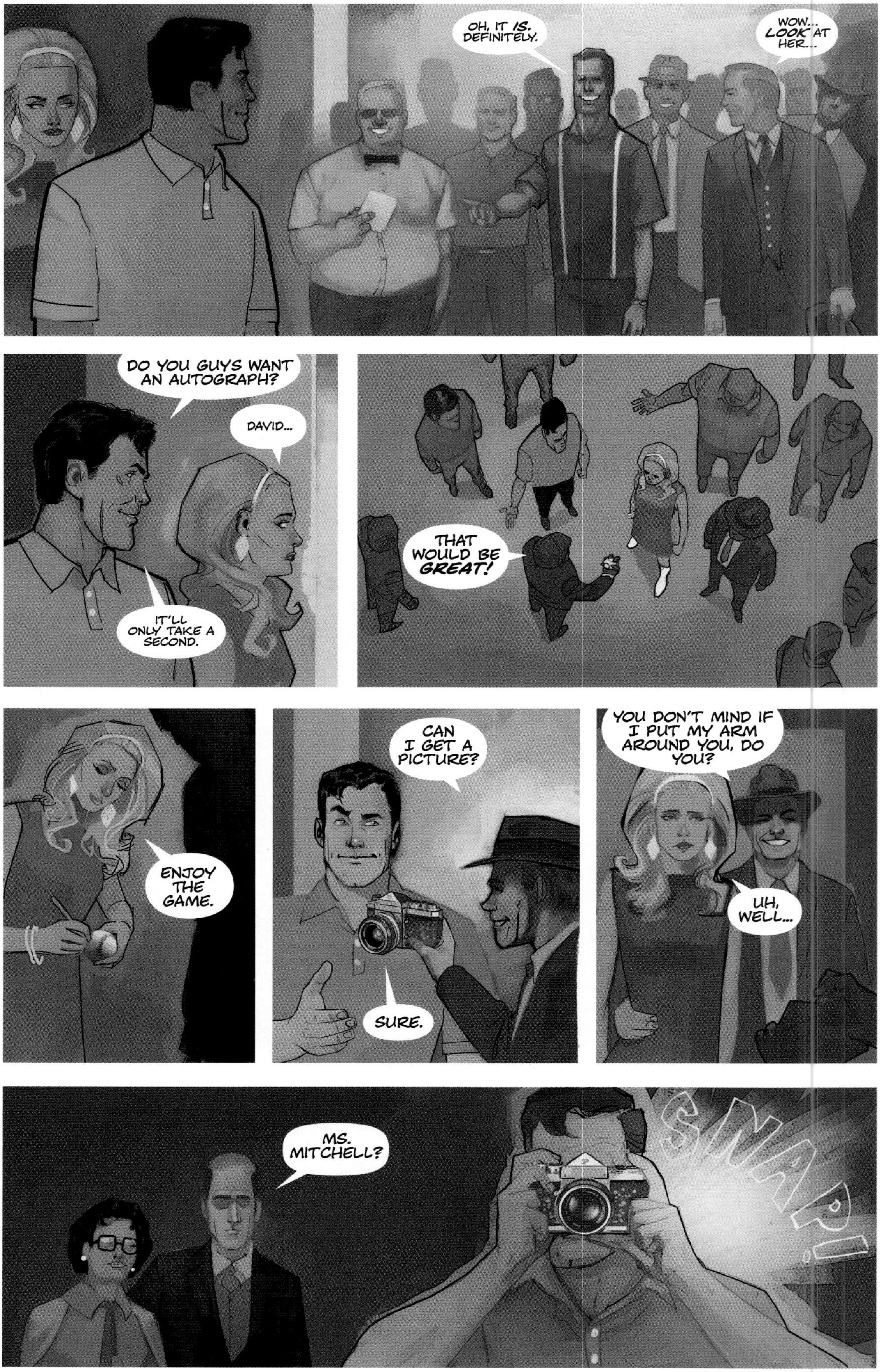
OH, IT *IS.* DEFINITELY.
WOW... *LOOK* AT HER...
DO YOU GUYS WANT AN AUTOGRAPH?
DAVID...
IT'LL ONLY TAKE A SECOND.
THAT WOULD BE *GREAT!*
ENJOY THE GAME.
CAN I GET A PICTURE?
SURE.
YOU DON'T MIND IF I PUT MY ARM AROUND YOU, DO YOU?
UH, WELL...
MS. MITCHELL?
SNAP!

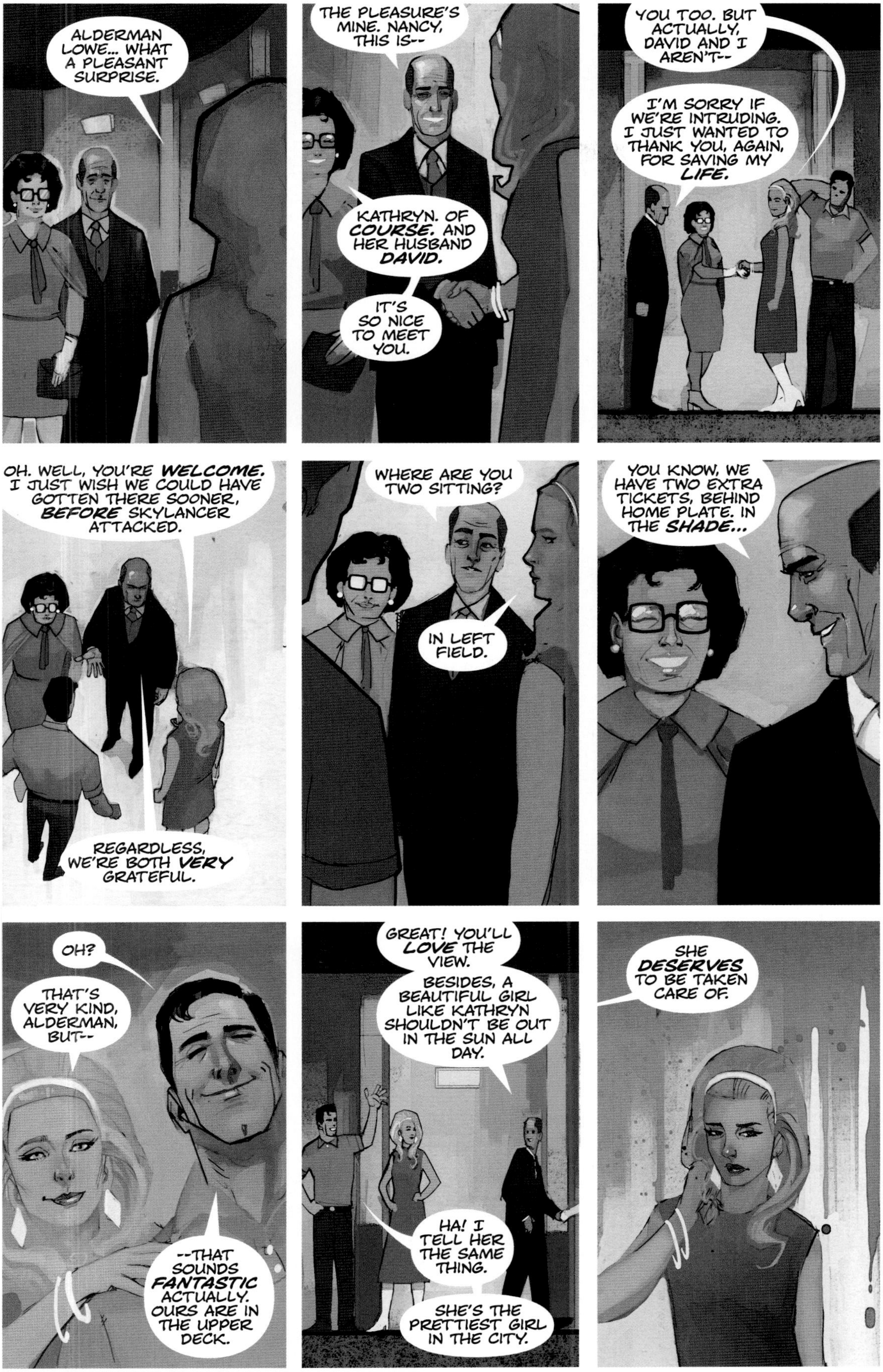
ALDERMAN LOWE... WHAT A PLEASANT SURPRISE.
THE PLEASURE'S MINE. NANCY, THIS IS--
KATHRYN. OF COURSE. AND HER HUSBAND DAVID.
IT'S SO NICE TO MEET YOU.
YOU TOO. BUT ACTUALLY, DAVID AND I AREN'T--
I'M SORRY IF WE'RE INTRUDING. I JUST WANTED TO THANK YOU, AGAIN, FOR SAVING MY LIFE.
OH. WELL, YOU'RE WELCOME. I JUST WISH WE COULD HAVE GOTTEN THERE SOONER, BEFORE SKYLANCER ATTACKED.
REGARDLESS, WE'RE BOTH VERY GRATEFUL.
WHERE ARE YOU TWO SITTING?
IN LEFT FIELD.
YOU KNOW, WE HAVE TWO EXTRA TICKETS, BEHIND HOME PLATE. IN THE SHADE...
OH?
THAT'S VERY KIND, ALDERMAN, BUT--
--THAT SOUNDS FANTASTIC ACTUALLY. OURS ARE IN THE UPPER DECK.
GREAT! YOU'LL LOVE THE VIEW.
BESIDES, A BEAUTIFUL GIRL LIKE KATHRYN SHOULDN'T BE OUT IN THE SUN ALL DAY.
HA! I TELL HER THE SAME THING.
SHE'S THE PRETTIEST GIRL IN THE CITY.
SHE DESERVES TO BE TAKEN CARE OF.

CHAPTER 3
Perception

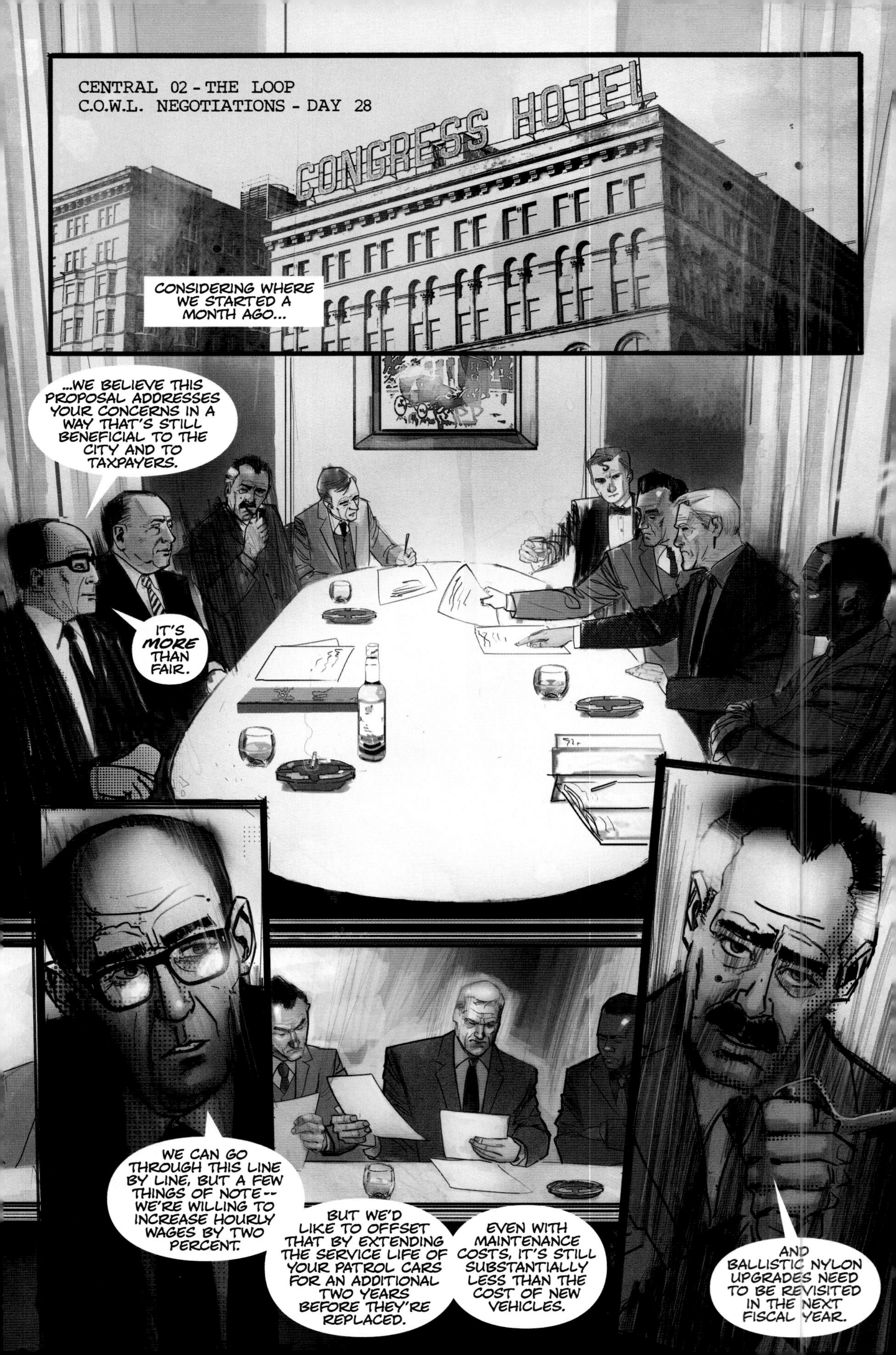
CENTRAL 02 - THE LOOP
C.O.W.L. NEGOTIATIONS - DAY 28
CONGRESS HOTEL
CONSIDERING WHERE WE STARTED A MONTH AGO...
...WE BELIEVE THIS PROPOSAL ADDRESSES YOUR CONCERNS IN A WAY THAT'S STILL BENEFICIAL TO THE CITY AND TO TAXPAYERS.
IT'S MORE THAN FAIR.
WE CAN GO THROUGH THIS LINE BY LINE, BUT A FEW THINGS OF NOTE-- WE'RE WILLING TO INCREASE HOURLY WAGES BY TWO PERCENT.
BUT WE'D LIKE TO OFFSET THAT BY EXTENDING THE SERVICE LIFE OF YOUR PATROL CARS FOR AN ADDITIONAL TWO YEARS BEFORE THEY'RE REPLACED.
EVEN WITH MAINTENANCE COSTS, IT'S STILL SUBSTANTIALLY LESS THAN THE COST OF NEW VEHICLES.
AND BALLISTIC NYLON UPGRADES NEED TO BE REVISITED IN THE NEXT FISCAL YEAR.

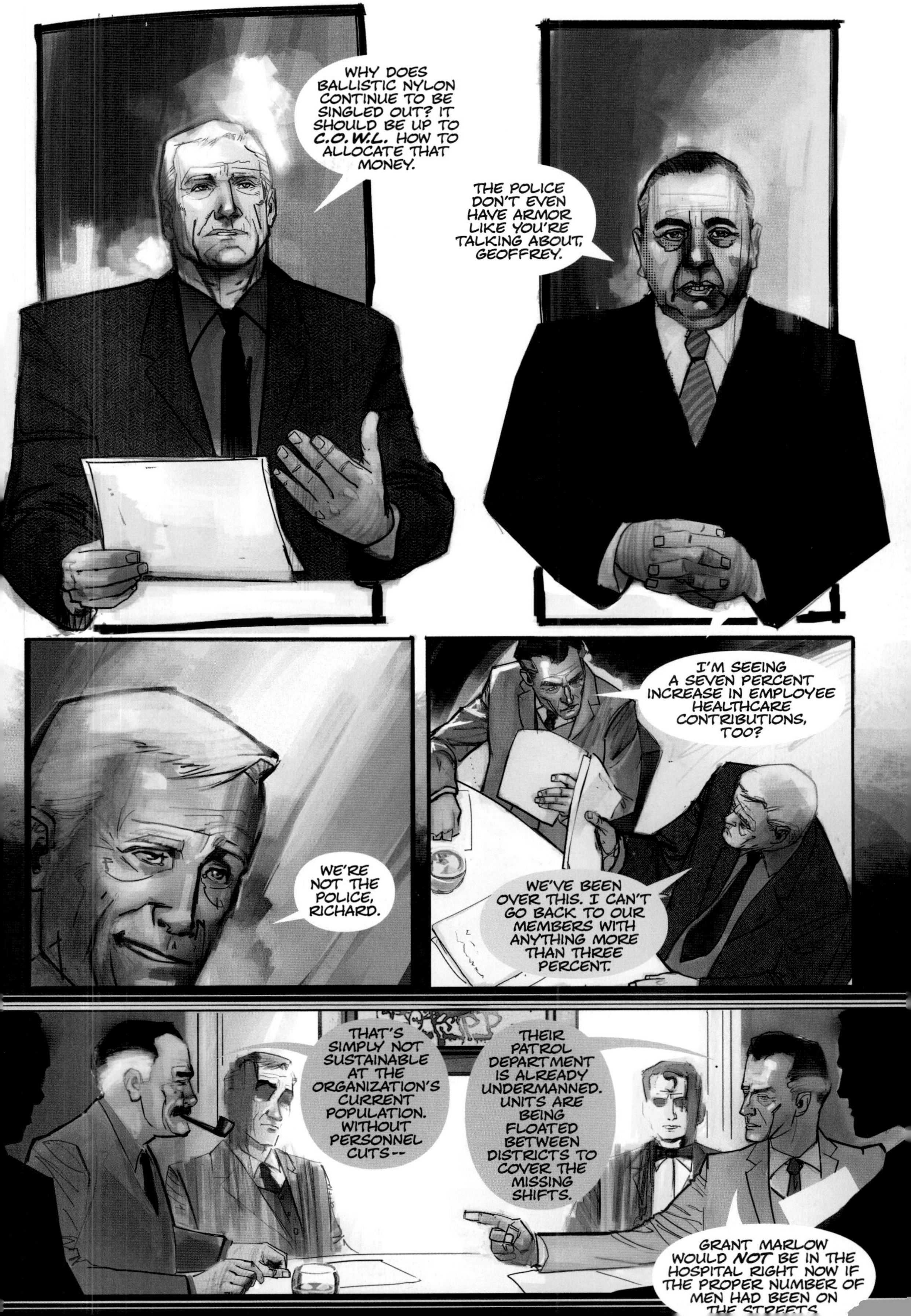

WHY DOES BALLISTIC NYLON CONTINUE TO BE SINGLED OUT? IT SHOULD BE UP TO C.O.W.L. HOW TO ALLOCATE THAT MONEY.
THE POLICE DON'T EVEN HAVE ARMOR LIKE YOU'RE TALKING ABOUT, GEOFFREY.
WE'RE NOT THE POLICE, RICHARD.
I'M SEEING A SEVEN PERCENT INCREASE IN EMPLOYEE HEALTHCARE CONTRIBUTIONS, TOO?
WE'VE BEEN OVER THIS. I CAN'T GO BACK TO OUR MEMBERS WITH ANYTHING MORE THAN THREE PERCENT.
THAT'S SIMPLY NOT SUSTAINABLE AT THE ORGANIZATION'S CURRENT POPULATION. WITHOUT PERSONNEL CUTS--
THEIR PATROL DEPARTMENT IS ALREADY UNDERMANNED. UNITS ARE BEING FLOATED BETWEEN DISTRICTS TO COVER THE MISSING SHIFTS.
GRANT MARLOW WOULD NOT BE IN THE HOSPITAL RIGHT NOW IF THE PROPER NUMBER OF MEN HAD BEEN ON

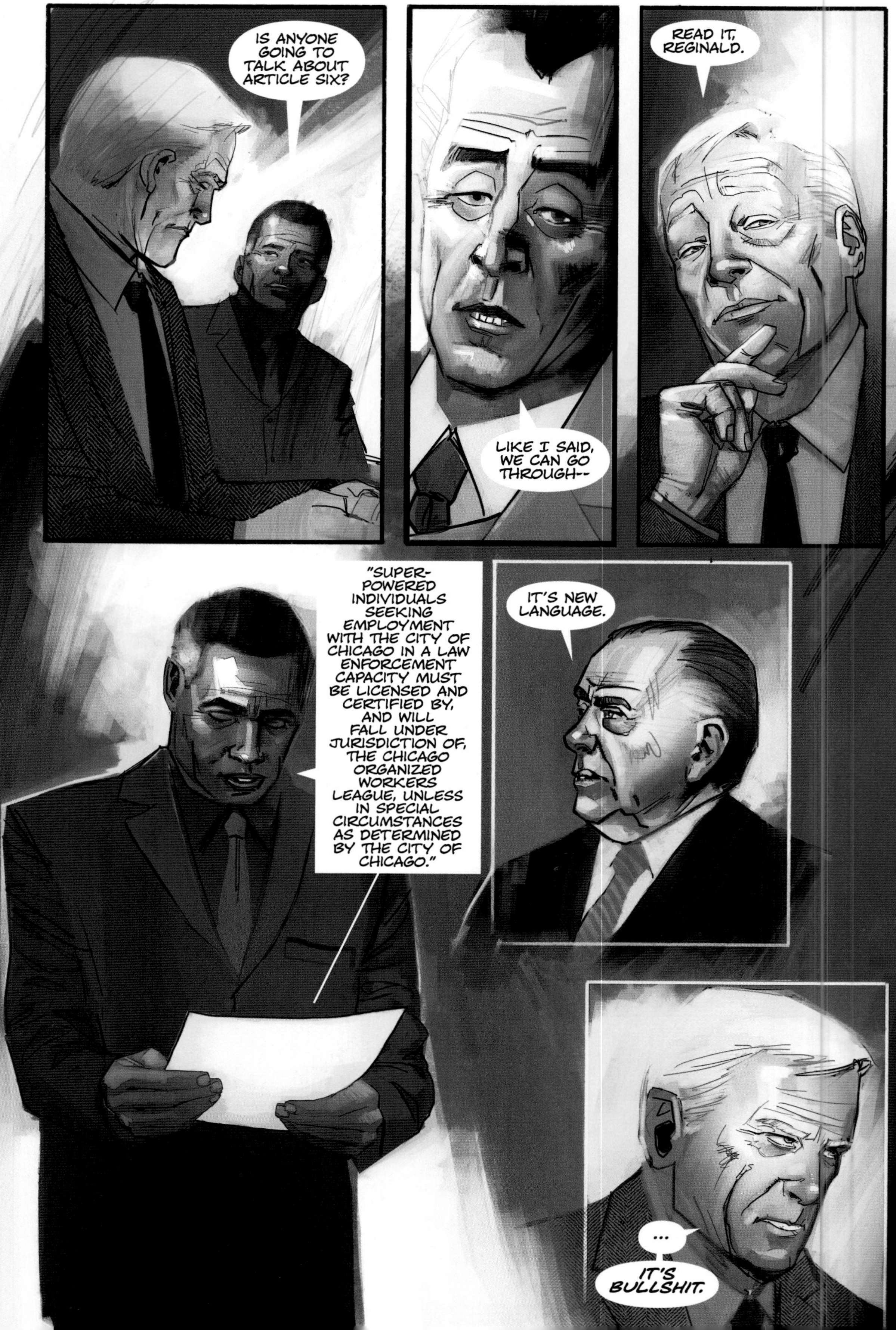
IS ANYONE GOING TO TALK ABOUT ARTICLE SIX?
LIKE I SAID, WE CAN GO THROUGH--
READ IT, REGINALD.
"SUPER-POWERED INDIVIDUALS SEEKING EMPLOYMENT WITH THE CITY OF CHICAGO IN A LAW ENFORCEMENT CAPACITY MUST BE LICENSED AND CERTIFIED BY, AND WILL FALL UNDER JURISDICTION OF, THE CHICAGO ORGANIZED WORKERS LEAGUE, UNLESS IN SPECIAL CIRCUMSTANCES AS DETERMINED BY THE CITY OF CHICAGO."
IT'S NEW LANGUAGE.
...
IT'S BULLSHIT.

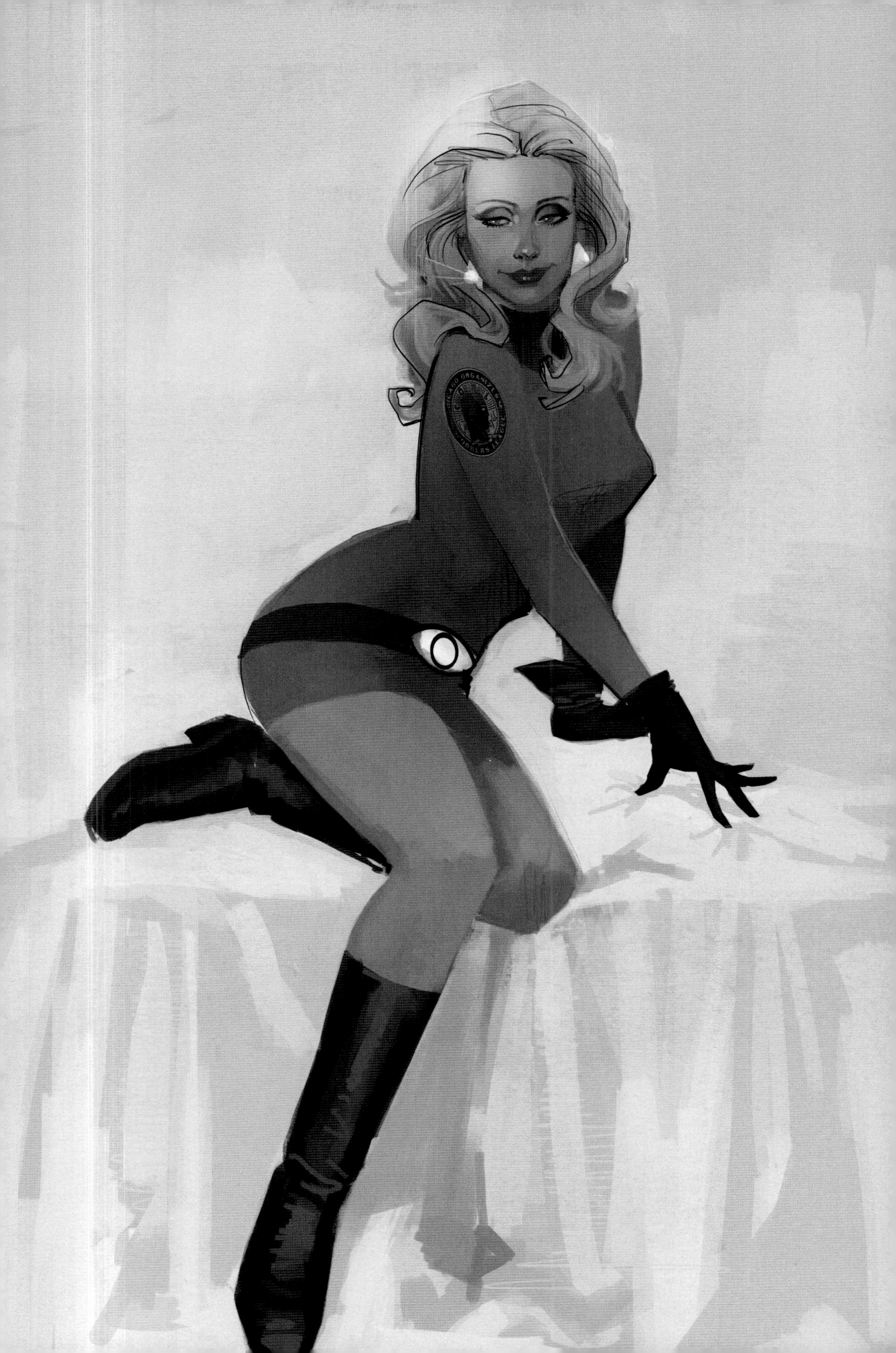

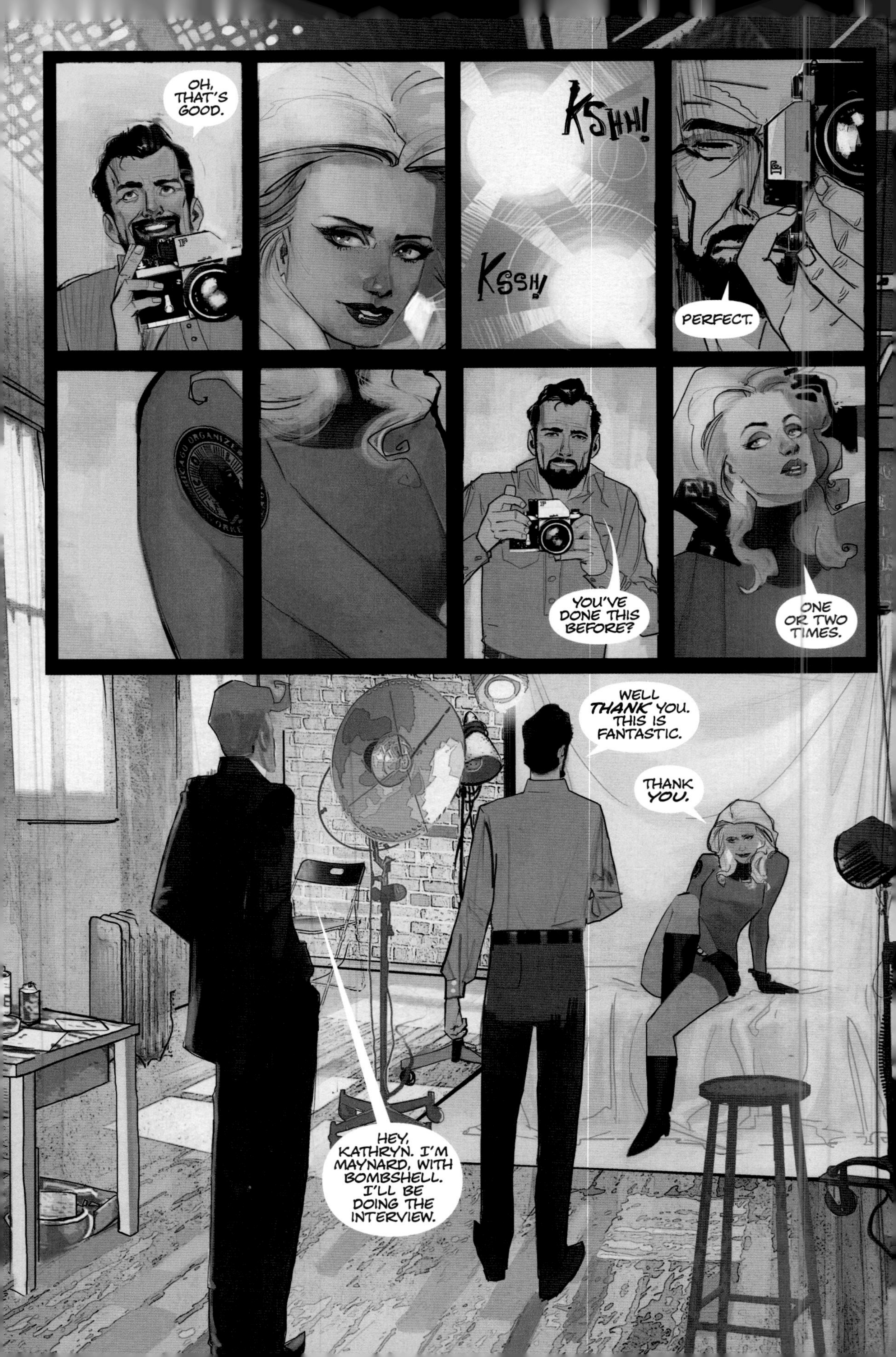
OH, THAT'S GOOD.
KSHH!
KSSH!
PERFECT.
YOU'VE DONE THIS BEFORE?
ONE OR TWO TIMES.
WELL *THANK* YOU. THIS IS FANTASTIC.
THANK *YOU.*
HEY, KATHRYN. I'M MAYNARD, WITH BOMBSHELL. I'LL BE DOING THE INTERVIEW.

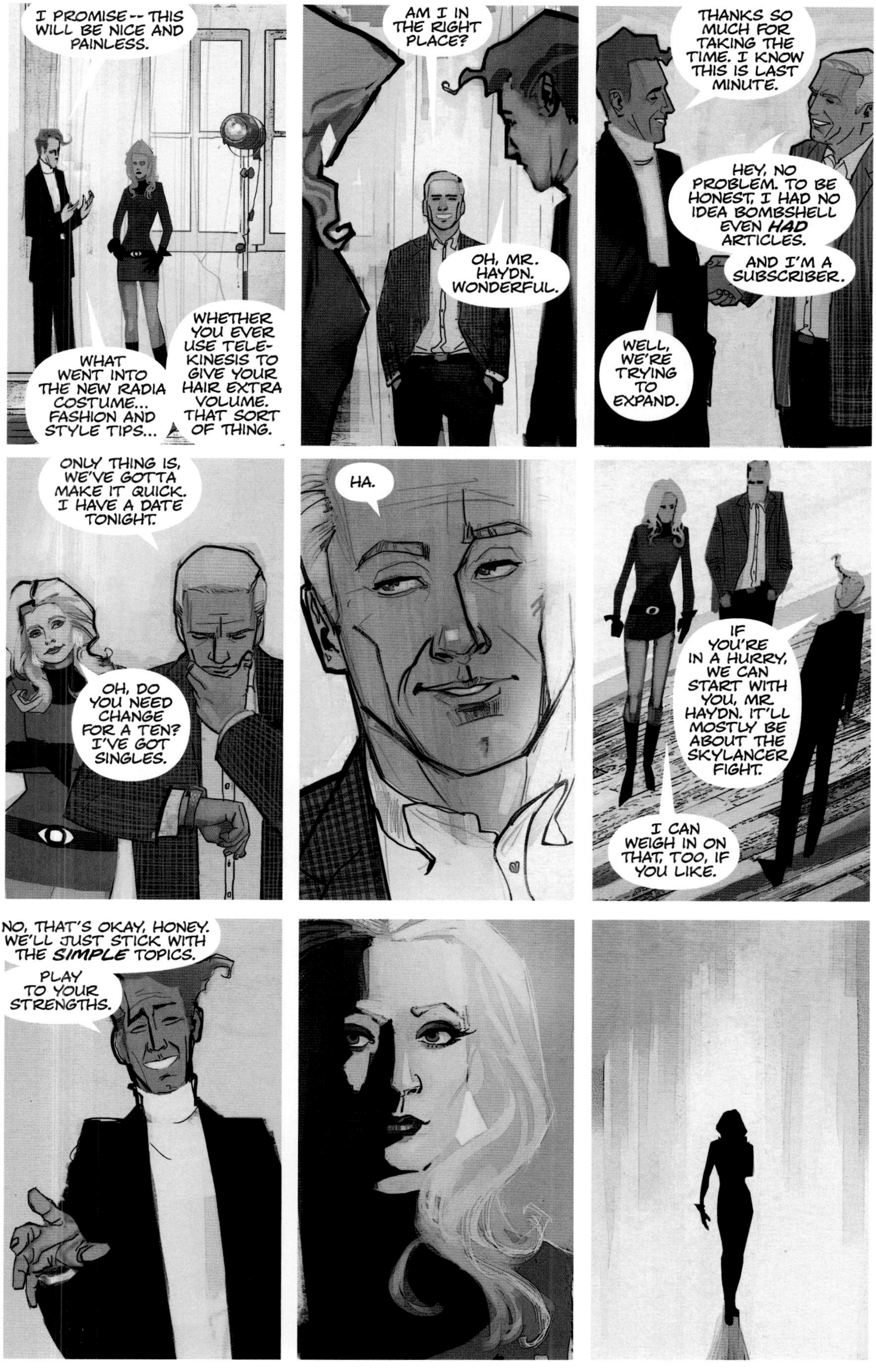
I PROMISE -- THIS WILL BE NICE AND PAINLESS.
WHAT WENT INTO THE NEW RADIA COSTUME... FASHION AND STYLE TIPS...
WHETHER YOU EVER USE TELE-KINESIS TO GIVE YOUR HAIR EXTRA VOLUME. THAT SORT OF THING.
AM I IN THE RIGHT PLACE?
OH, MR. HAYDN. WONDERFUL.
THANKS SO MUCH FOR TAKING THE TIME. I KNOW THIS IS LAST MINUTE.
HEY, NO PROBLEM. TO BE HONEST, I HAD NO IDEA BOMBSHELL EVEN HAD ARTICLES.
AND I'M A SUBSCRIBER.
WELL, WE'RE TRYING TO EXPAND.
ONLY THING IS, WE'VE GOTTA MAKE IT QUICK. I HAVE A DATE TONIGHT.
OH, DO YOU NEED CHANGE FOR A TEN? I'VE GOT SINGLES.
HA.
IF YOU'RE IN A HURRY, WE CAN START WITH YOU, MR. HAYDN. IT'LL MOSTLY BE ABOUT THE SKYLANCER FIGHT.
I CAN WEIGH IN ON THAT, TOO, IF YOU LIKE.
NO, THAT'S OKAY, HONEY. WE'LL JUST STICK WITH THE SIMPLE TOPICS.
PLAY TO YOUR STRENGTHS.

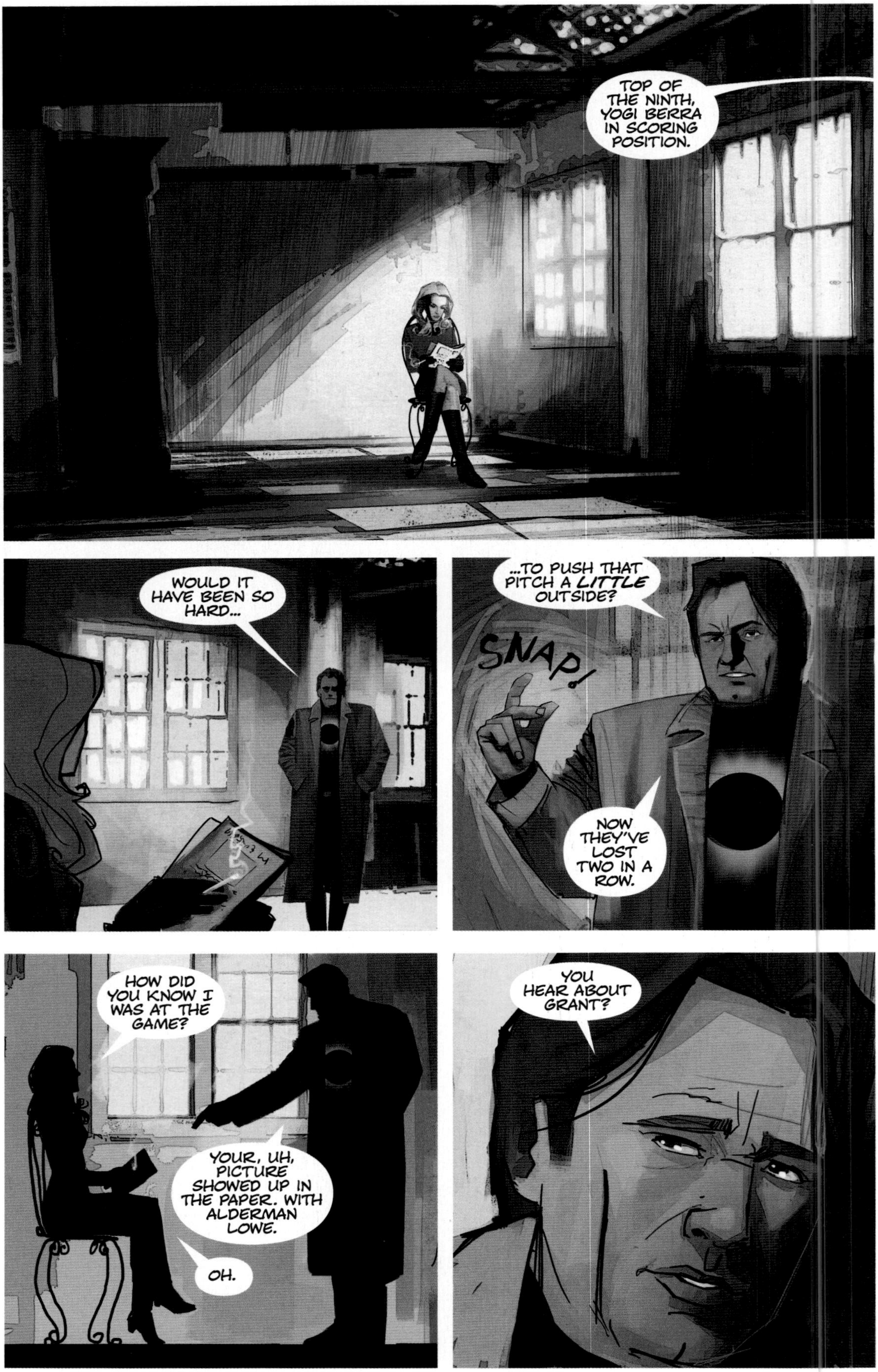
TOP OF THE NINTH, YOGI BERRA IN SCORING POSITION.
WOULD IT HAVE BEEN SO HARD...
...TO PUSH THAT PITCH A *LITTLE* OUTSIDE?
SNAP!
NOW THEY'VE LOST TWO IN A ROW.
HOW DID YOU KNOW I WAS AT THE GAME?
YOUR, UH, PICTURE SHOWED UP IN THE PAPER. WITH ALDERMAN LOWE.
OH.
YOU HEAR ABOUT GRANT?

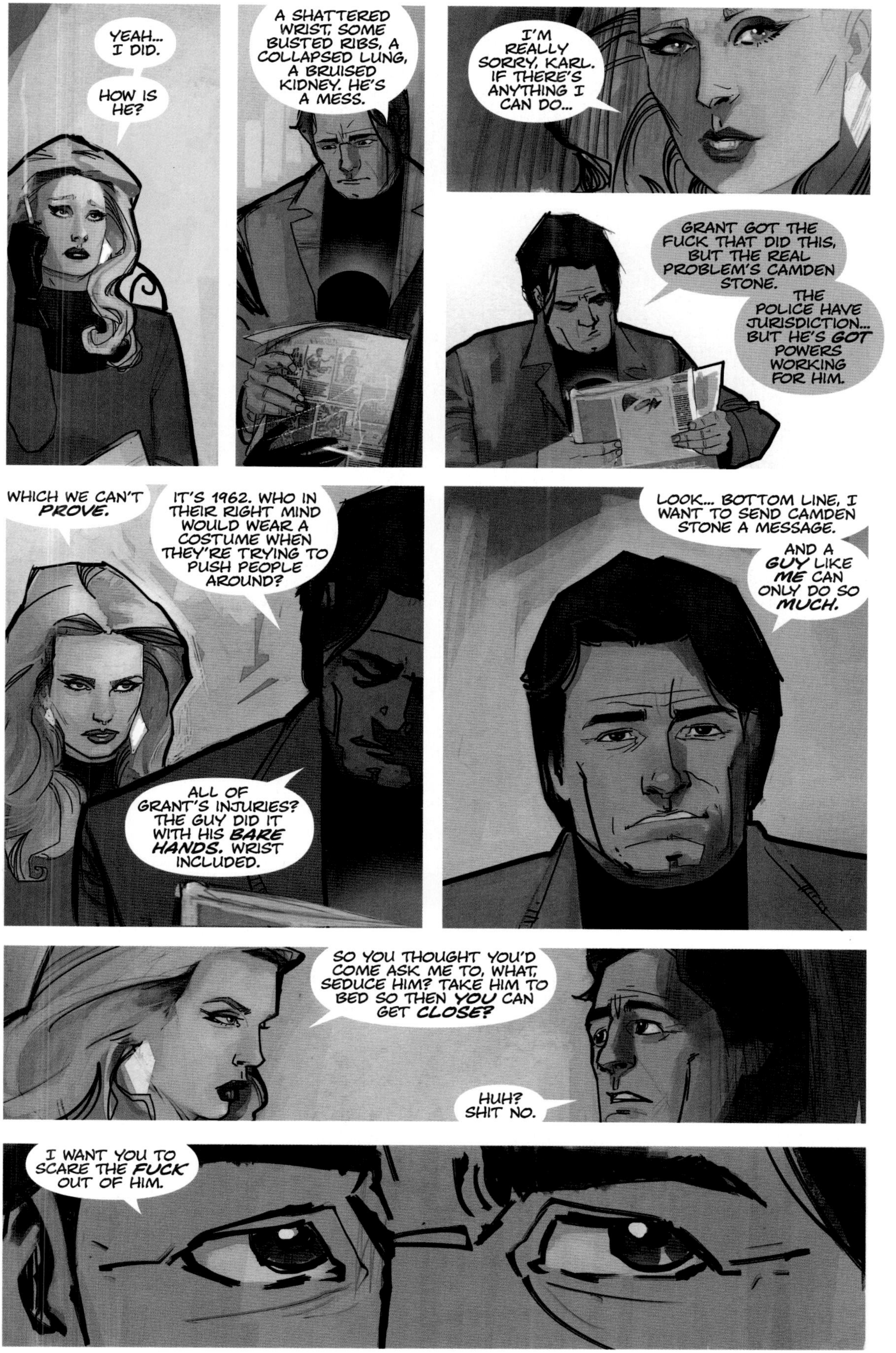
YEAH... I DID.
HOW IS HE?
A SHATTERED WRIST, SOME BUSTED RIBS, A COLLAPSED LUNG, A BRUISED KIDNEY. HE'S A MESS.
I'M REALLY SORRY, KARL. IF THERE'S ANYTHING I CAN DO...
GRANT GOT THE FUCK THAT DID THIS, BUT THE REAL PROBLEM'S CAMDEN STONE.
THE POLICE HAVE JURISDICTION... BUT HE'S GOT POWERS WORKING FOR HIM.
WHICH WE CAN'T PROVE.
IT'S 1962. WHO IN THEIR RIGHT MIND WOULD WEAR A COSTUME WHEN THEY'RE TRYING TO PUSH PEOPLE AROUND?
ALL OF GRANT'S INJURIES? THE GUY DID IT WITH HIS BARE HANDS. WRIST INCLUDED.
LOOK... BOTTOM LINE, I WANT TO SEND CAMDEN STONE A MESSAGE.
AND A GUY LIKE ME CAN ONLY DO SO MUCH.
SO YOU THOUGHT YOU'D COME ASK ME TO, WHAT, SEDUCE HIM? TAKE HIM TO BED SO THEN YOU CAN GET CLOSE?
HUH? SHIT NO.
I WANT YOU TO SCARE THE FUCK OUT OF HIM.

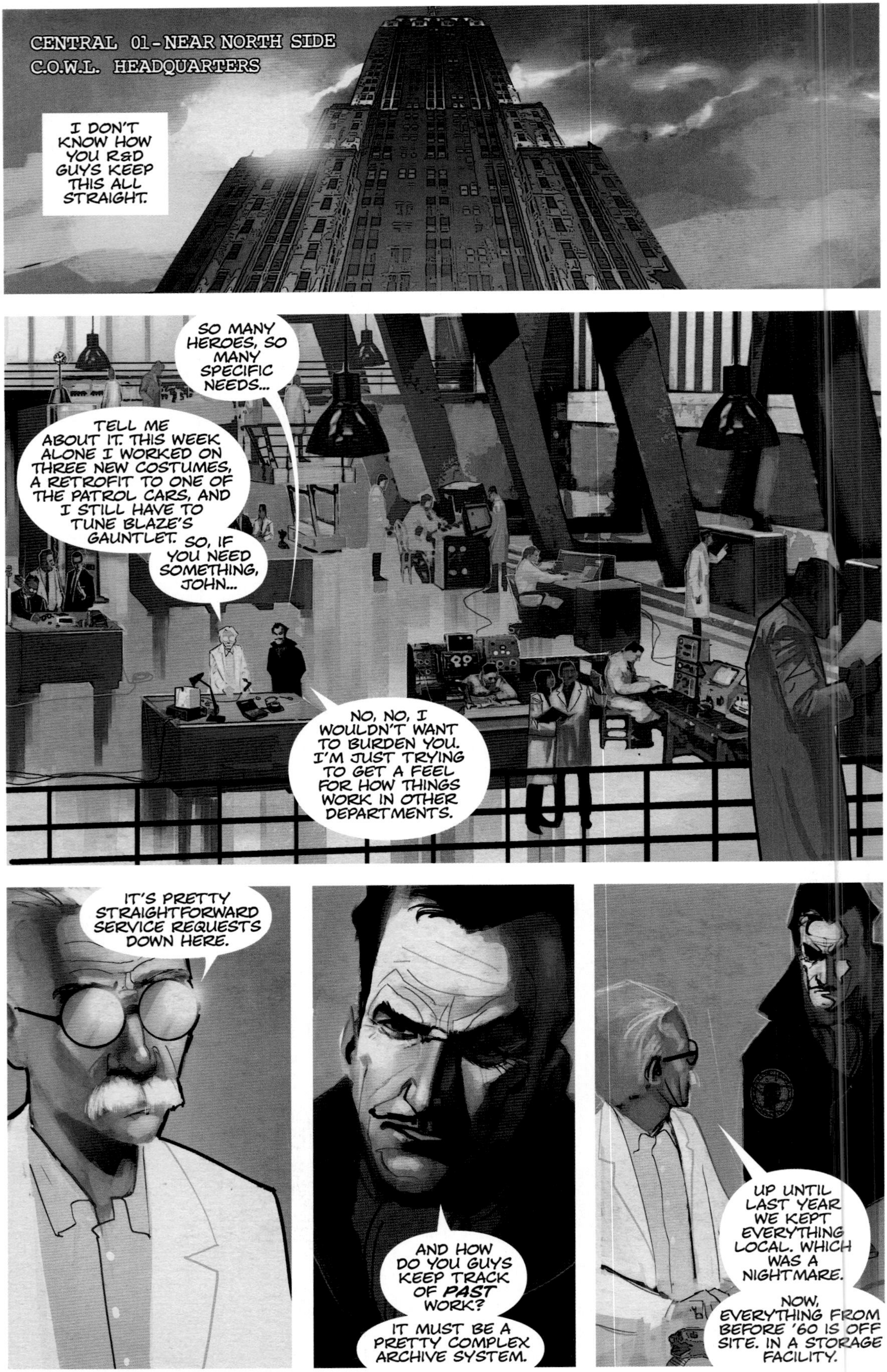
CENTRAL 01-NEAR NORTH SIDE
C.O.W.L. HEADQUARTERS
I DON'T KNOW HOW YOU R&D GUYS KEEP THIS ALL STRAIGHT.
SO MANY HEROES, SO MANY SPECIFIC NEEDS...
TELL ME ABOUT IT. THIS WEEK ALONE I WORKED ON THREE NEW COSTUMES, A RETROFIT TO ONE OF THE PATROL CARS, AND I STILL HAVE TO TUNE BLAZE'S GAUNTLET.
SO, IF YOU NEED SOMETHING, JOHN...
NO, NO, I WOULDN'T WANT TO BURDEN YOU. I'M JUST TRYING TO GET A FEEL FOR HOW THINGS WORK IN OTHER DEPARTMENTS.
IT'S PRETTY STRAIGHTFORWARD SERVICE REQUESTS DOWN HERE.
AND HOW DO YOU GUYS KEEP TRACK OF PAST WORK?
IT MUST BE A PRETTY COMPLEX ARCHIVE SYSTEM.
UP UNTIL LAST YEAR WE KEPT EVERYTHING LOCAL. WHICH WAS A NIGHTMARE.
NOW, EVERYTHING FROM BEFORE '60 IS OFF SITE. IN A STORAGE FACILITY.

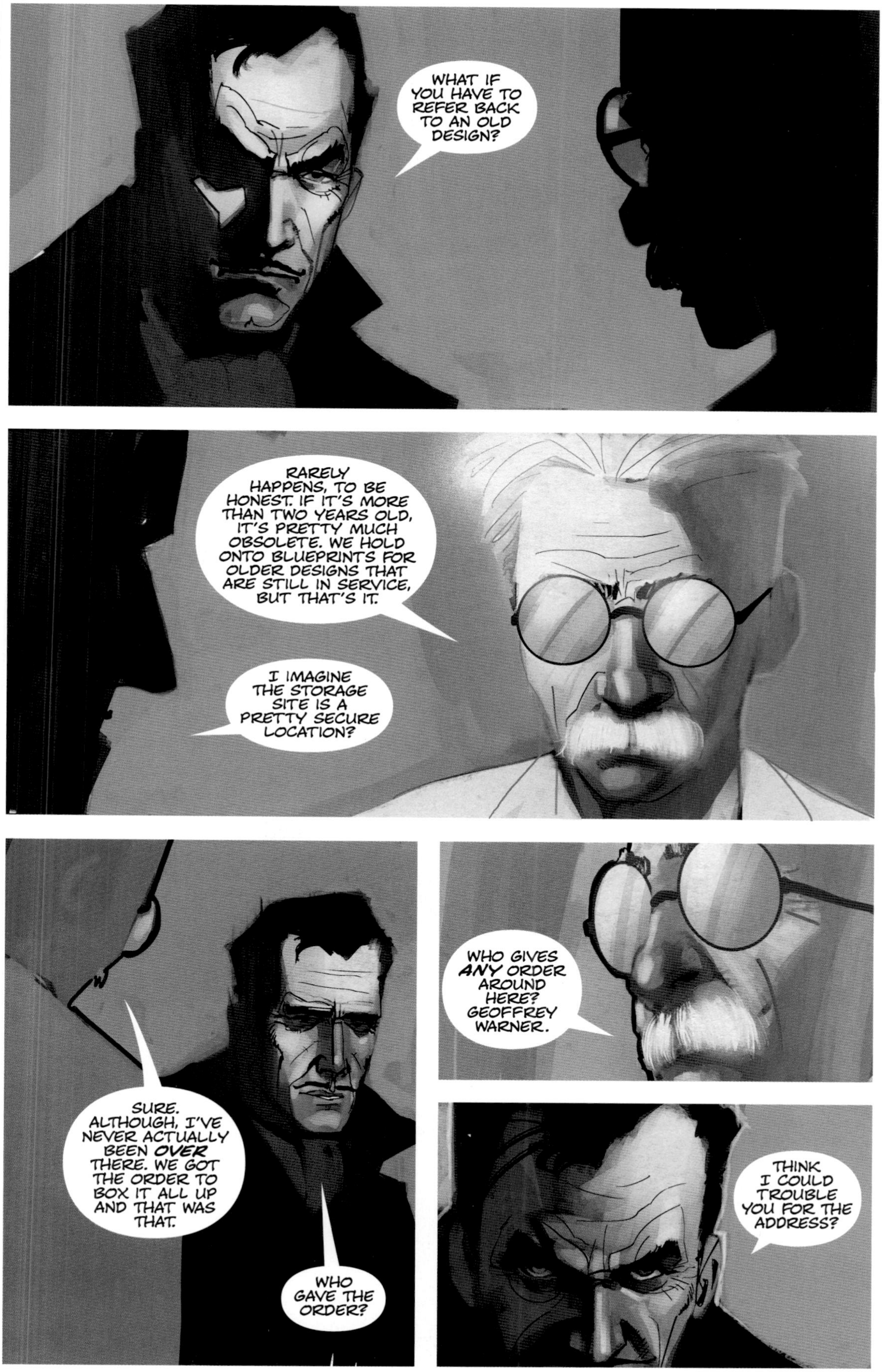
WHAT IF YOU HAVE TO REFER BACK TO AN OLD DESIGN?
RARELY HAPPENS, TO BE HONEST. IF IT'S MORE THAN TWO YEARS OLD, IT'S PRETTY MUCH OBSOLETE. WE HOLD ONTO BLUEPRINTS FOR OLDER DESIGNS THAT ARE STILL IN SERVICE, BUT THAT'S IT.
I IMAGINE THE STORAGE SITE IS A PRETTY SECURE LOCATION?
SURE. ALTHOUGH, I'VE NEVER ACTUALLY BEEN OVER THERE. WE GOT THE ORDER TO BOX IT ALL UP AND THAT WAS THAT.
WHO GAVE THE ORDER?
WHO GIVES ANY ORDER AROUND HERE? GEOFFREY WARNER.
THINK I COULD TROUBLE YOU FOR THE ADDRESS?

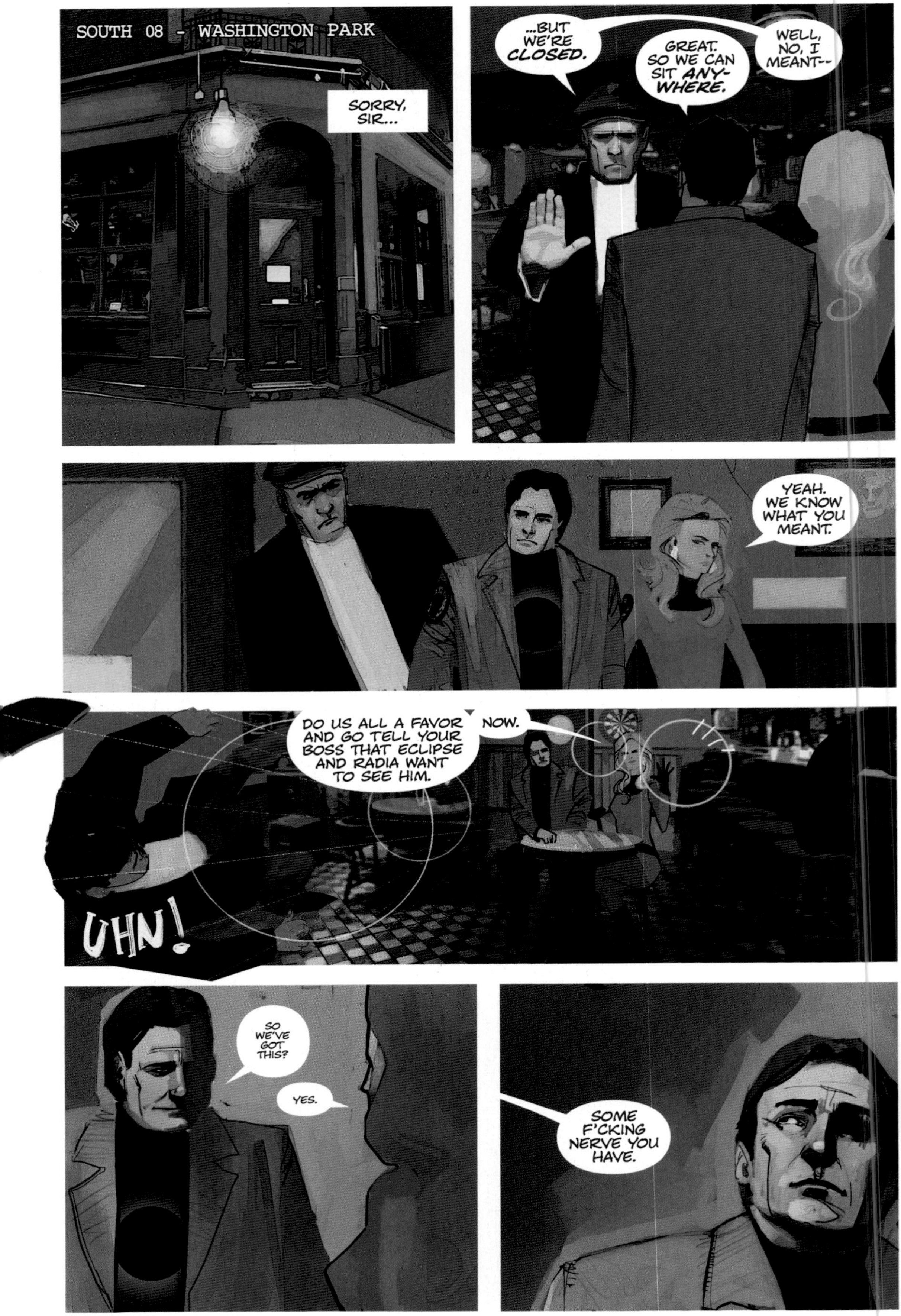
SOUTH 08 - WASHINGTON PARK
SORRY, SIR...
...BUT WE'RE CLOSED.
GREAT. SO WE CAN SIT ANYWHERE.
WELL, NO, I MEANT--
YEAH. WE KNOW WHAT YOU MEANT.
DO US ALL A FAVOR AND GO TELL YOUR BOSS THAT ECLIPSE AND RADIA WANT TO SEE HIM.
NOW.
UHN!
SO WE'VE GOT THIS?
YES.
SOME F'CKING NERVE YOU HAVE.

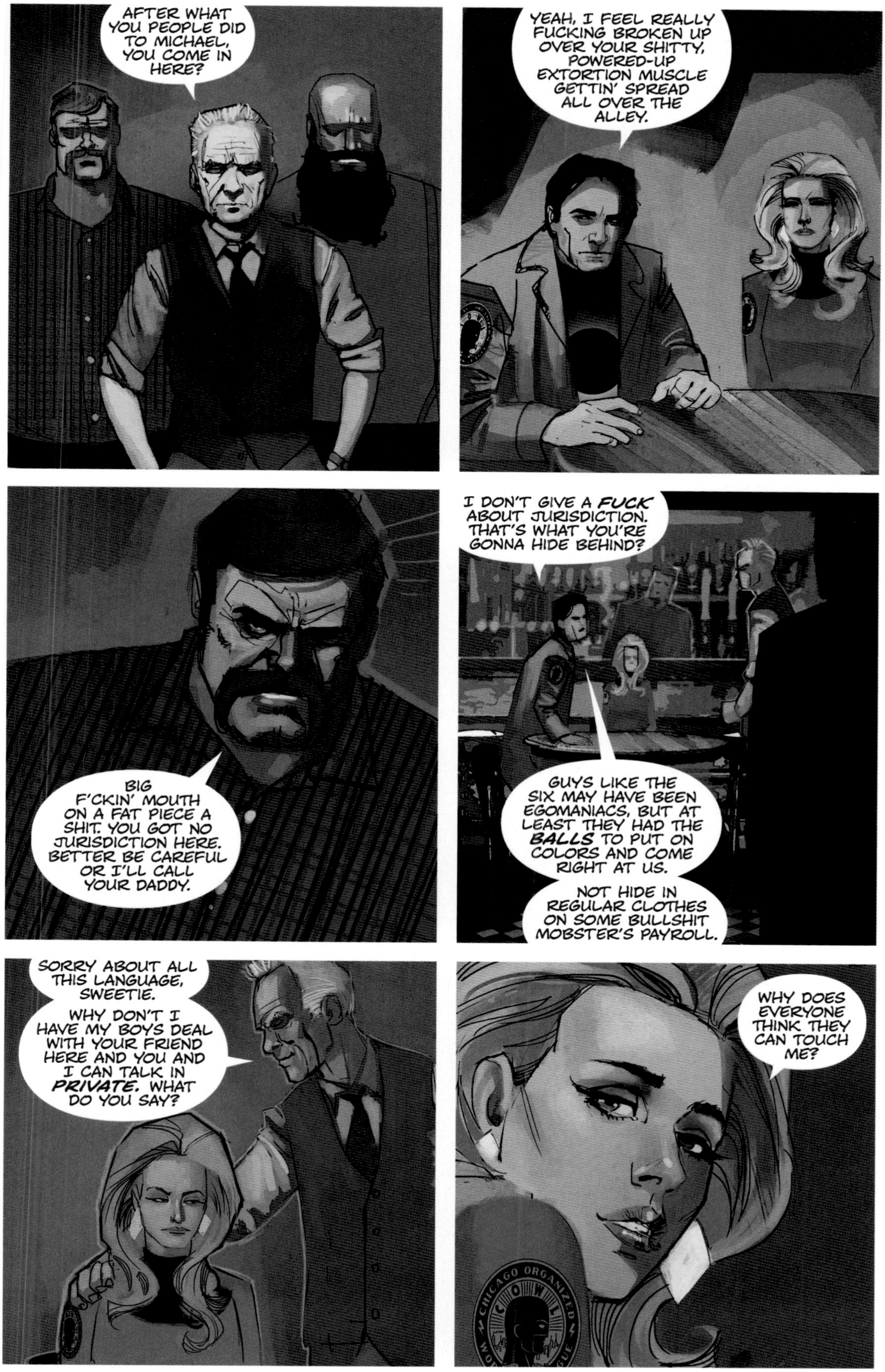
AFTER WHAT YOU PEOPLE DID TO MICHAEL, YOU COME IN HERE?
YEAH, I FEEL REALLY FUCKING BROKEN UP OVER YOUR SHITTY, POWERED-UP EXTORTION MUSCLE GETTIN' SPREAD ALL OVER THE ALLEY.
BIG F'CKIN' MOUTH ON A FAT PIECE A SHIT. YOU GOT NO JURISDICTION HERE. BETTER BE CAREFUL OR I'LL CALL YOUR DADDY.
I DON'T GIVE A FUCK ABOUT JURISDICTION. THAT'S WHAT YOU'RE GONNA HIDE BEHIND?
GUYS LIKE THE SIX MAY HAVE BEEN EGOMANIACS, BUT AT LEAST THEY HAD THE BALLS TO PUT ON COLORS AND COME RIGHT AT US.
NOT HIDE IN REGULAR CLOTHES ON SOME BULLSHIT MOBSTER'S PAYROLL.
SORRY ABOUT ALL THIS LANGUAGE, SWEETIE.
WHY DON'T I HAVE MY BOYS DEAL WITH YOUR FRIEND HERE AND YOU AND I CAN TALK IN PRIVATE. WHAT DO YOU SAY?
WHY DOES EVERYONE THINK THEY CAN TOUCH ME?
CHICAGO ORGANIZED

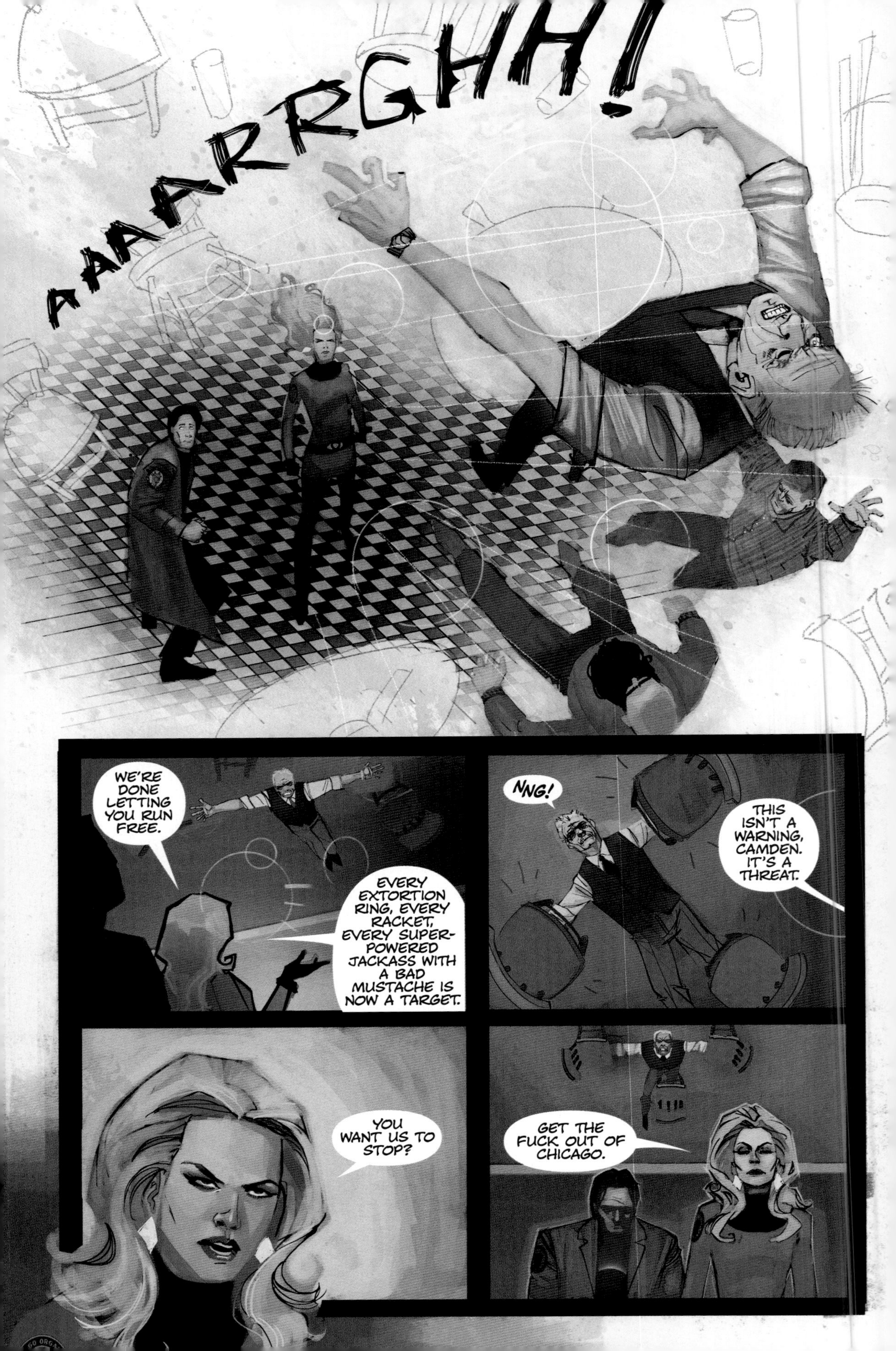
AAAARRGHH!
WE'RE DONE LETTING YOU RUN FREE.
EVERY EXTORTION RING, EVERY RACKET, EVERY SUPER-POWERED JACKASS WITH A BAD MUSTACHE IS NOW A TARGET.
NNG!
THIS ISN'T A WARNING, CAMDEN. IT'S A THREAT.
YOU WANT US TO STOP?
GET THE FUCK OUT OF CHICAGO.

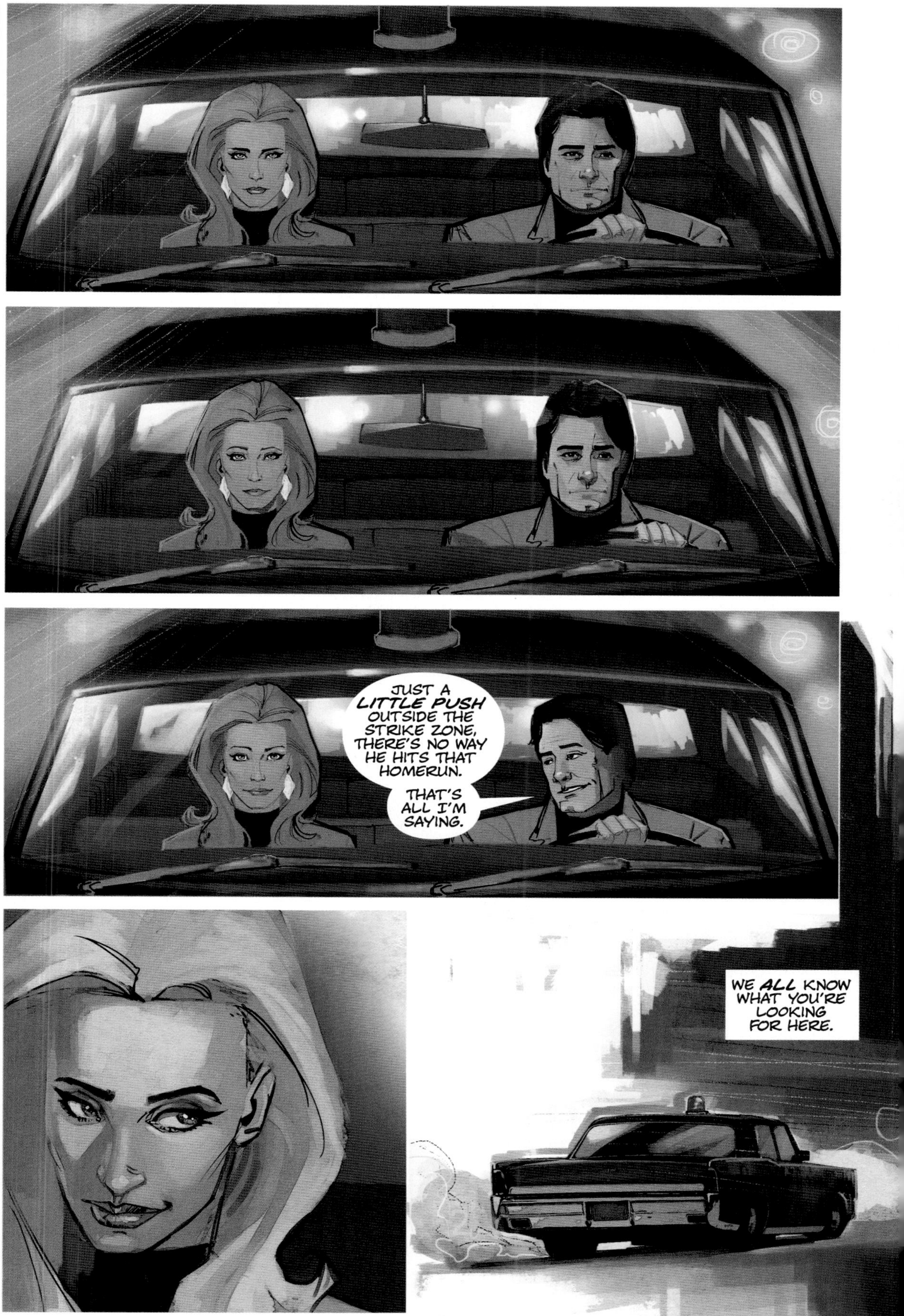
JUST A LITTLE PUSH OUTSIDE THE STRIKE ZONE, THERE'S NO WAY HE HITS THAT HOMERUN.
THAT'S ALL I'M SAYING.
WE ALL KNOW WHAT YOU'RE LOOKING FOR HERE.

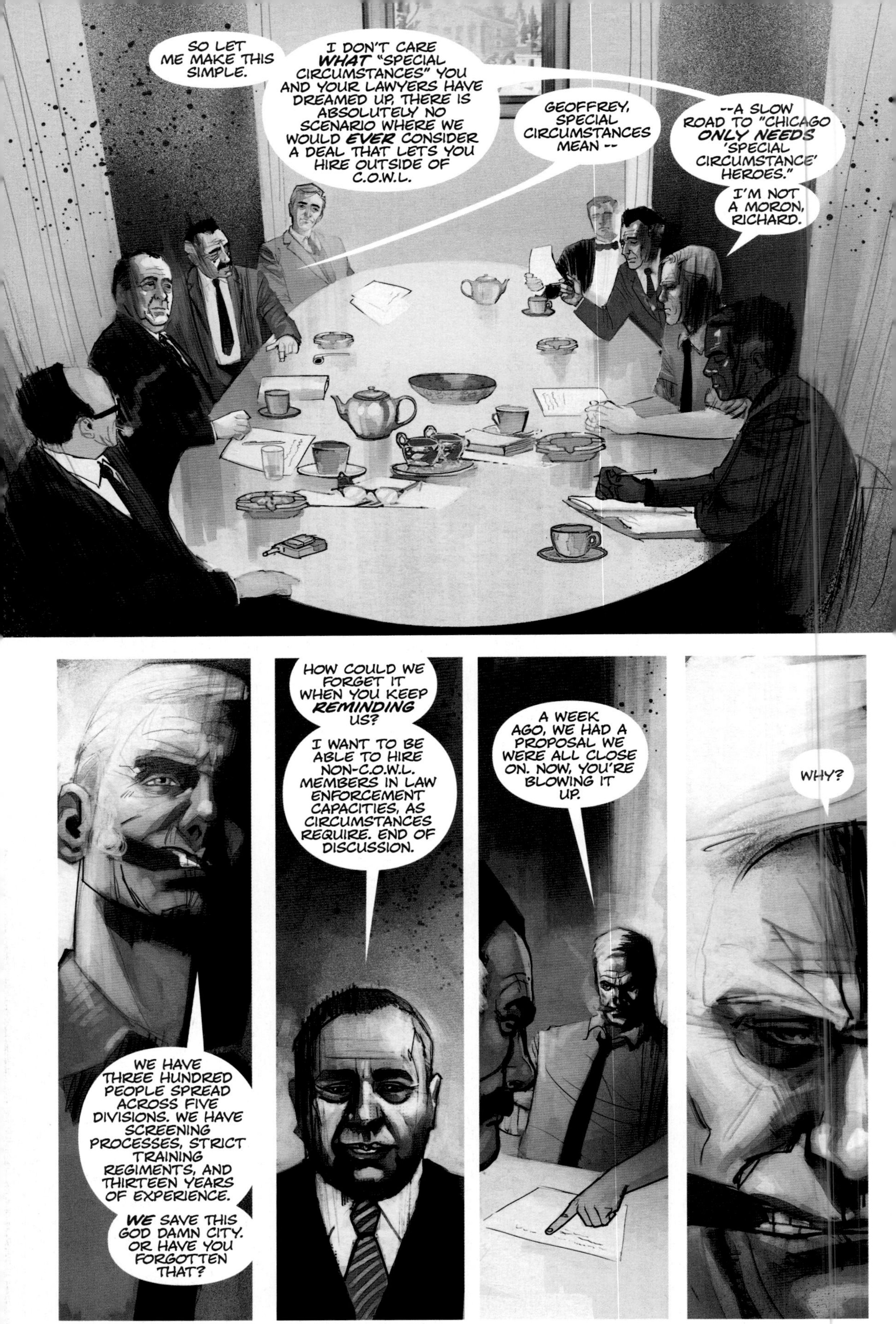
SO LET ME MAKE THIS SIMPLE.
I DON'T CARE WHAT "SPECIAL CIRCUMSTANCES" YOU AND YOUR LAWYERS HAVE DREAMED UP, THERE IS ABSOLUTELY NO SCENARIO WHERE WE WOULD EVER CONSIDER A DEAL THAT LETS YOU HIRE OUTSIDE OF C.O.W.L.
GEOFFREY, SPECIAL CIRCUMSTANCES MEAN --
--A SLOW ROAD TO "CHICAGO ONLY NEEDS 'SPECIAL CIRCUMSTANCE' HEROES."
I'M NOT A MORON, RICHARD.
WE HAVE THREE HUNDRED PEOPLE SPREAD ACROSS FIVE DIVISIONS. WE HAVE SCREENING PROCESSES, STRICT TRAINING REGIMENTS, AND THIRTEEN YEARS OF EXPERIENCE.
WE SAVE THIS GOD DAMN CITY. OR HAVE YOU FORGOTTEN THAT?
HOW COULD WE FORGET IT WHEN YOU KEEP REMINDING US?
I WANT TO BE ABLE TO HIRE NON-C.O.W.L. MEMBERS IN LAW ENFORCEMENT CAPACITIES, AS CIRCUMSTANCES REQUIRE. END OF DISCUSSION.
A WEEK AGO, WE HAD A PROPOSAL WE WERE ALL CLOSE ON. NOW, YOU'RE BLOWING IT UP.
WHY?

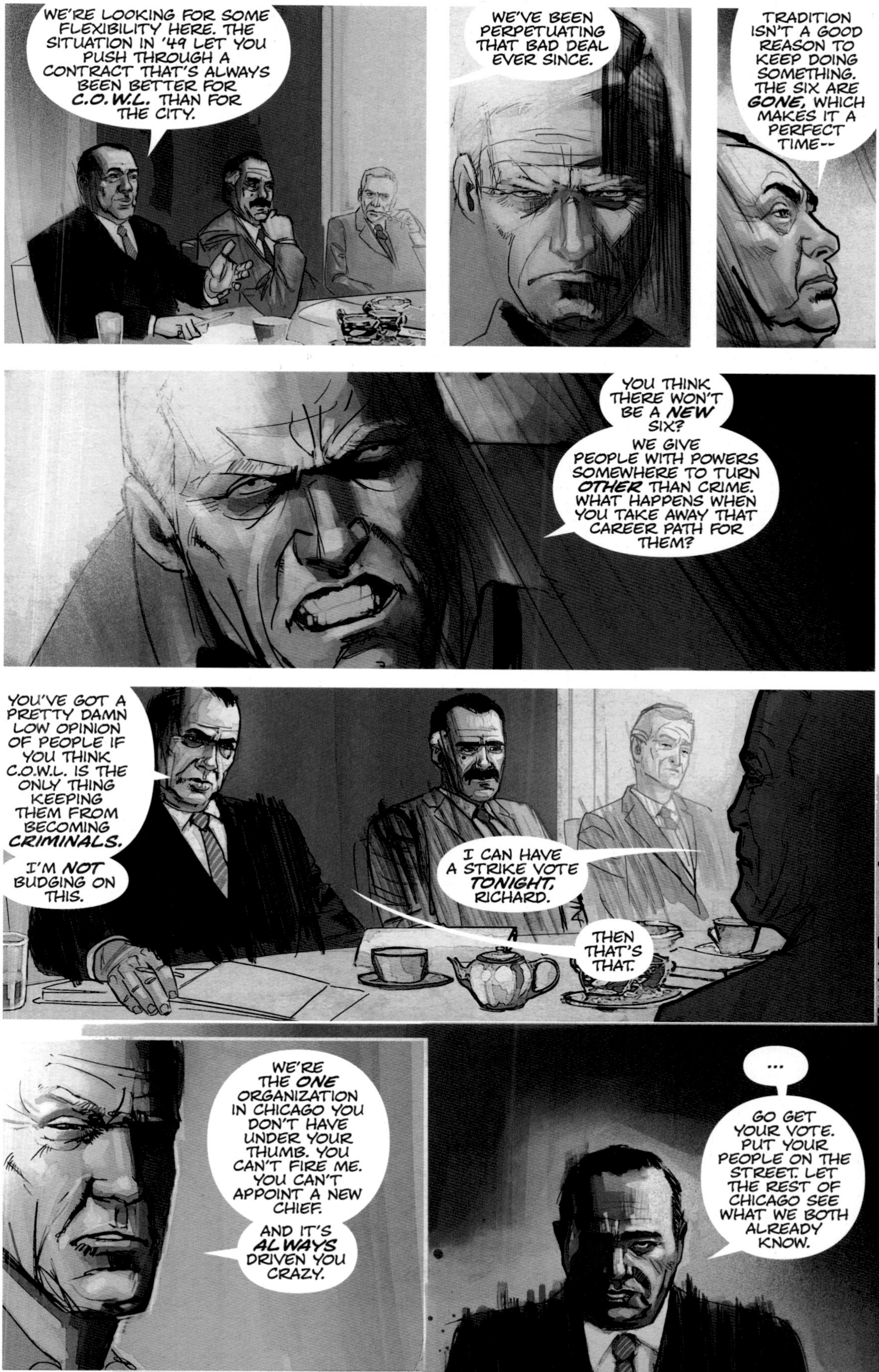
WE'RE LOOKING FOR SOME FLEXIBILITY HERE. THE SITUATION IN '49 LET YOU PUSH THROUGH A CONTRACT THAT'S ALWAYS BEEN BETTER FOR C.O.W.L. THAN FOR THE CITY.
WE'VE BEEN PERPETUATING THAT BAD DEAL EVER SINCE.
TRADITION ISN'T A GOOD REASON TO KEEP DOING SOMETHING. THE SIX ARE GONE, WHICH MAKES IT A PERFECT TIME--
YOU THINK THERE WON'T BE A NEW SIX?
WE GIVE PEOPLE WITH POWERS SOMEWHERE TO TURN OTHER THAN CRIME. WHAT HAPPENS WHEN YOU TAKE AWAY THAT CAREER PATH FOR THEM?
YOU'VE GOT A PRETTY DAMN LOW OPINION OF PEOPLE IF YOU THINK C.O.W.L. IS THE ONLY THING KEEPING THEM FROM BECOMING CRIMINALS.
I'M NOT BUDGING ON THIS.
I CAN HAVE A STRIKE VOTE TONIGHT, RICHARD.
THEN THAT'S THAT.
WE'RE THE ONE ORGANIZATION IN CHICAGO YOU DON'T HAVE UNDER YOUR THUMB. YOU CAN'T FIRE ME. YOU CAN'T APPOINT A NEW CHIEF.
AND IT'S ALWAYS DRIVEN YOU CRAZY.
...
GO GET YOUR VOTE. PUT YOUR PEOPLE ON THE STREET. LET THE REST OF CHICAGO SEE WHAT WE BOTH ALREADY KNOW.

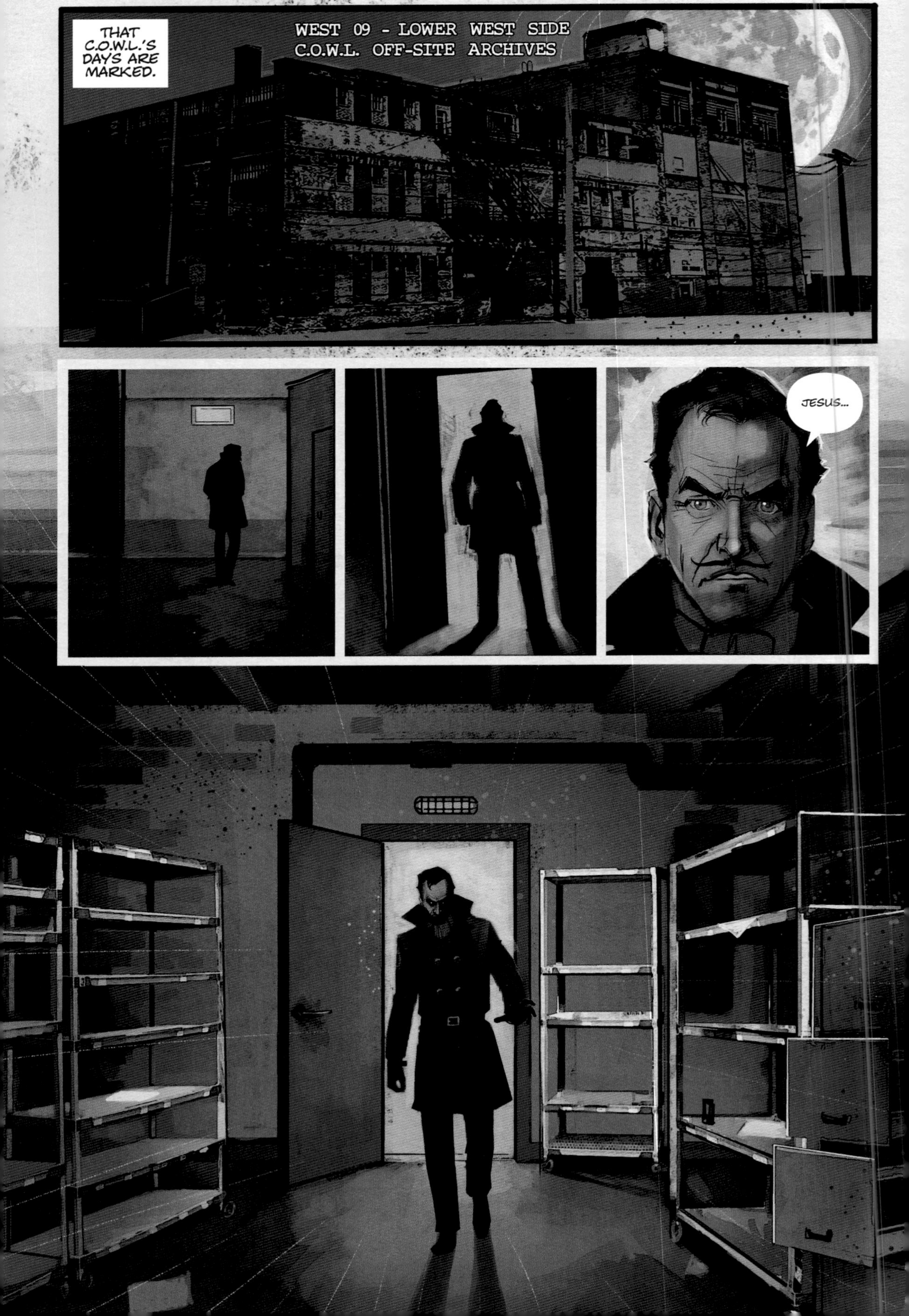
THAT C.O.W.L.'S DAYS ARE MARKED.
WEST 09 - LOWER WEST SIDE
C.O.W.L. OFF-SITE ARCHIVES
JESUS...

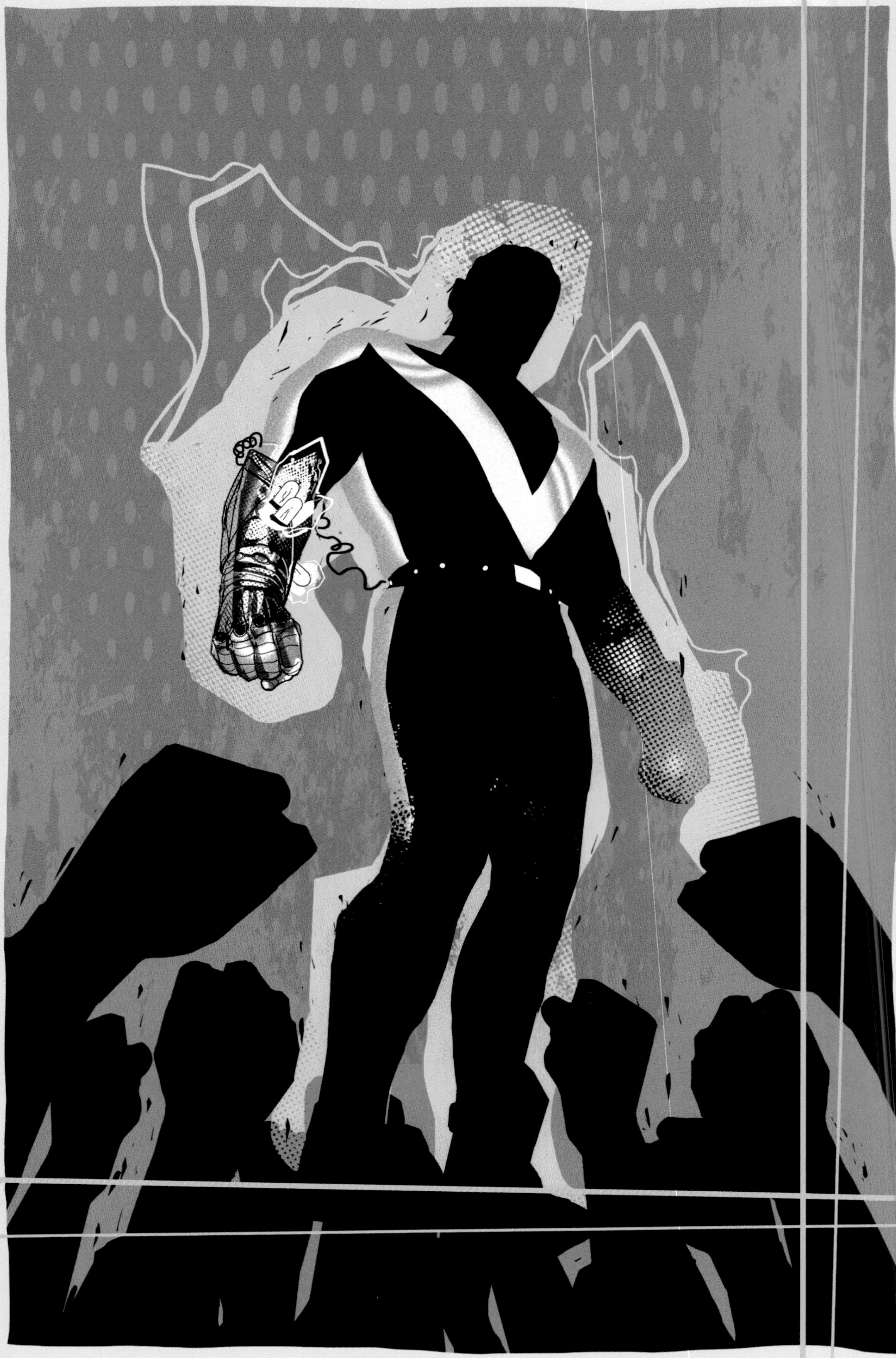

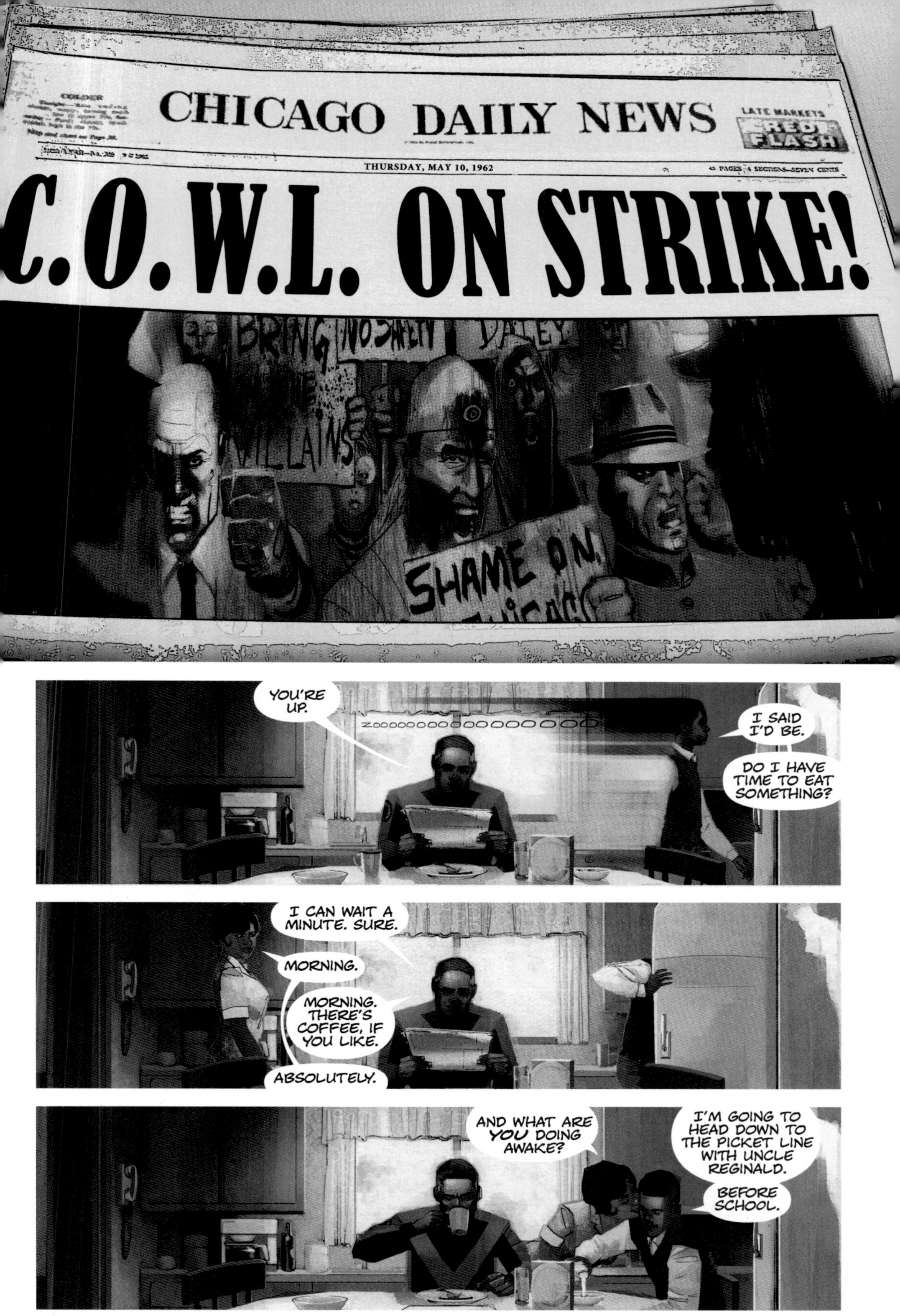
COLDER
CHICAGO DAILY NEWS
LATE MARKETS
RED FLASH
THURSDAY, MAY 10, 1962
C.O.W.L. ON STRIKE!
BRING
VILLAINS
DALEY
SHAME ON
YOU'RE UP.
ZOOOOOOOOOOOOOOOOOOO
I SAID I'D BE.
DO I HAVE TIME TO EAT SOMETHING?
I CAN WAIT A MINUTE. SURE.
MORNING.
MORNING. THERE'S COFFEE, IF YOU LIKE.
ABSOLUTELY.
AND WHAT ARE YOU DOING AWAKE?
I'M GOING TO HEAD DOWN TO THE PICKET LINE WITH UNCLE REGINALD.
BEFORE SCHOOL.

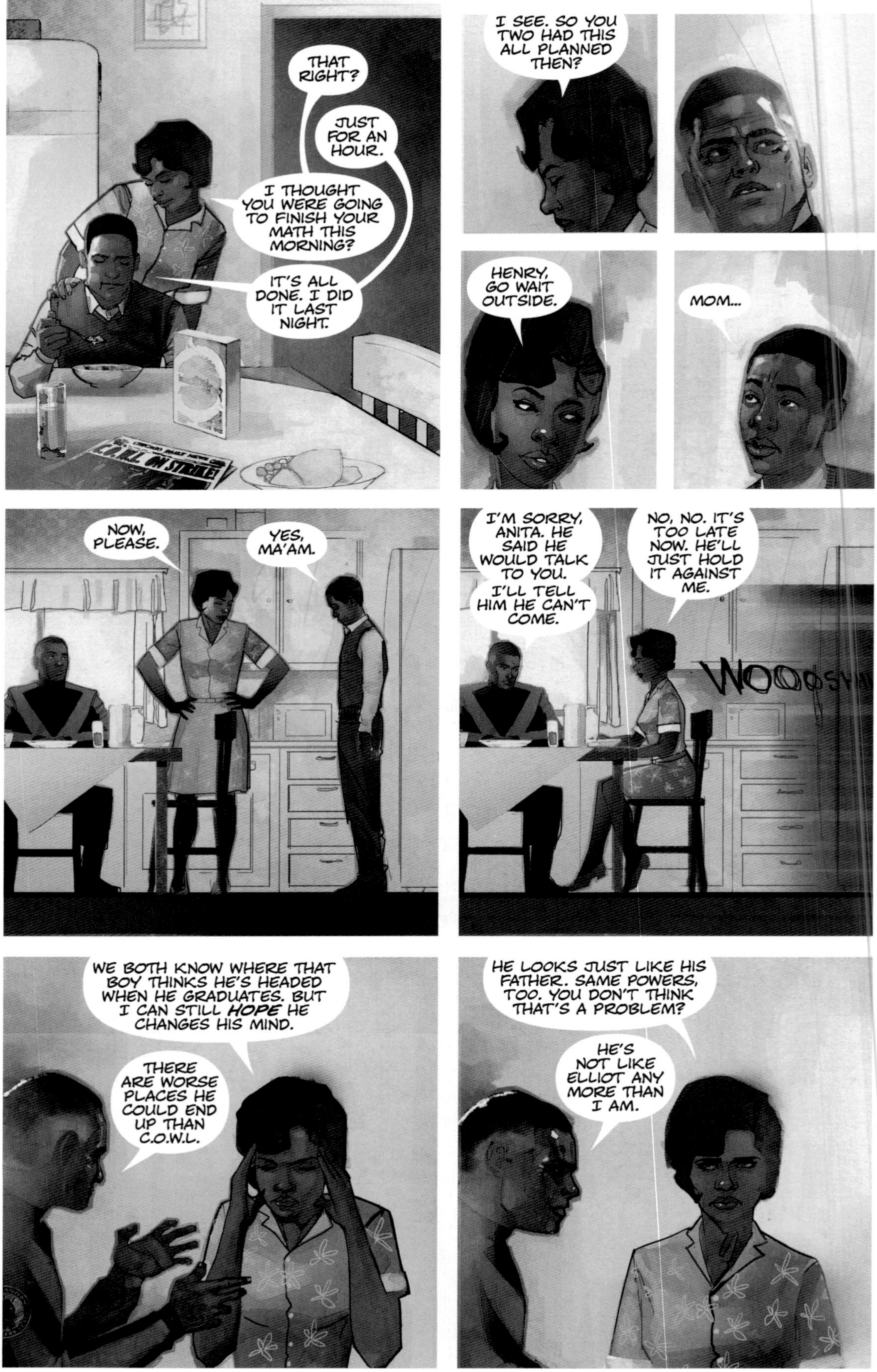
THAT RIGHT?
JUST FOR AN HOUR.
I THOUGHT YOU WERE GOING TO FINISH YOUR MATH THIS MORNING?
IT'S ALL DONE. I DID IT LAST NIGHT.
C.O.W.L. ON STRIKE!
I SEE. SO YOU TWO HAD THIS ALL PLANNED THEN?
HENRY, GO WAIT OUTSIDE.
MOM...
NOW, PLEASE.
YES, MA'AM.
I'M SORRY, ANITA. HE SAID HE WOULD TALK TO YOU.
I'LL TELL HIM HE CAN'T COME.
NO, NO. IT'S TOO LATE NOW. HE'LL JUST HOLD IT AGAINST ME.
WE BOTH KNOW WHERE THAT BOY THINKS HE'S HEADED WHEN HE GRADUATES. BUT I CAN STILL *HOPE* HE CHANGES HIS MIND.
THERE ARE WORSE PLACES HE COULD END UP THAN C.O.W.L.
HE LOOKS JUST LIKE HIS FATHER. SAME POWERS, TOO. YOU DON'T THINK THAT'S A PROBLEM?
HE'S NOT LIKE ELLIOT ANY MORE THAN I AM.

BESIDES, GEOFFREY AND I NEED AS MANY PEOPLE ON THE PICKET LINE AS POSSIBLE. IT'S FINE.

...

GEOFFREY AND YOU. DO YOU THINK HE'D WORD IT LIKE THAT?

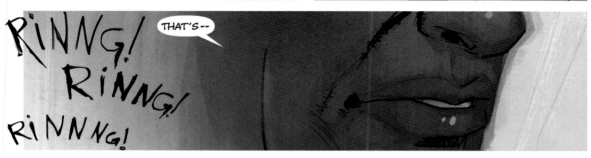

RINNG!
RINNG!
RINNNG!

THAT'S--

HELLO?

GOOD, I'M GLAD I CAUGHT YOU AT HOME.

GEOFFREY? I WAS JUST HEADING TO CITY HALL.

THAT CAN WAIT.

WHAT'S GOING ON?

THERE'S A PROBLEM I NEED YOU TO HANDLE.

CHAPTER 4
Unity

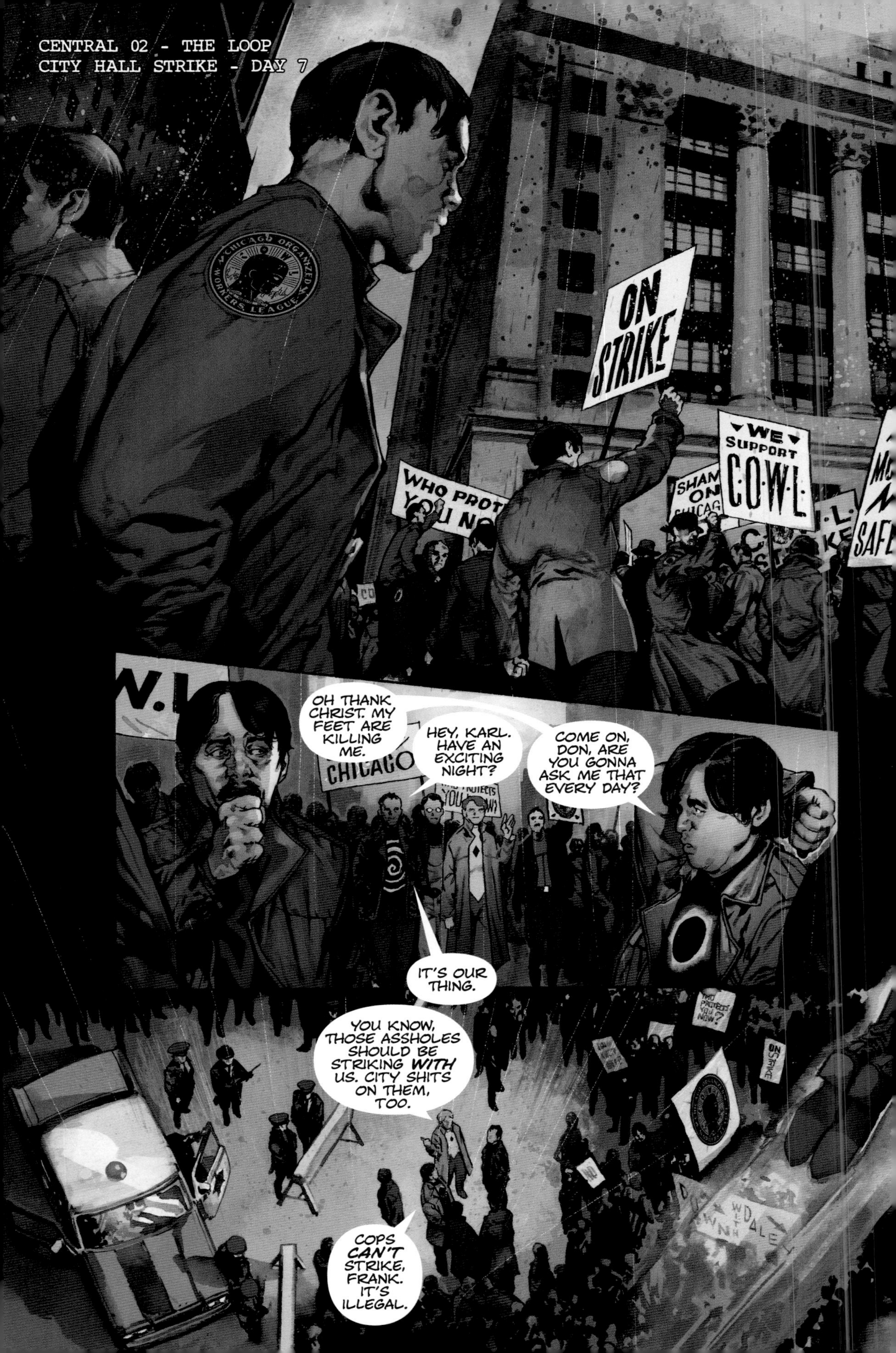

CENTRAL 02 - THE LOOP
CITY HALL STRIKE - DAY 7
ON STRIKE
WE SUPPORT C.O.W.L
WHO PROTECTS YOU NOW
OH THANK CHRIST. MY FEET ARE KILLING ME.
HEY, KARL. HAVE AN EXCITING NIGHT?
COME ON, DON, ARE YOU GONNA ASK ME THAT EVERY DAY?
IT'S OUR THING.
YOU KNOW, THOSE ASSHOLES SHOULD BE STRIKING *WITH* US. CITY SHITS ON THEM, TOO.
COPS *CAN'T* STRIKE, FRANK. IT'S ILLEGAL.

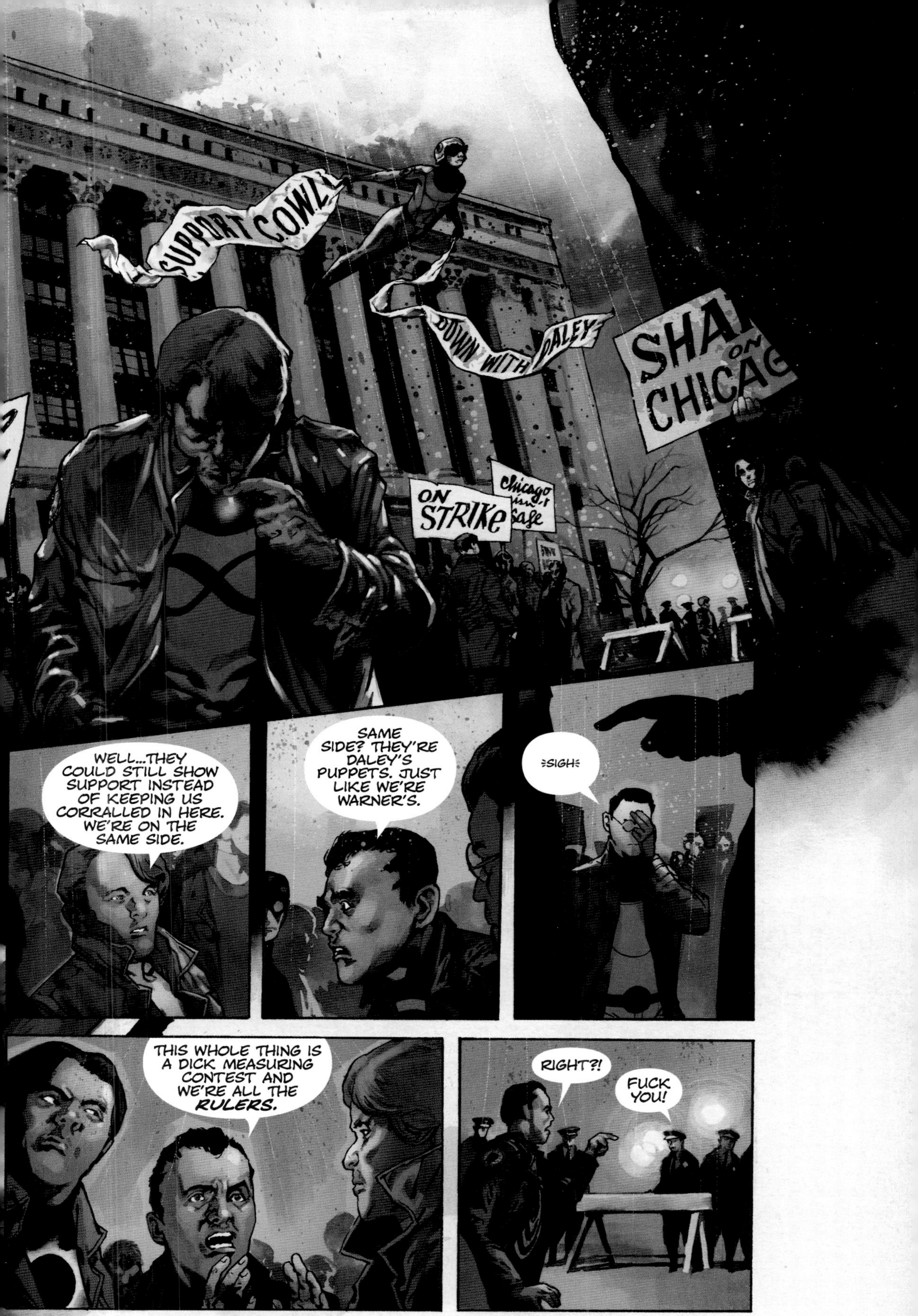
SUPPORT C.O.W.L.!
DOWN WITH DALEY
ON STRIKE
WELL...THEY COULD STILL SHOW SUPPORT INSTEAD OF KEEPING US CORRALLED IN HERE. WE'RE ON THE SAME SIDE.
SAME SIDE? THEY'RE DALEY'S PUPPETS. JUST LIKE WE'RE WARNER'S.
SIGH
THIS WHOLE THING IS A DICK MEASURING CONTEST AND WE'RE ALL THE RULERS.
RIGHT?!
FUCK YOU!

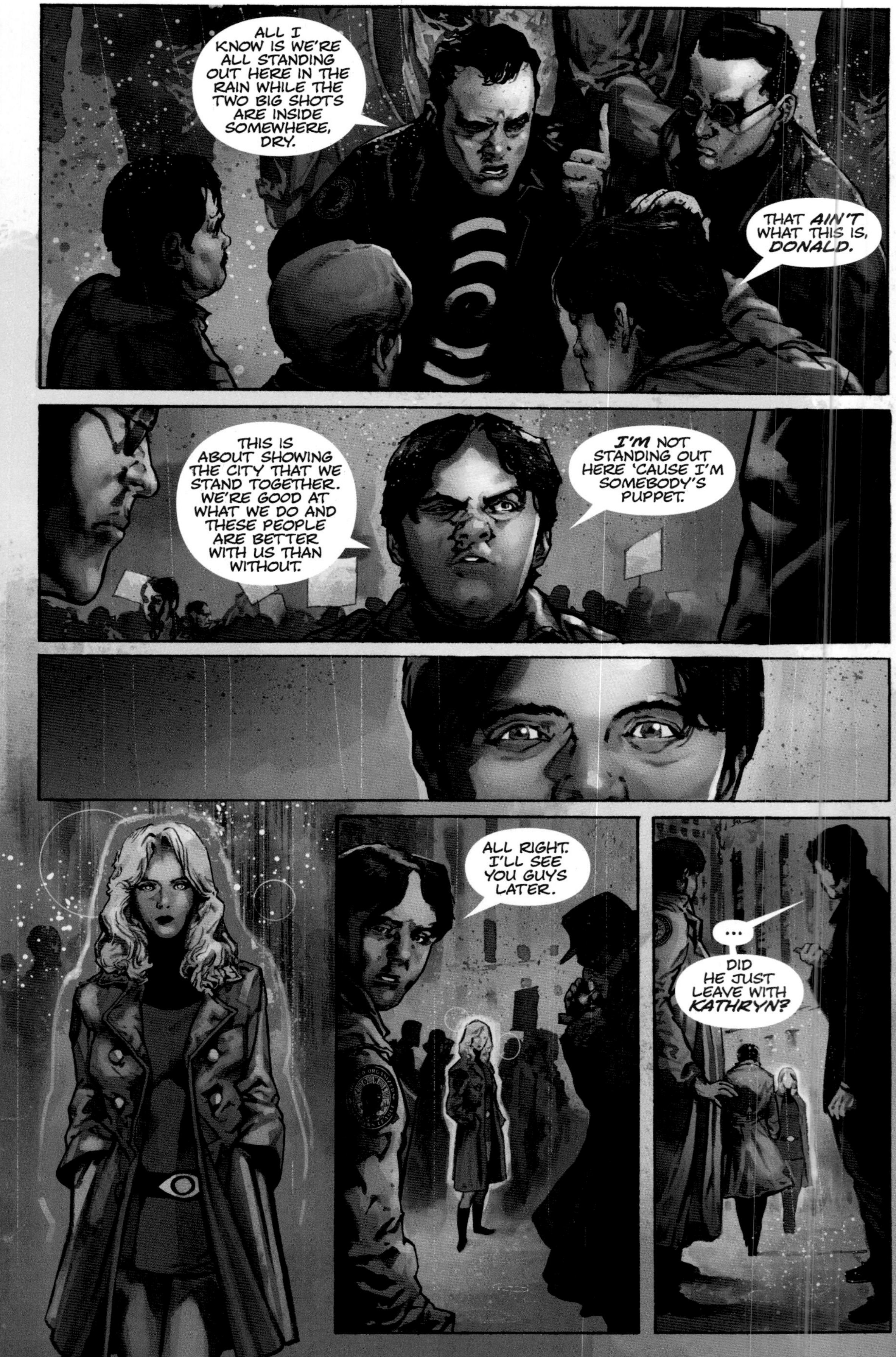
ALL I KNOW IS WE'RE ALL STANDING OUT HERE IN THE RAIN WHILE THE TWO BIG SHOTS ARE INSIDE SOMEWHERE, DRY.
THAT *AIN'T* WHAT THIS IS, *DONALD.*
THIS IS ABOUT SHOWING THE CITY THAT WE STAND TOGETHER. WE'RE GOOD AT WHAT WE DO AND THESE PEOPLE ARE BETTER WITH US THAN WITHOUT.
I'M NOT STANDING OUT HERE 'CAUSE I'M SOMEBODY'S PUPPET.
ALL RIGHT. I'LL SEE YOU GUYS LATER.
...
DID HE JUST LEAVE WITH *KATHRYN?*

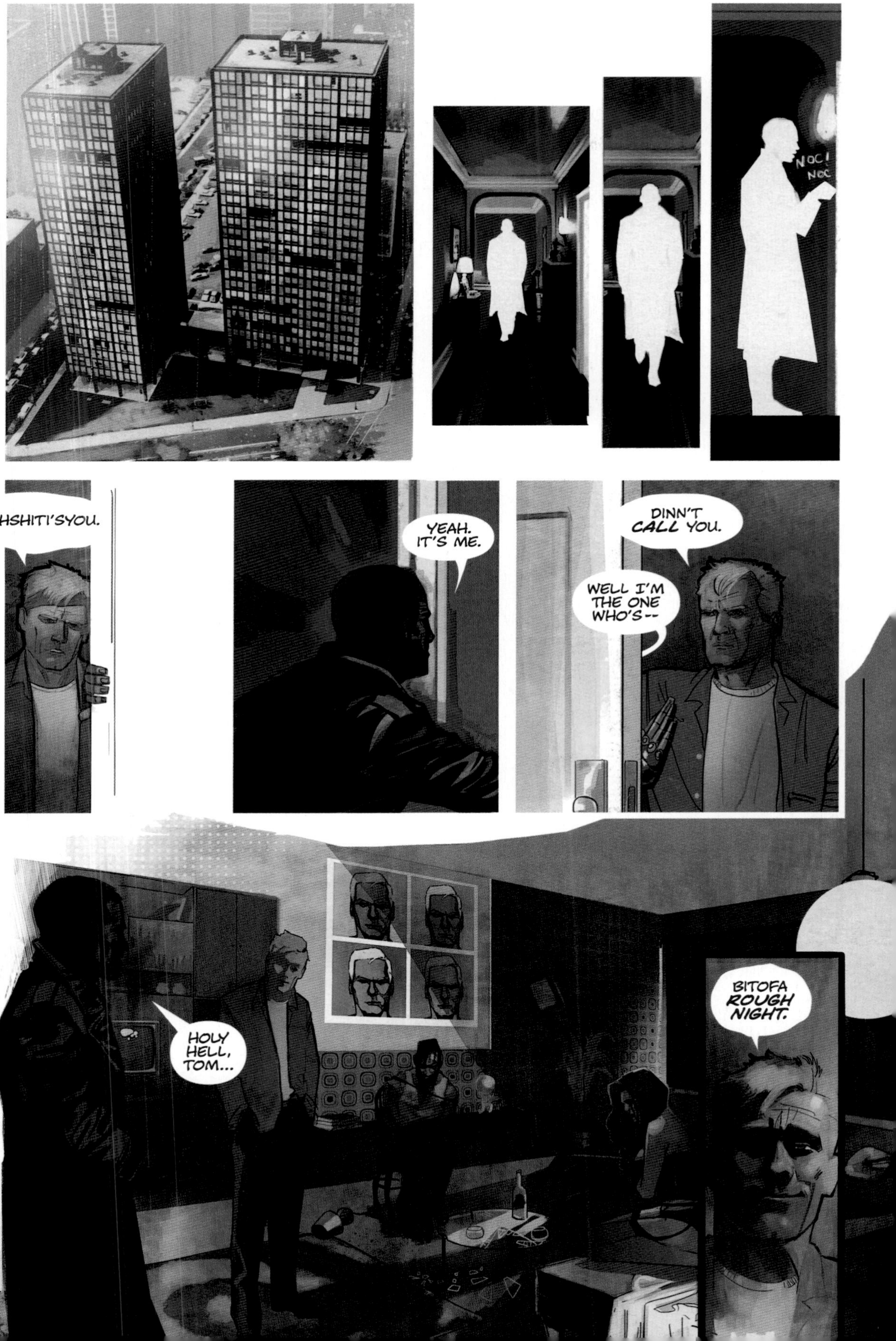
NOC! NOC
OHSHITI'SYOU.
YEAH. IT'S ME.
DINN'T CALL YOU.
WELL I'M THE ONE WHO'S--
HOLY HELL, TOM...
BITOFA ROUGH NIGHT.

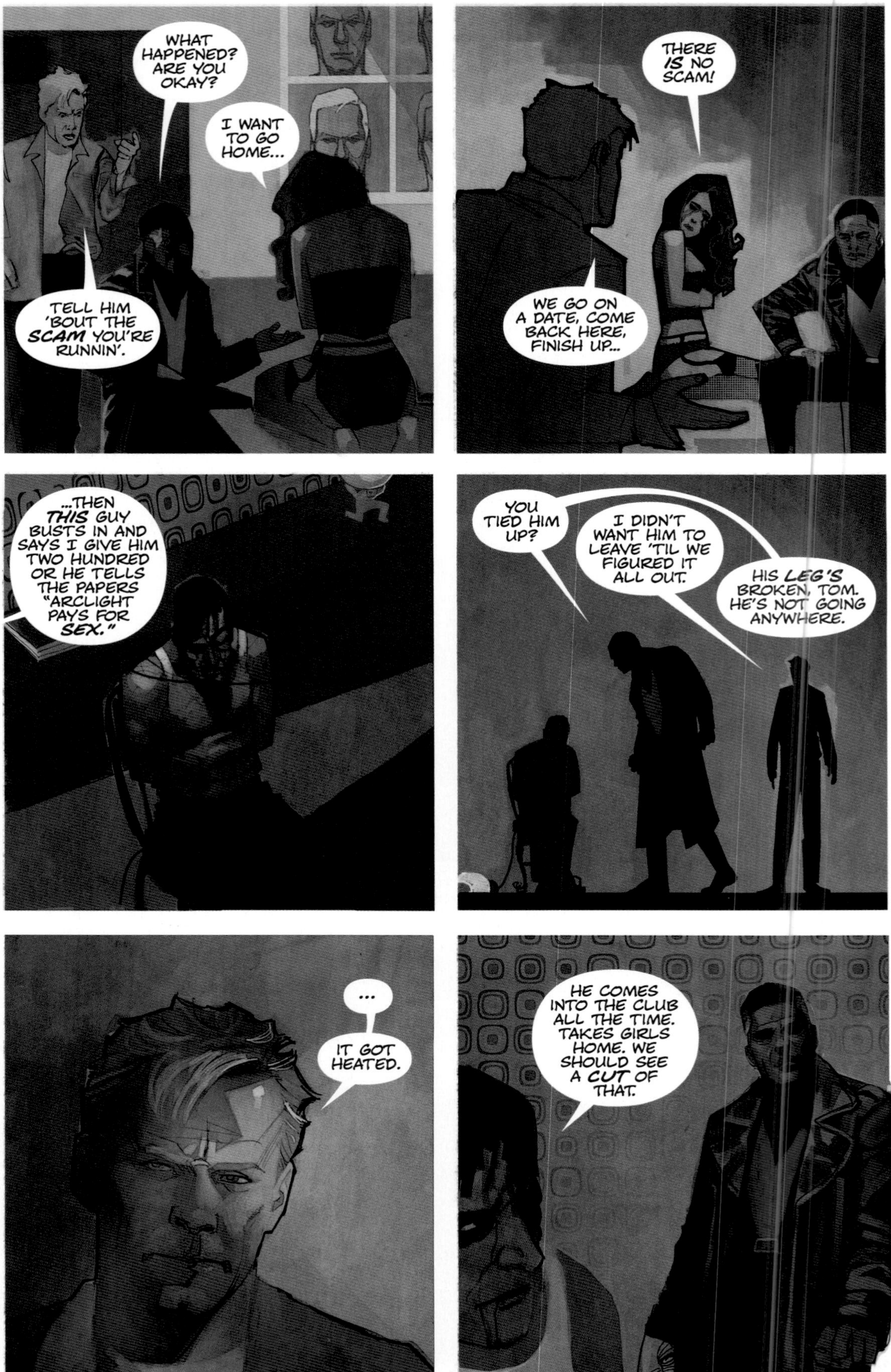
WHAT HAPPENED? ARE YOU OKAY?
I WANT TO GO HOME...
TELL HIM 'BOUT THE SCAM YOU'RE RUNNIN'.
THERE IS NO SCAM!
WE GO ON A DATE, COME BACK HERE, FINISH UP...
...THEN THIS GUY BUSTS IN AND SAYS I GIVE HIM TWO HUNDRED OR HE TELLS THE PAPERS "ARCLIGHT PAYS FOR SEX."
YOU TIED HIM UP?
I DIDN'T WANT HIM TO LEAVE 'TIL WE FIGURED IT ALL OUT.
HIS LEG'S BROKEN, TOM. HE'S NOT GOING ANYWHERE.
...
IT GOT HEATED.
HE COMES INTO THE CLUB ALL THE TIME. TAKES GIRLS HOME. WE SHOULD SEE A CUT OF THAT.

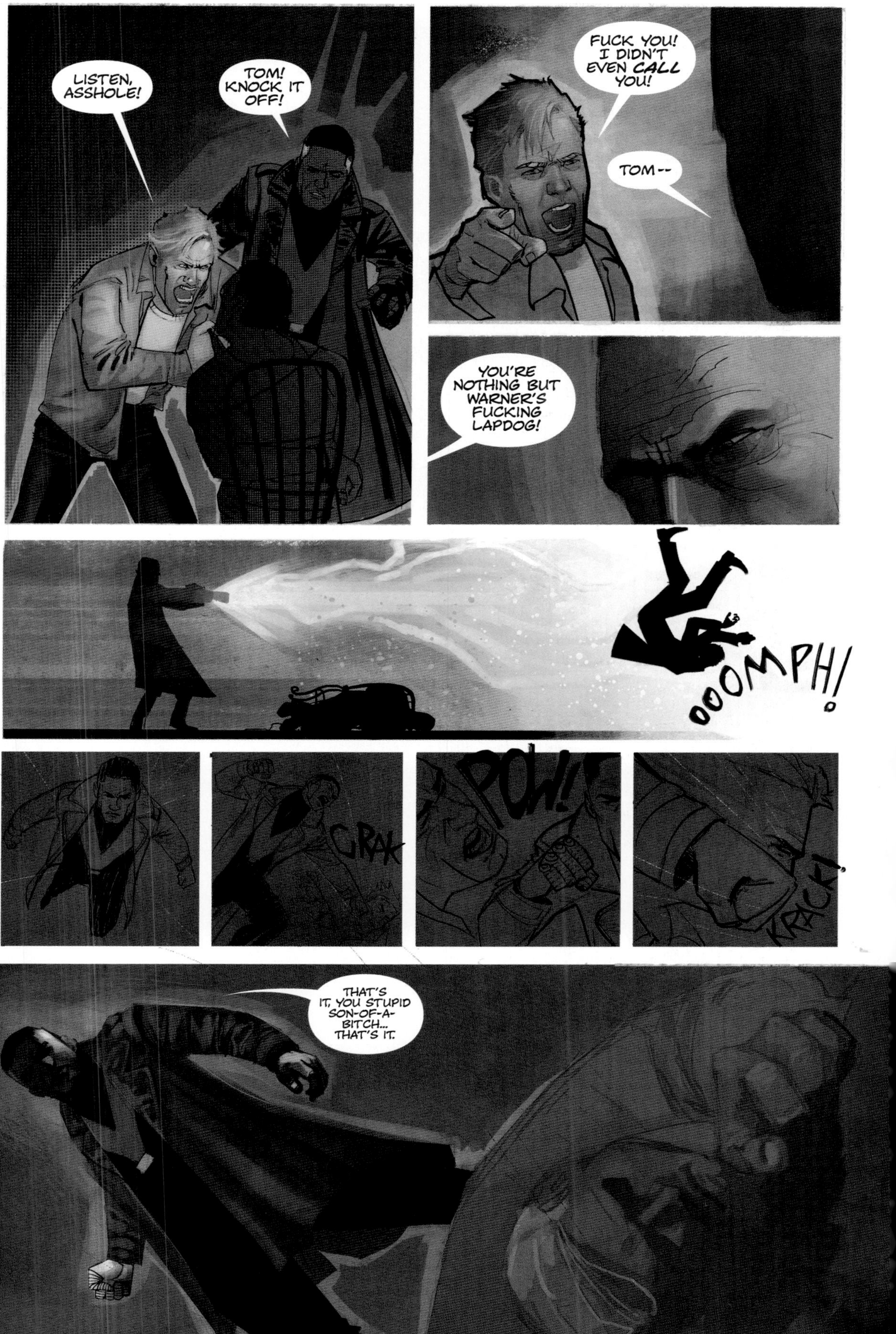
LISTEN, ASSHOLE!
TOM! KNOCK IT OFF!
FUCK YOU! I DIDN'T EVEN CALL YOU!
TOM--
YOU'RE NOTHING BUT WARNER'S FUCKING LAPDOG!
OOOMPH!
GRAK
POW!
KRACK!
THAT'S IT, YOU STUPID SON-OF-A-BITCH... THAT'S IT.

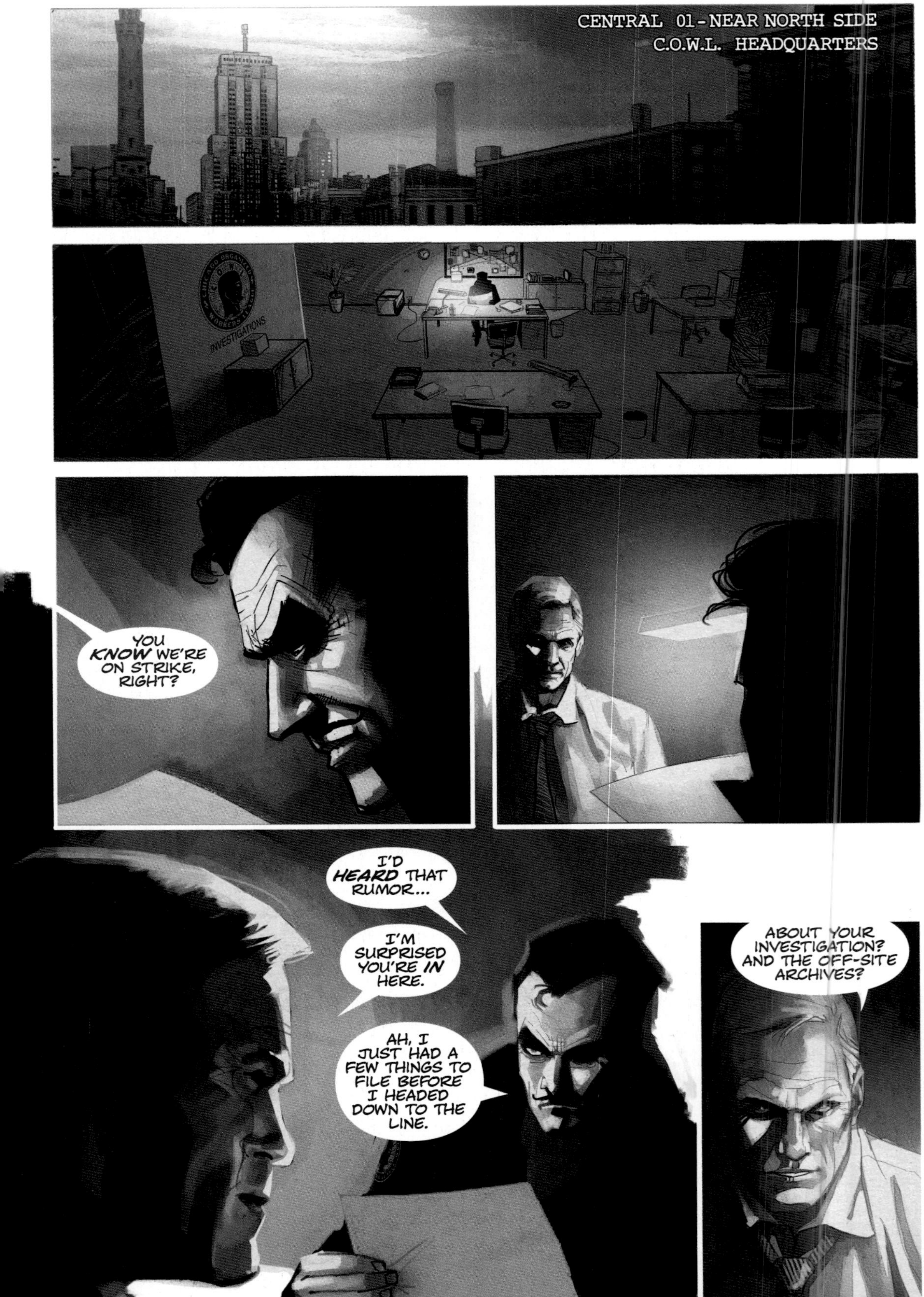
CENTRAL 01-NEAR NORTH SIDE
C.O.W.L. HEADQUARTERS
INVESTIGATIONS
YOU KNOW WE'RE ON STRIKE, RIGHT?
I'D HEARD THAT RUMOR...
I'M SURPRISED YOU'RE IN HERE.
AH, I JUST HAD A FEW THINGS TO FILE BEFORE I HEADED DOWN TO THE LINE.
ABOUT YOUR INVESTIGATION? AND THE OFF-SITE ARCHIVES?

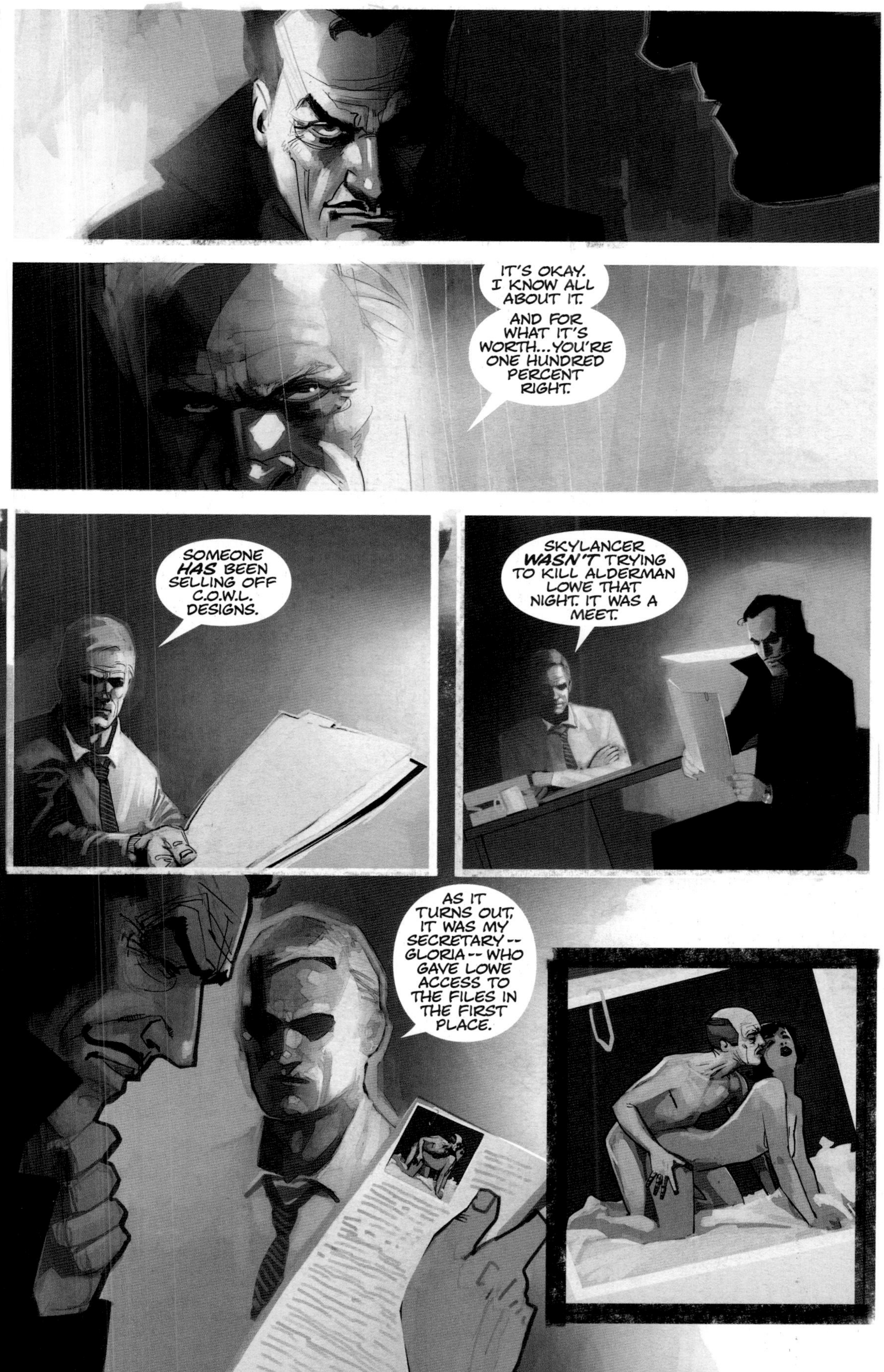
IT'S OKAY. I KNOW ALL ABOUT IT.
AND FOR WHAT IT'S WORTH...YOU'RE ONE HUNDRED PERCENT RIGHT.
SOMEONE HAS BEEN SELLING OFF C.O.W.L. DESIGNS.
SKYLANCER WASN'T TRYING TO KILL ALDERMAN LOWE THAT NIGHT. IT WAS A MEET.
AS IT TURNS OUT, IT WAS MY SECRETARY-- GLORIA-- WHO GAVE LOWE ACCESS TO THE FILES IN THE FIRST PLACE.

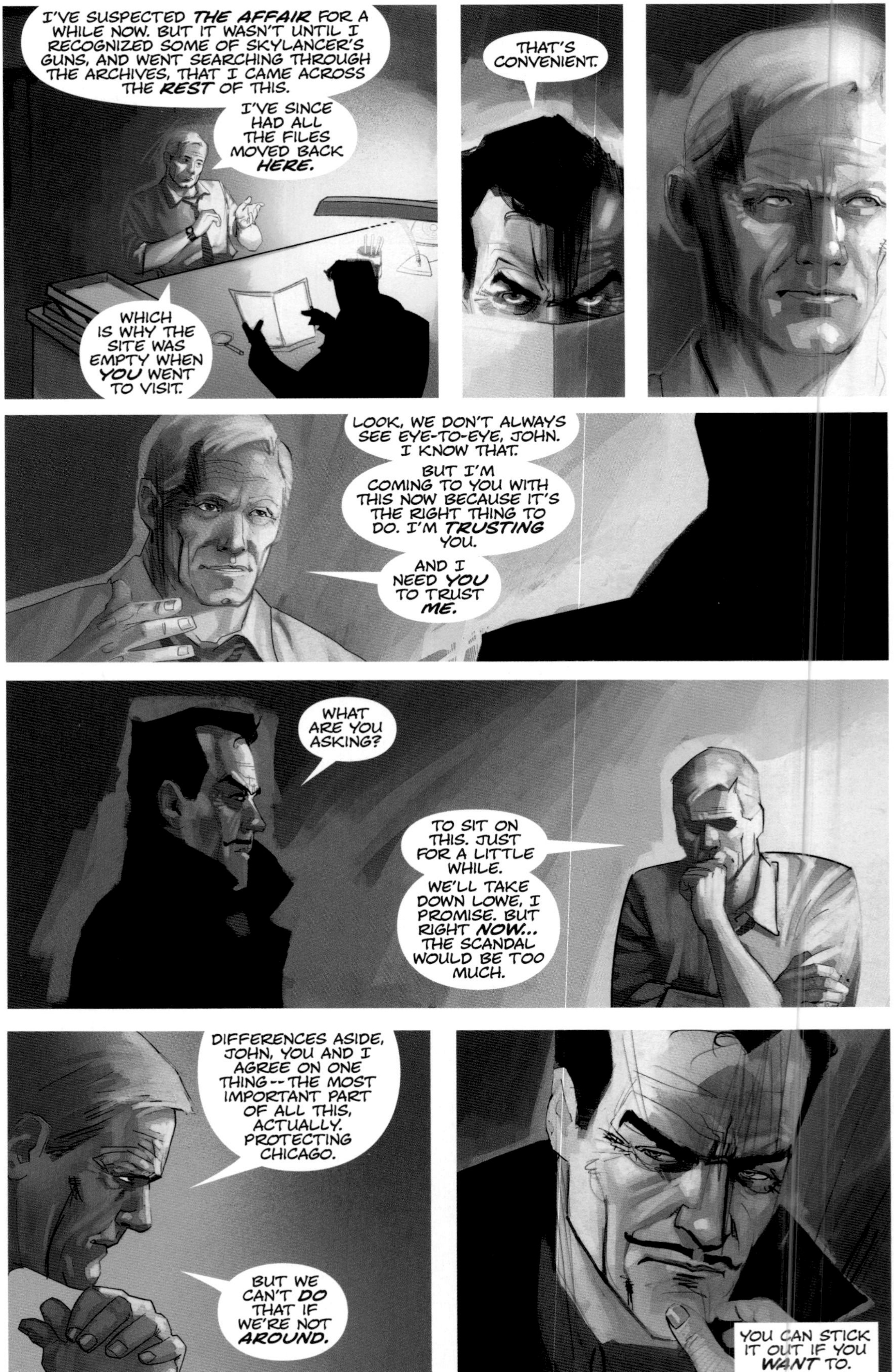
I'VE SUSPECTED THE AFFAIR FOR A WHILE NOW. BUT IT WASN'T UNTIL I RECOGNIZED SOME OF SKYLANCER'S GUNS, AND WENT SEARCHING THROUGH THE ARCHIVES, THAT I CAME ACROSS THE REST OF THIS.
I'VE SINCE HAD ALL THE FILES MOVED BACK HERE.
WHICH IS WHY THE SITE WAS EMPTY WHEN YOU WENT TO VISIT.
THAT'S CONVENIENT.
LOOK, WE DON'T ALWAYS SEE EYE-TO-EYE, JOHN. I KNOW THAT.
BUT I'M COMING TO YOU WITH THIS NOW BECAUSE IT'S THE RIGHT THING TO DO. I'M TRUSTING YOU.
AND I NEED YOU TO TRUST ME.
WHAT ARE YOU ASKING?
TO SIT ON THIS. JUST FOR A LITTLE WHILE.
WE'LL TAKE DOWN LOWE, I PROMISE. BUT RIGHT NOW... THE SCANDAL WOULD BE TOO MUCH.
DIFFERENCES ASIDE, JOHN, YOU AND I AGREE ON ONE THING--THE MOST IMPORTANT PART OF ALL THIS, ACTUALLY. PROTECTING CHICAGO.
BUT WE CAN'T DO THAT IF WE'RE NOT AROUND.
YOU CAN STICK IT OUT IF YOU WANT TO.

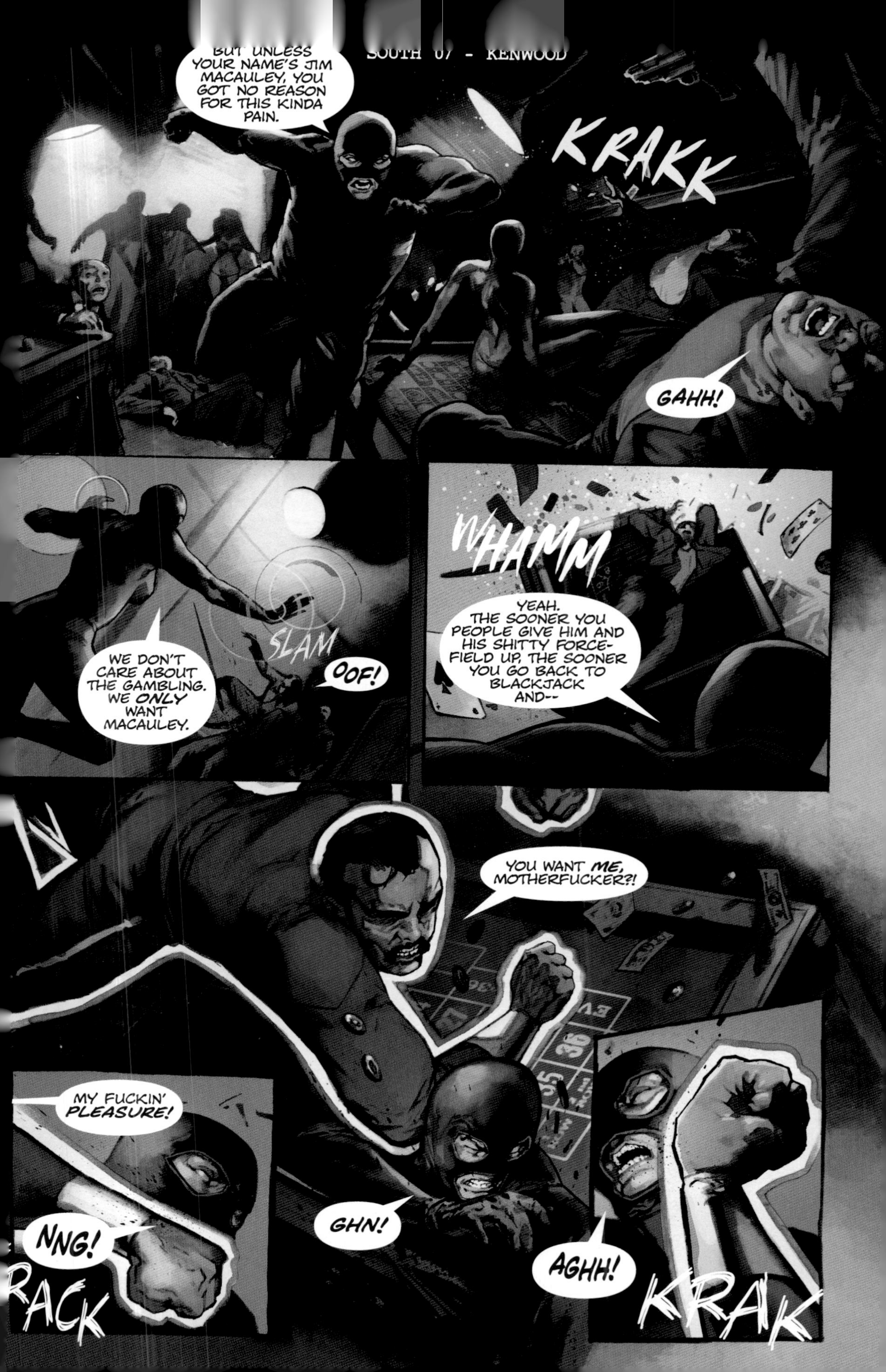

SOUTH 07 - KENWOOD
BUT UNLESS YOUR NAME'S JIM MACAULEY, YOU GOT NO REASON FOR THIS KINDA PAIN.
KRAKK
GAHH!
WE DON'T CARE ABOUT THE GAMBLING. WE ONLY WANT MACAULEY.
SLAM
OOF!
WHAMM
YEAH. THE SOONER YOU PEOPLE GIVE HIM AND HIS SHITTY FORCE-FIELD UP, THE SOONER YOU GO BACK TO BLACKJACK AND--
YOU WANT ME, MOTHERFUCKER?!
MY FUCKIN' PLEASURE!
NNG!
RACK
GHN!
AGHH!
KRAK

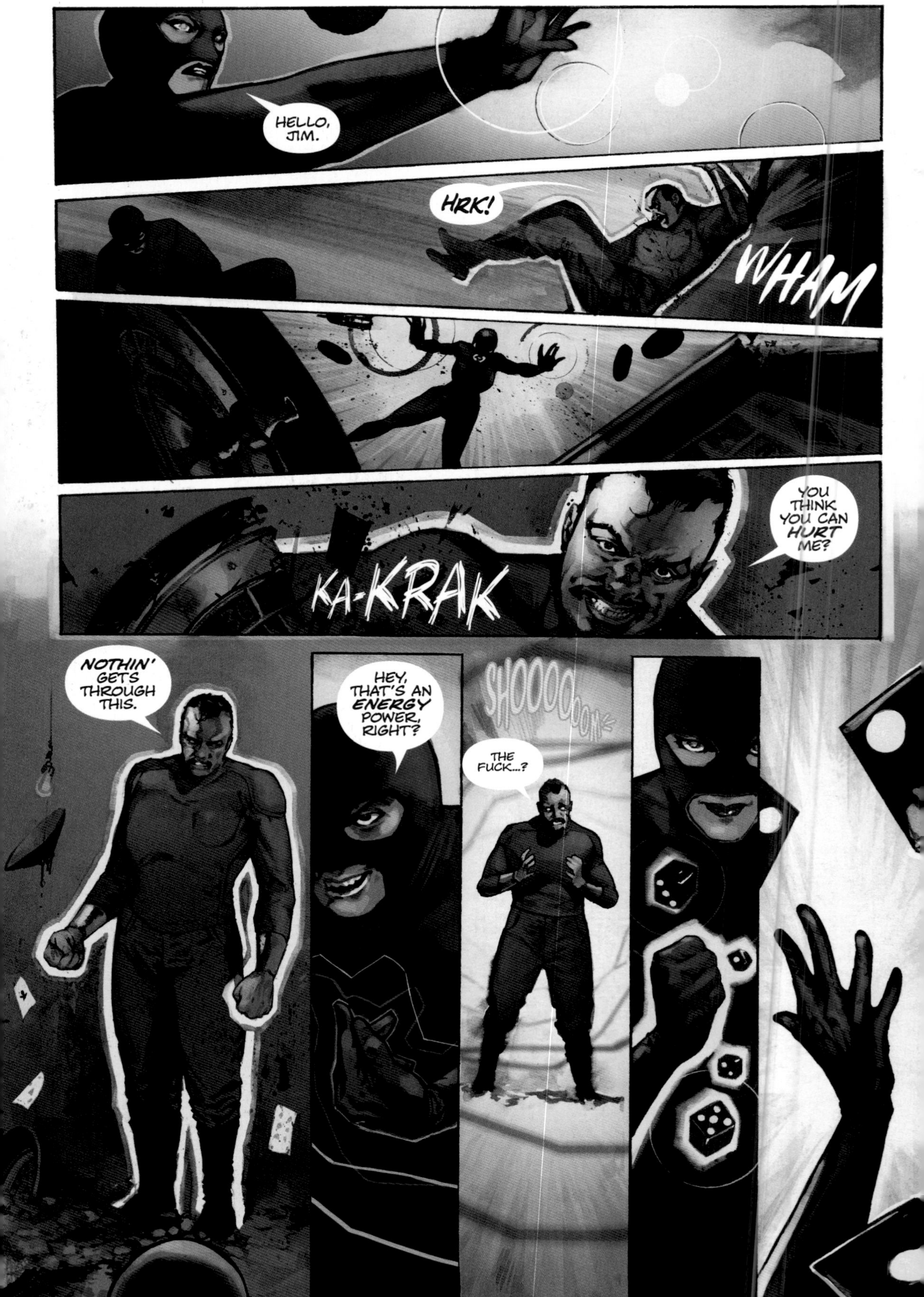
HELLO, JIM.
HRK!
WHAM
YOU THINK YOU CAN HURT ME?
KA-KRAK
NOTHIN' GETS THROUGH THIS.
HEY, THAT'S AN ENERGY POWER, RIGHT?
SHOOOOOOOM
THE FUCK...?

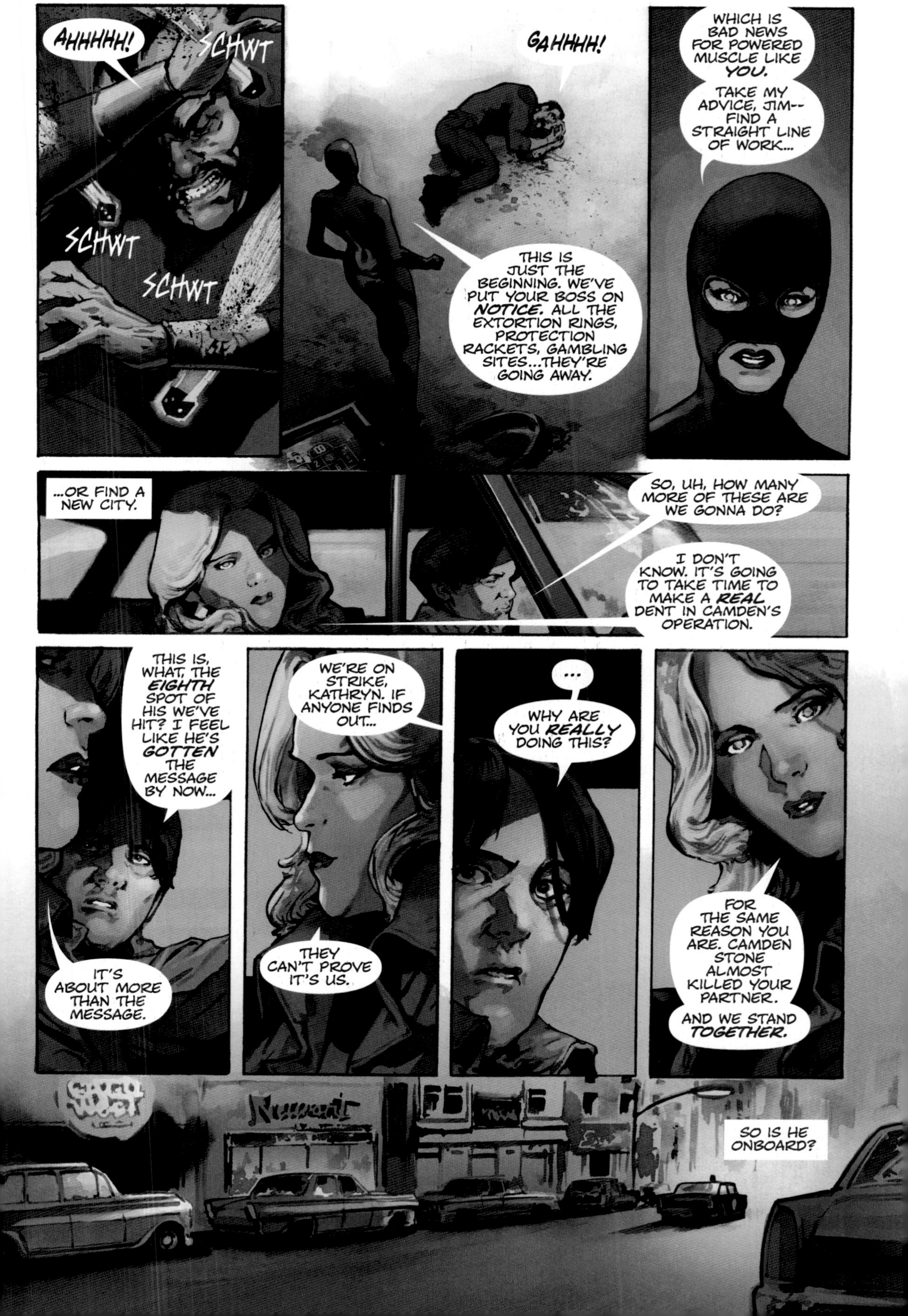
AHHHHH!
SCHWT
SCHWT
SCHWT
GAHHHH!
THIS IS JUST THE BEGINNING. WE'VE PUT YOUR BOSS ON NOTICE. ALL THE EXTORTION RINGS, PROTECTION RACKETS, GAMBLING SITES...THEY'RE GOING AWAY.
WHICH IS BAD NEWS FOR POWERED MUSCLE LIKE YOU.
TAKE MY ADVICE, JIM-- FIND A STRAIGHT LINE OF WORK...
...OR FIND A NEW CITY.
SO, UH, HOW MANY MORE OF THESE ARE WE GONNA DO?
I DON'T KNOW. IT'S GOING TO TAKE TIME TO MAKE A REAL DENT IN CAMDEN'S OPERATION.
THIS IS, WHAT, THE EIGHTH SPOT OF HIS WE'VE HIT? I FEEL LIKE HE'S GOTTEN THE MESSAGE BY NOW...
IT'S ABOUT MORE THAN THE MESSAGE.
WE'RE ON STRIKE, KATHRYN. IF ANYONE FINDS OUT...
THEY CAN'T PROVE IT'S US.
...
WHY ARE YOU REALLY DOING THIS?
FOR THE SAME REASON YOU ARE. CAMDEN STONE ALMOST KILLED YOUR PARTNER.
AND WE STAND TOGETHER.
SO IS HE ONBOARD?

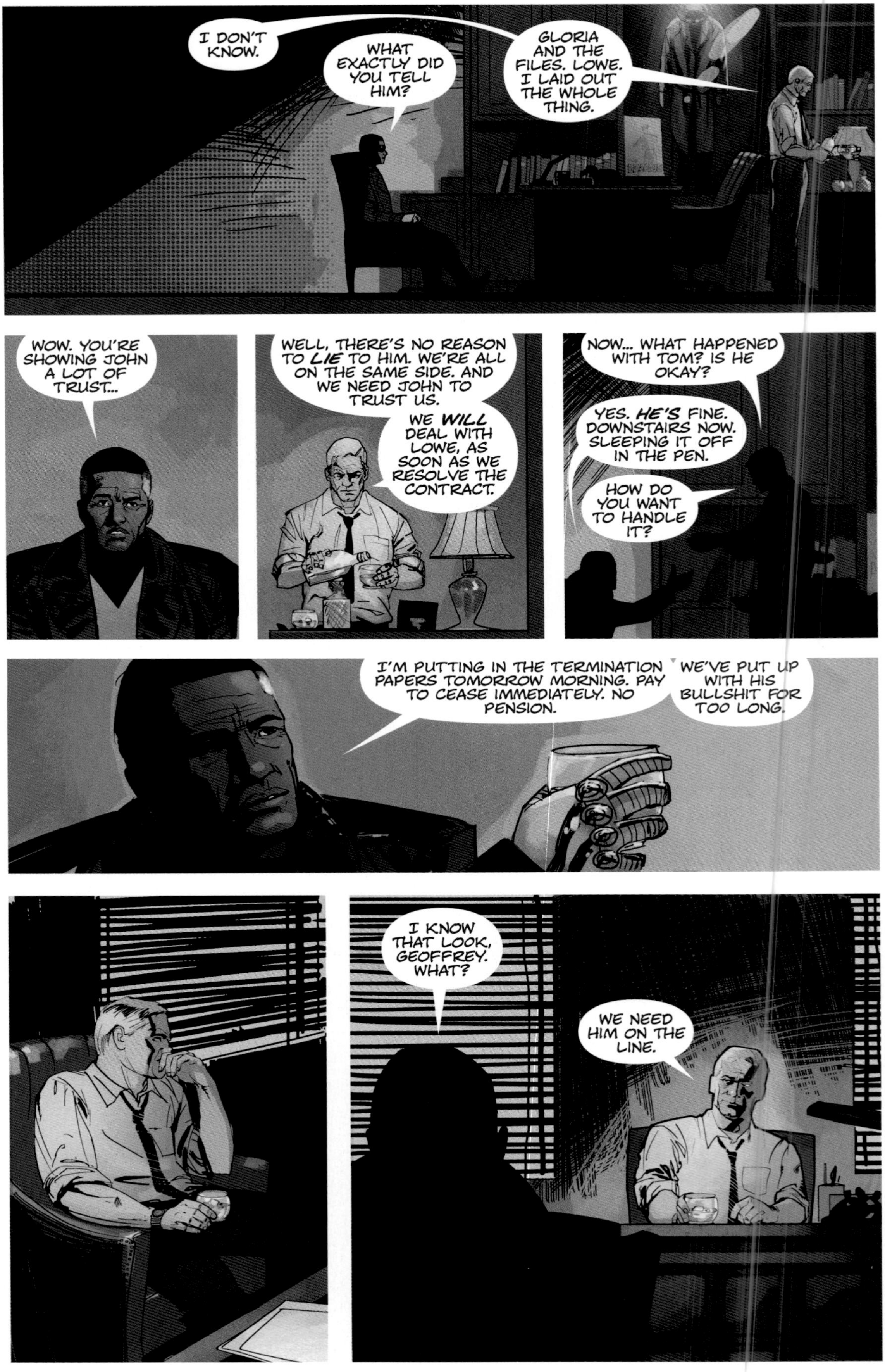
I DON'T KNOW.
WHAT EXACTLY DID YOU TELL HIM?
GLORIA AND THE FILES. LOWE. I LAID OUT THE WHOLE THING.
WOW. YOU'RE SHOWING JOHN A LOT OF TRUST...
WELL, THERE'S NO REASON TO LIE TO HIM. WE'RE ALL ON THE SAME SIDE. AND WE NEED JOHN TO TRUST US.
WE WILL DEAL WITH LOWE, AS SOON AS WE RESOLVE THE CONTRACT.
NOW... WHAT HAPPENED WITH TOM? IS HE OKAY?
YES. HE'S FINE. DOWNSTAIRS NOW. SLEEPING IT OFF IN THE PEN.
HOW DO YOU WANT TO HANDLE IT?
I'M PUTTING IN THE TERMINATION PAPERS TOMORROW MORNING. PAY TO CEASE IMMEDIATELY. NO PENSION.
WE'VE PUT UP WITH HIS BULLSHIT FOR TOO LONG.
I KNOW THAT LOOK, GEOFFREY. WHAT?
WE NEED HIM ON THE LINE.

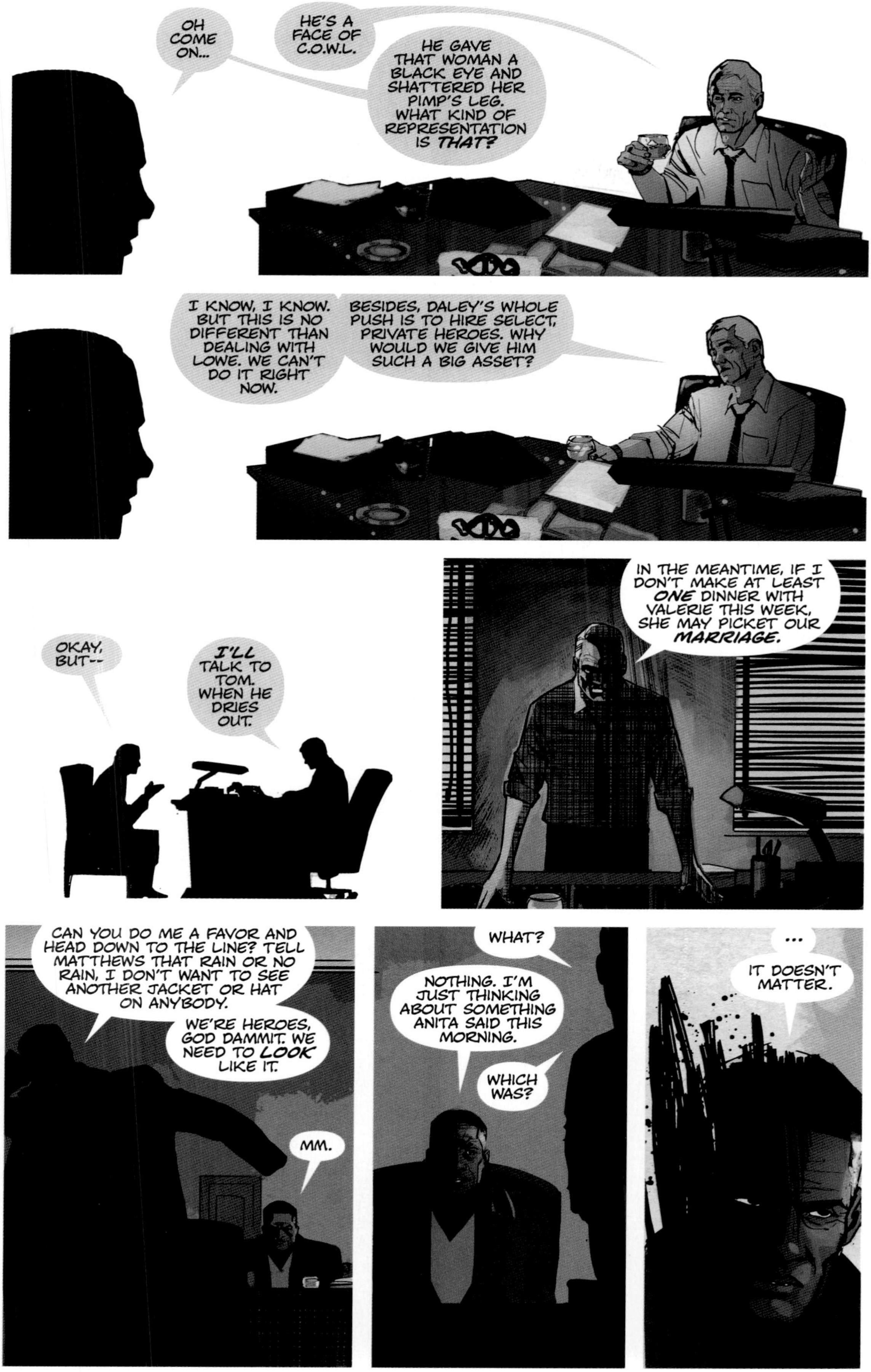
OH COME ON...
HE'S A FACE OF C.O.W.L.
HE GAVE THAT WOMAN A BLACK EYE AND SHATTERED HER PIMP'S LEG. WHAT KIND OF REPRESENTATION IS *THAT?*
I KNOW, I KNOW. BUT THIS IS NO DIFFERENT THAN DEALING WITH LOWE. WE CAN'T DO IT RIGHT NOW.
BESIDES, DALEY'S WHOLE PUSH IS TO HIRE SELECT, PRIVATE HEROES. WHY WOULD WE GIVE HIM SUCH A BIG ASSET?
OKAY, BUT--
I'LL TALK TO TOM. WHEN HE DRIES OUT.
IN THE MEANTIME, IF I DON'T MAKE AT LEAST *ONE* DINNER WITH VALERIE THIS WEEK, SHE MAY PICKET OUR *MARRIAGE.*
CAN YOU DO ME A FAVOR AND HEAD DOWN TO THE LINE? TELL MATTHEWS THAT RAIN OR NO RAIN, I DON'T WANT TO SEE ANOTHER JACKET OR HAT ON ANYBODY.
WE'RE HEROES, GOD DAMMIT. WE NEED TO *LOOK* LIKE IT.
MM.
WHAT?
NOTHING. I'M JUST THINKING ABOUT SOMETHING ANITA SAID THIS MORNING.
WHICH WAS?
...
IT DOESN'T MATTER.

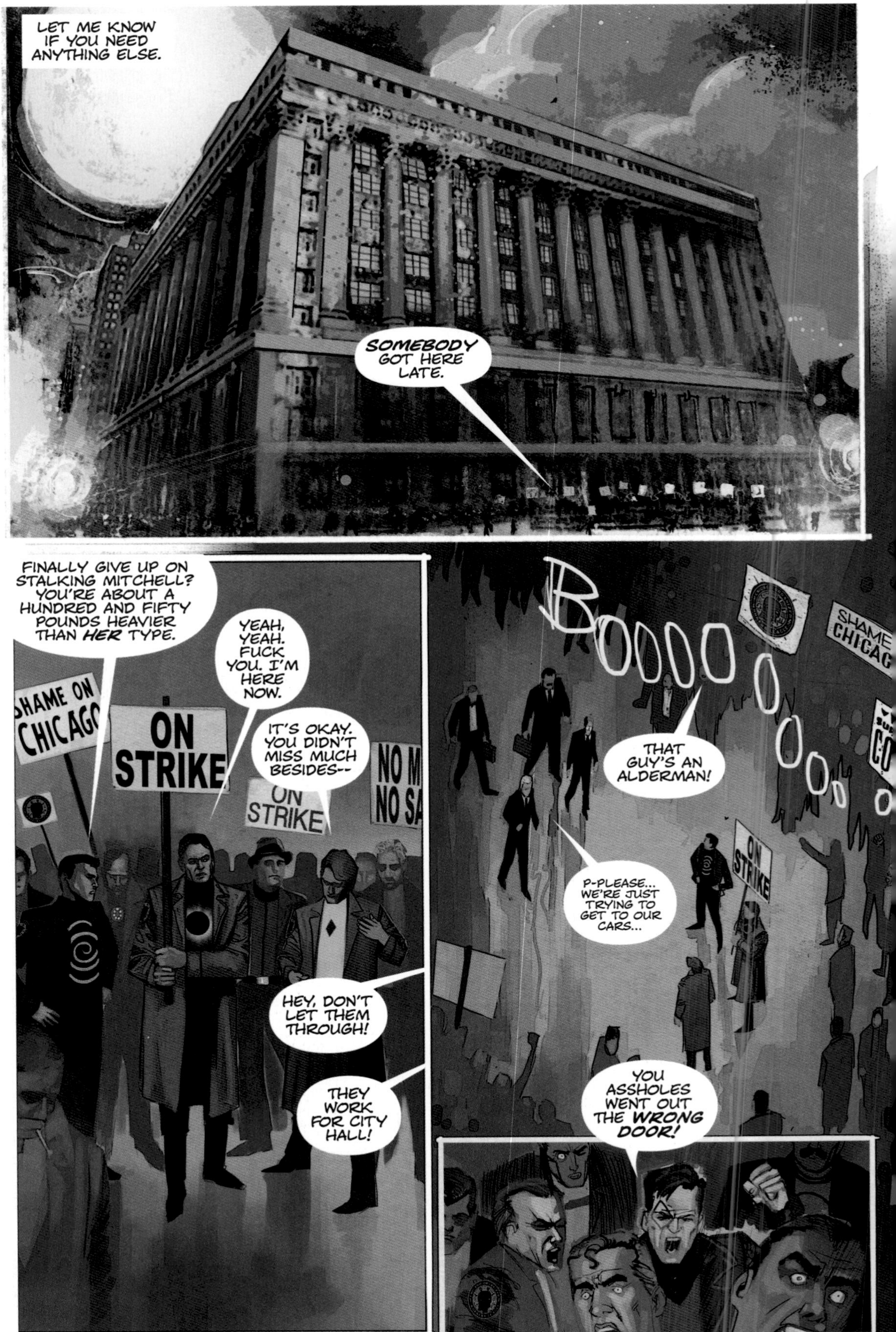
LET ME KNOW IF YOU NEED ANYTHING ELSE.
SOMEBODY GOT HERE LATE.
FINALLY GIVE UP ON STALKING MITCHELL? YOU'RE ABOUT A HUNDRED AND FIFTY POUNDS HEAVIER THAN HER TYPE.
YEAH, YEAH. FUCK YOU. I'M HERE NOW.
IT'S OKAY. YOU DIDN'T MISS MUCH BESIDES--
ON STRIKE
ON STRIKE
HEY, DON'T LET THEM THROUGH!
THEY WORK FOR CITY HALL!
BOOOOOOOOOO
THAT GUY'S AN ALDERMAN!
P-PLEASE... WE'RE JUST TRYING TO GET TO OUR CARS...
ON STRIKE
YOU ASSHOLES WENT OUT THE WRONG DOOR!

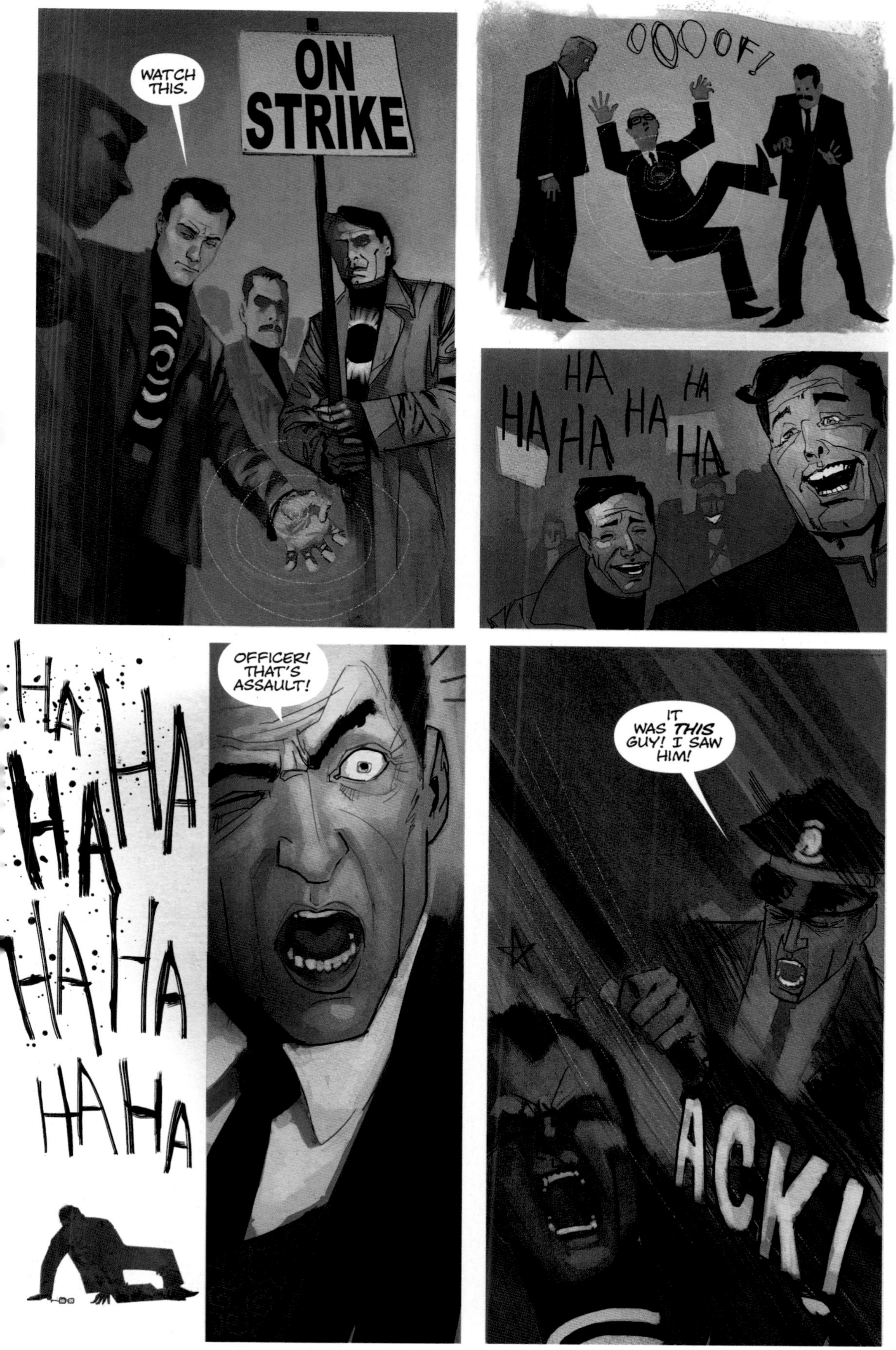
WATCH THIS.
ON STRIKE
OOOOOF!
HA HA HA HA HA HA HA
HA HA HA HA HA HA HA HA
OFFICER! THAT'S ASSAULT!
IT WAS *THIS* GUY! I SAW HIM!
ACK!

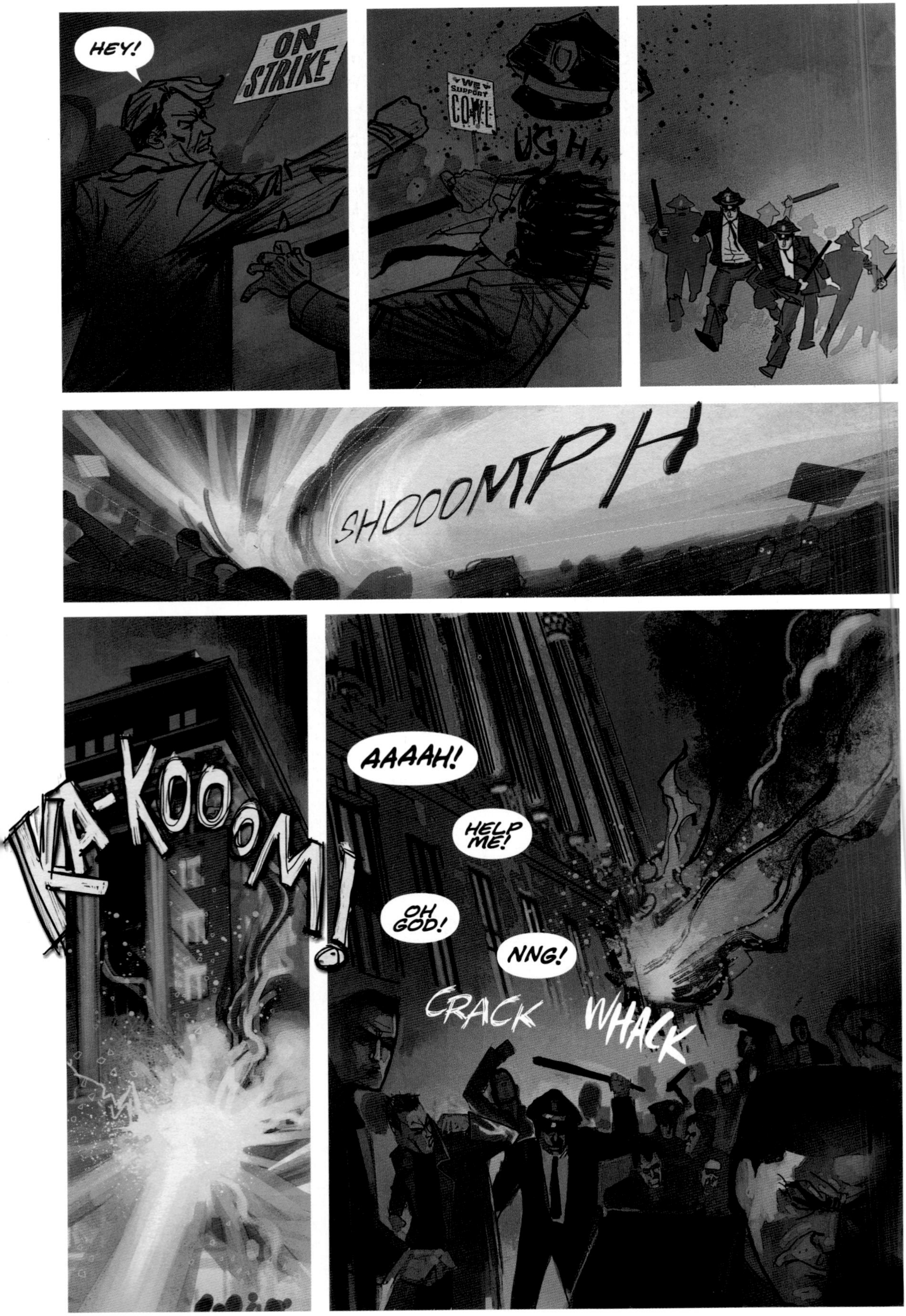
HEY!
ON STRIKE
WE SUPPORT COWL
UGHH
SHOOOMPH
KA-KOOOM!
AAAAH!
HELP ME!
OH GOD!
NNG!
CRACK
WHACK

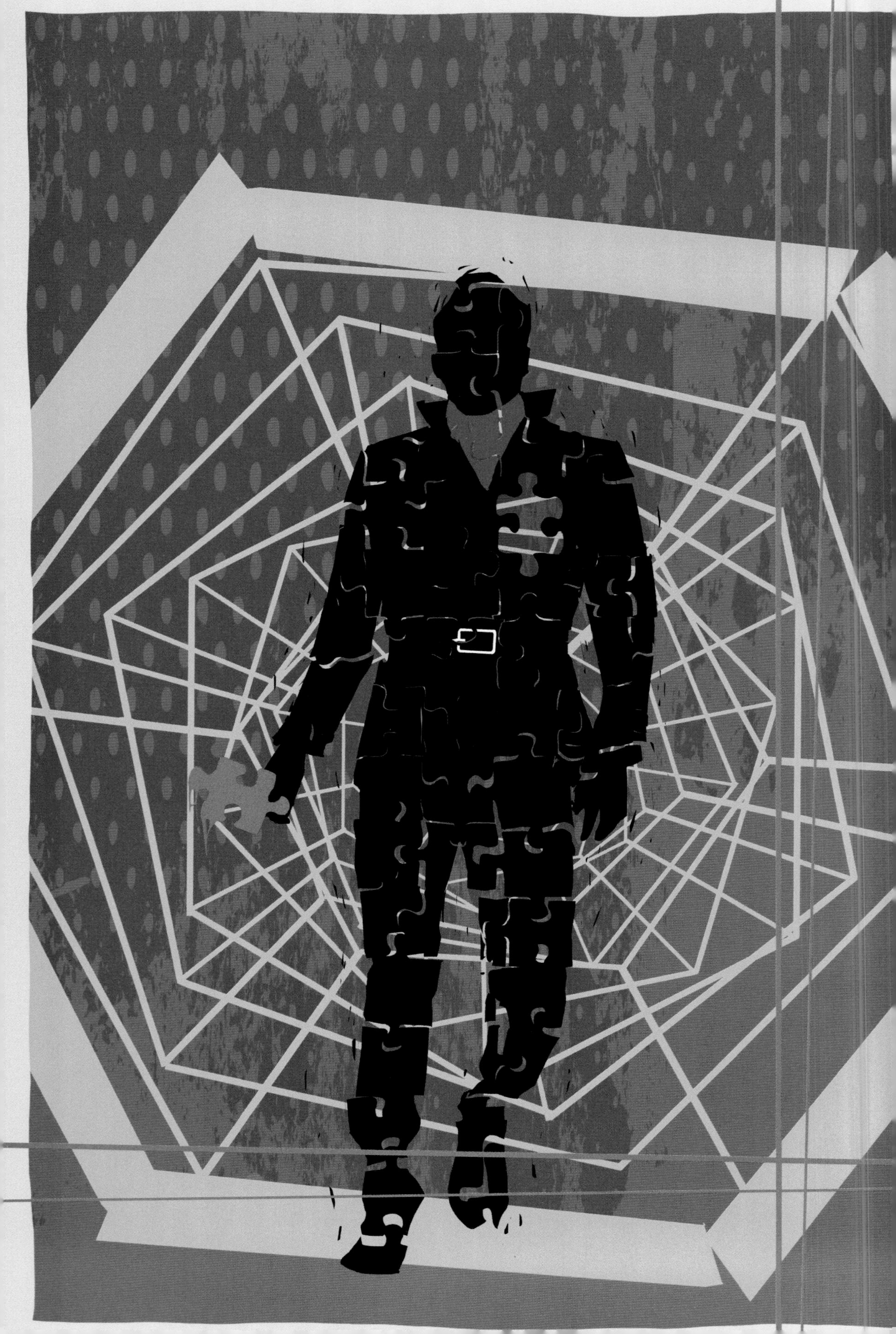

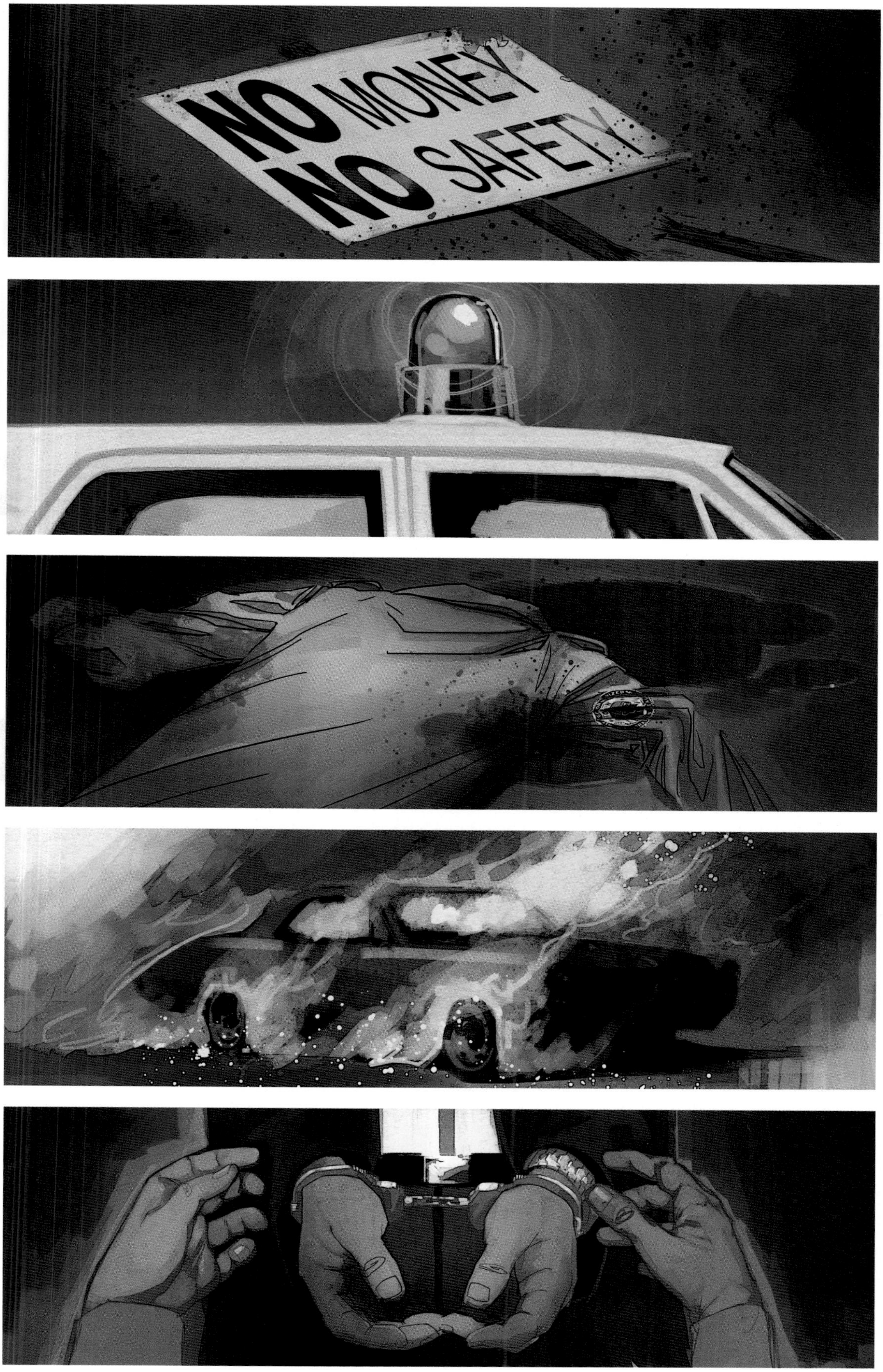
NO MONEY
NO SAFETY

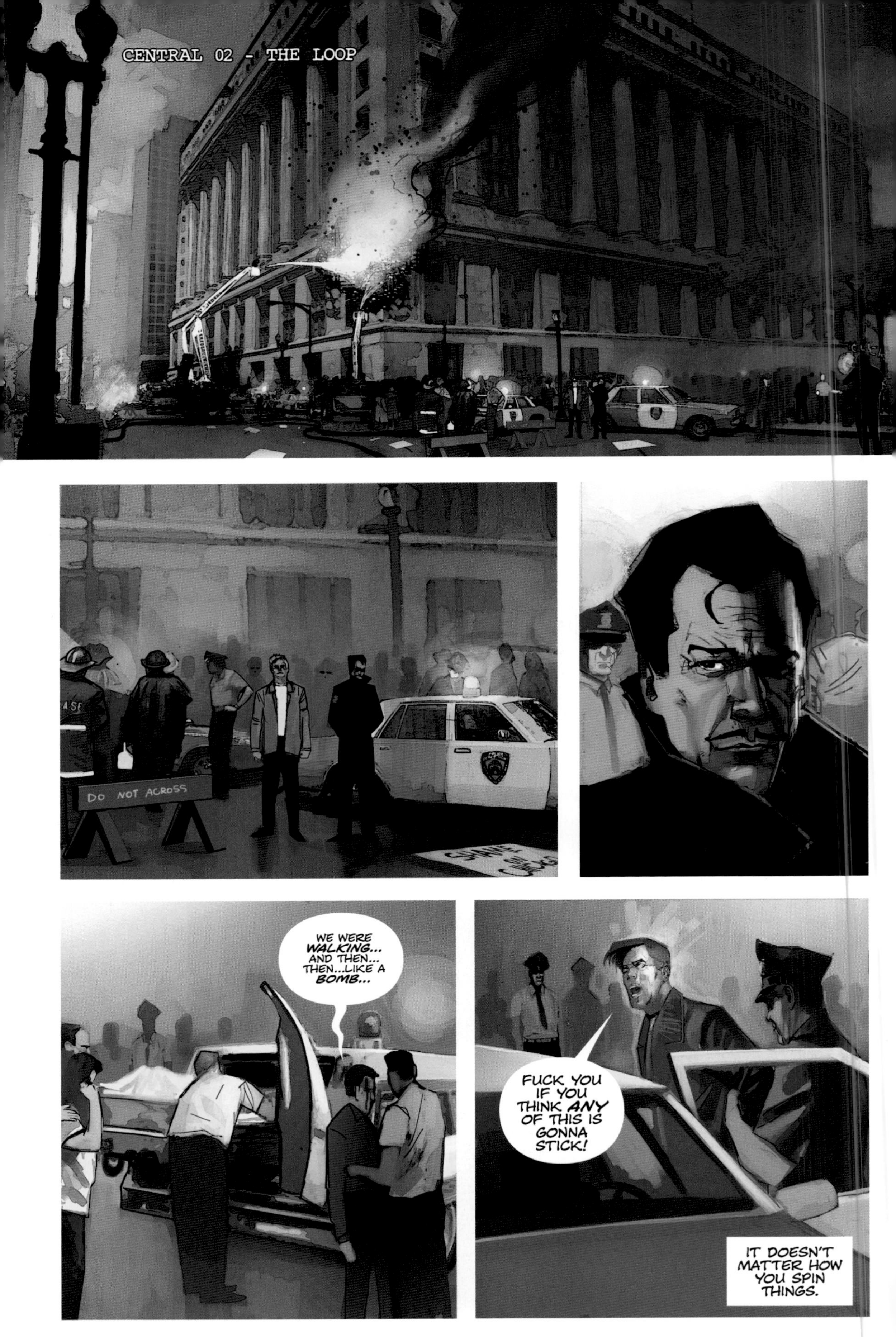
CENTRAL 02 - THE LOOP
DO NOT ACROSS
WE WERE *WALKING*... AND THEN... THEN...LIKE A *BOMB*...
FUCK YOU IF YOU THINK *ANY* OF THIS IS GONNA STICK!
IT DOESN'T MATTER HOW YOU SPIN THINGS.

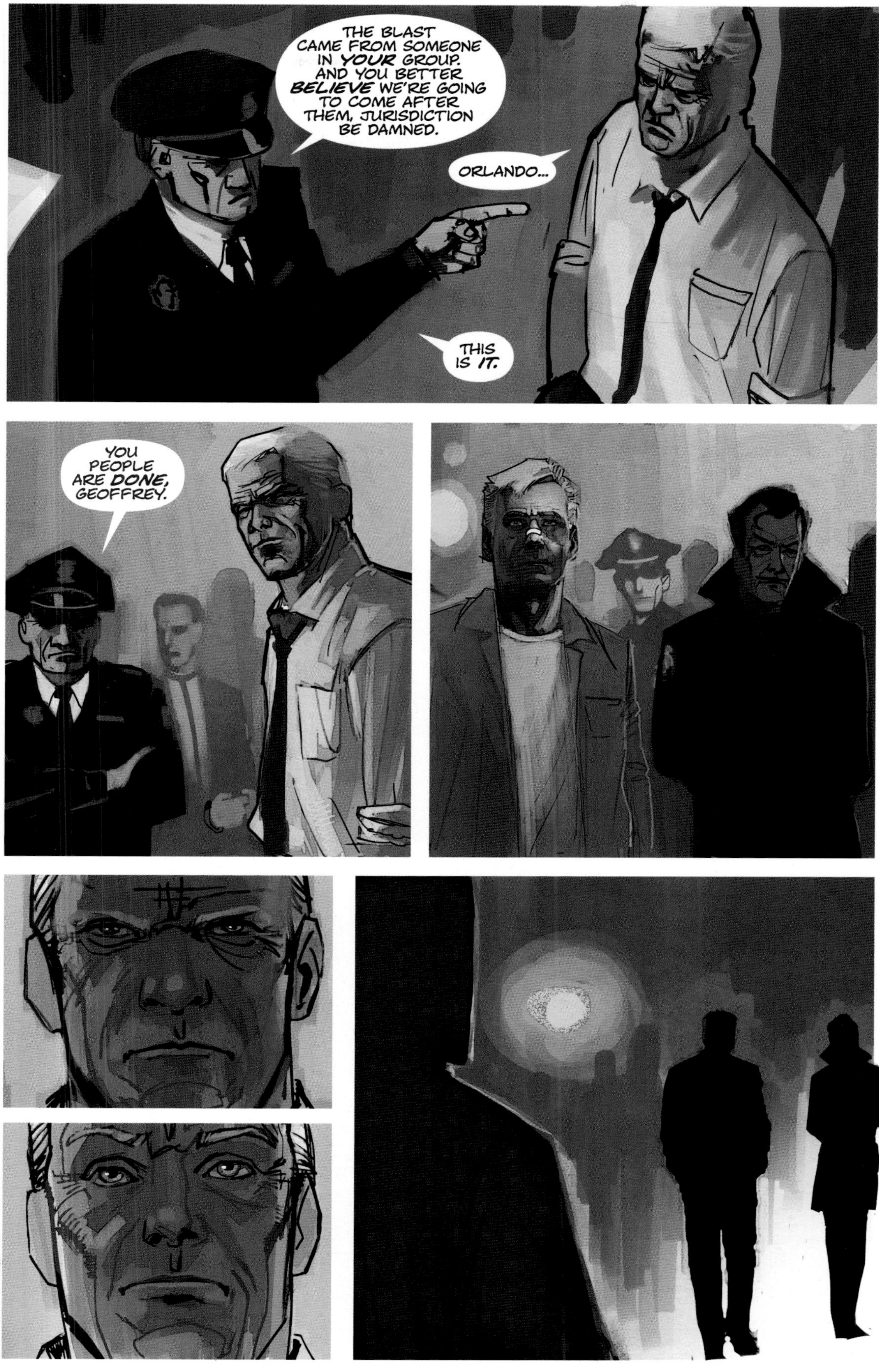
THE BLAST CAME FROM SOMEONE IN YOUR GROUP. AND YOU BETTER BELIEVE WE'RE GOING TO COME AFTER THEM, JURISDICTION BE DAMNED.
ORLANDO...
THIS IS IT.
YOU PEOPLE ARE DONE, GEOFFREY.

CHAPTER 5
Sacrifice

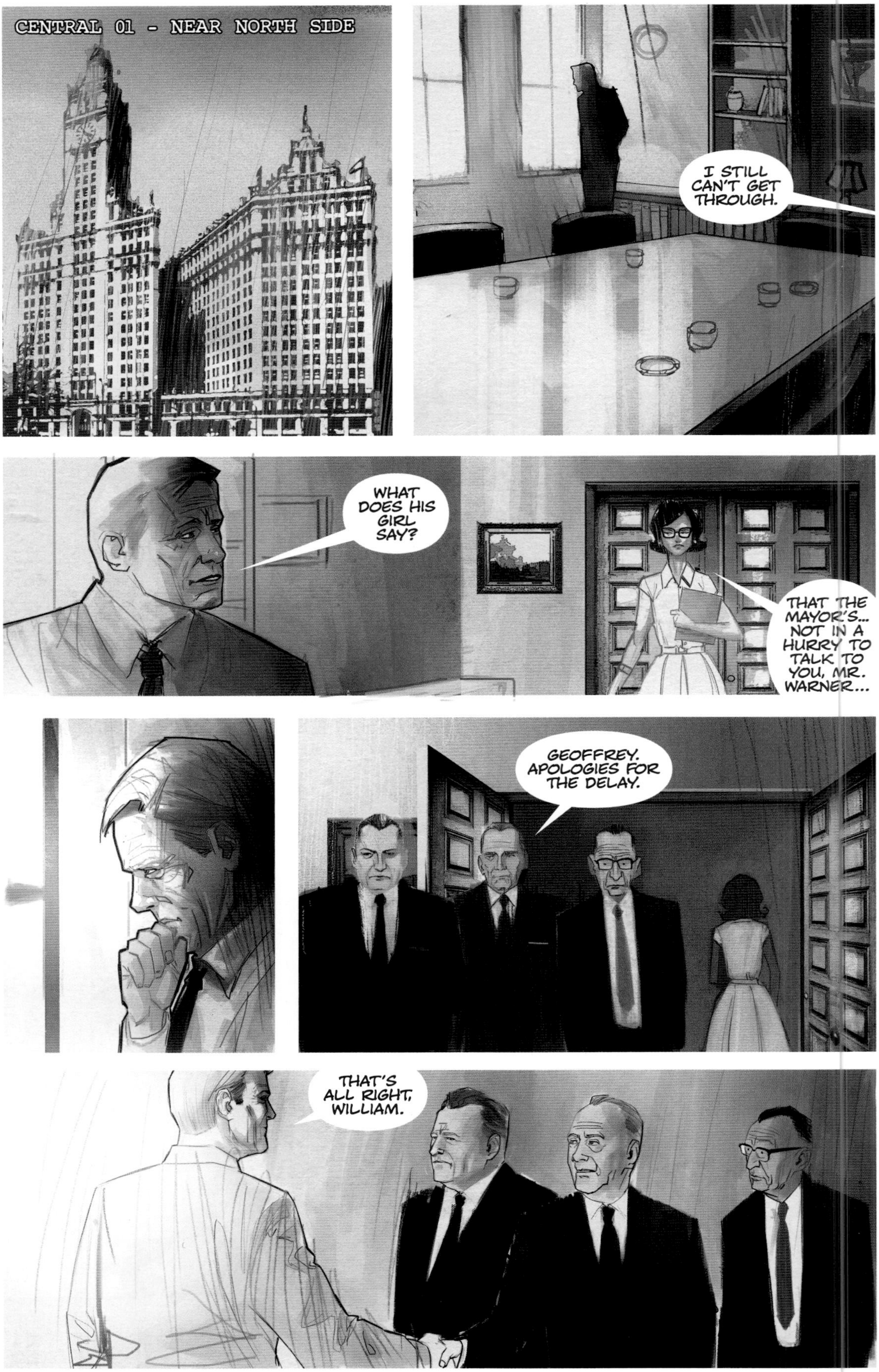
CENTRAL 01 - NEAR NORTH SIDE
I STILL CAN'T GET THROUGH.
WHAT DOES HIS GIRL SAY?
THAT THE MAYOR'S... NOT IN A HURRY TO TALK TO YOU, MR. WARNER...
GEOFFREY. APOLOGIES FOR THE DELAY.
THAT'S ALL RIGHT, WILLIAM.

YOU HAVE A LOT OF DUCKS TO LINE UP, SO WE'LL KEEP THIS SHORT.

THE BRICKLAYERS AND RAIL WORKERS ARE OUT, AND AFTER TALKING TO JOHN AND BILL HERE... BOTH THE TEACHERS AND SERVICE EMPLOYEES ARE PULLING THEIR SUPPORT, TOO.

WHAT?

THERE WERE PEOPLE *IN* THE BUILDING... NOT TO SAY ANYTHING OF THE ONES ON THE STREET. YOU'RE FORTUNATE NO ONE'S *DEAD.*

SULLIVAN AND I DON'T SEE EYE-TO-EYE ON MUCH, BUT WE'RE IN AGREEMENT HERE.

AND I'M SURE YOUR RELATIONSHIP WITH THE MAYOR HAS NOTHING TO DO WITH IT.

TAKE IT HOWEVER YOU'D LIKE.

WHAT ABOUT YOU, JOHN?

THE SCHOOL BOARD CONTRACTS ARE UP NEXT YEAR...

SO THE CITY'S TWO MOST POWERFUL UNIONS ARE WALKING AWAY, HANGING US OUT TO DRY.

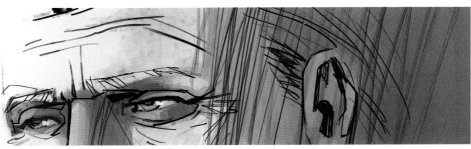

WHAT GOOD IS HAVING A LABOR FEDERATION IF WE'RE NOT ALL IN IT *TOGETHER?*

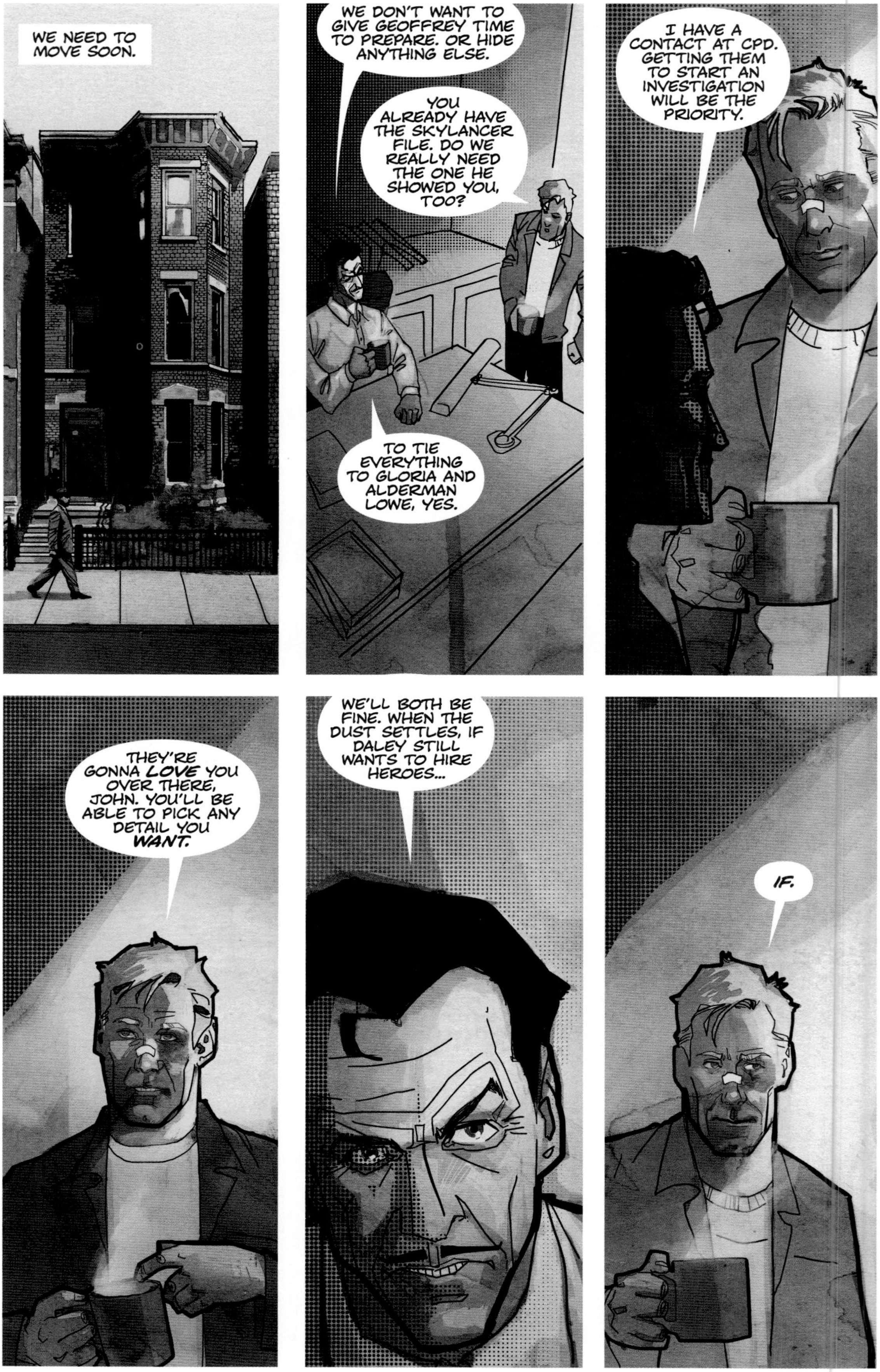

WE NEED TO MOVE SOON.
WE DON'T WANT TO GIVE GEOFFREY TIME TO PREPARE. OR HIDE ANYTHING ELSE.
YOU ALREADY HAVE THE SKYLANCER FILE. DO WE REALLY NEED THE ONE HE SHOWED YOU, TOO?
TO TIE EVERYTHING TO GLORIA AND ALDERMAN LOWE, YES.
I HAVE A CONTACT AT CPD. GETTING THEM TO START AN INVESTIGATION WILL BE THE PRIORITY.
THEY'RE GONNA LOVE YOU OVER THERE, JOHN. YOU'LL BE ABLE TO PICK ANY DETAIL YOU WANT.
WE'LL BOTH BE FINE. WHEN THE DUST SETTLES, IF DALEY STILL WANTS TO HIRE HEROES...
IF.

THERE'RE ALWAYS OTHER CITIES, TOO, TOM. OR THE MILITARY.

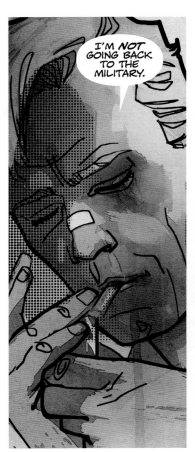

I'M *NOT* GOING BACK TO THE MILITARY.

BUT SCREW IT. I HAVE YOUR BACK.

AGAIN.

AFTER FIVE YEARS AND EVERYTHING I'VE PUT INTO THIS PLACE, THEY ACT LIKE I'M JUST AN EMBARRASSMENT.

THEY WANT ME TO BE OUT IN FRONT, BUT GOD FORBID I HAVE AN OPINION.

I'M TIRED OF "GEOFFREY WARNER KNOWS BEST." FUCK *HIM*. FUCK C.O.W.L.

MCFETRIDGE HAS THE SERVICE WORKERS PULLING THEIR SUPPORT.

AND FEWKES IS DOING THE SAME THING WITH THE TEACHERS.

WE STOOD WITH *BOTH* OF THEM IN '56 AND '58. NOW THEY'RE TURNING THEIR *BACKS.*

WOW...

I NEED ANOTHER PIECE. TO RUN TOMORROW, IF POSSIBLE. RALLY WHATEVER SUPPORT WE CAN.

I DON'T KNOW THAT I CAN DO THAT.

IF NOT FOR THE MORNING, THEN THE EVENING EDITION. WE CAN MAKE THAT DEADLINE WITHOUT A PROBLEM.

NO, I MEAN... ANYTHING I WRITE NOW... IT LOOKS LIKE I'M DEFENDING WHAT HAPPENED. I'LL LOSE MY CREDIBILITY.

CREDIBILITY?

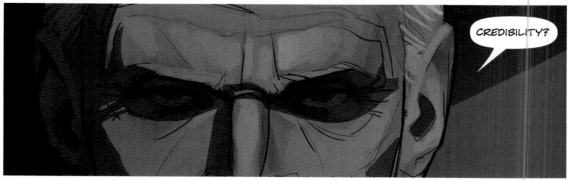

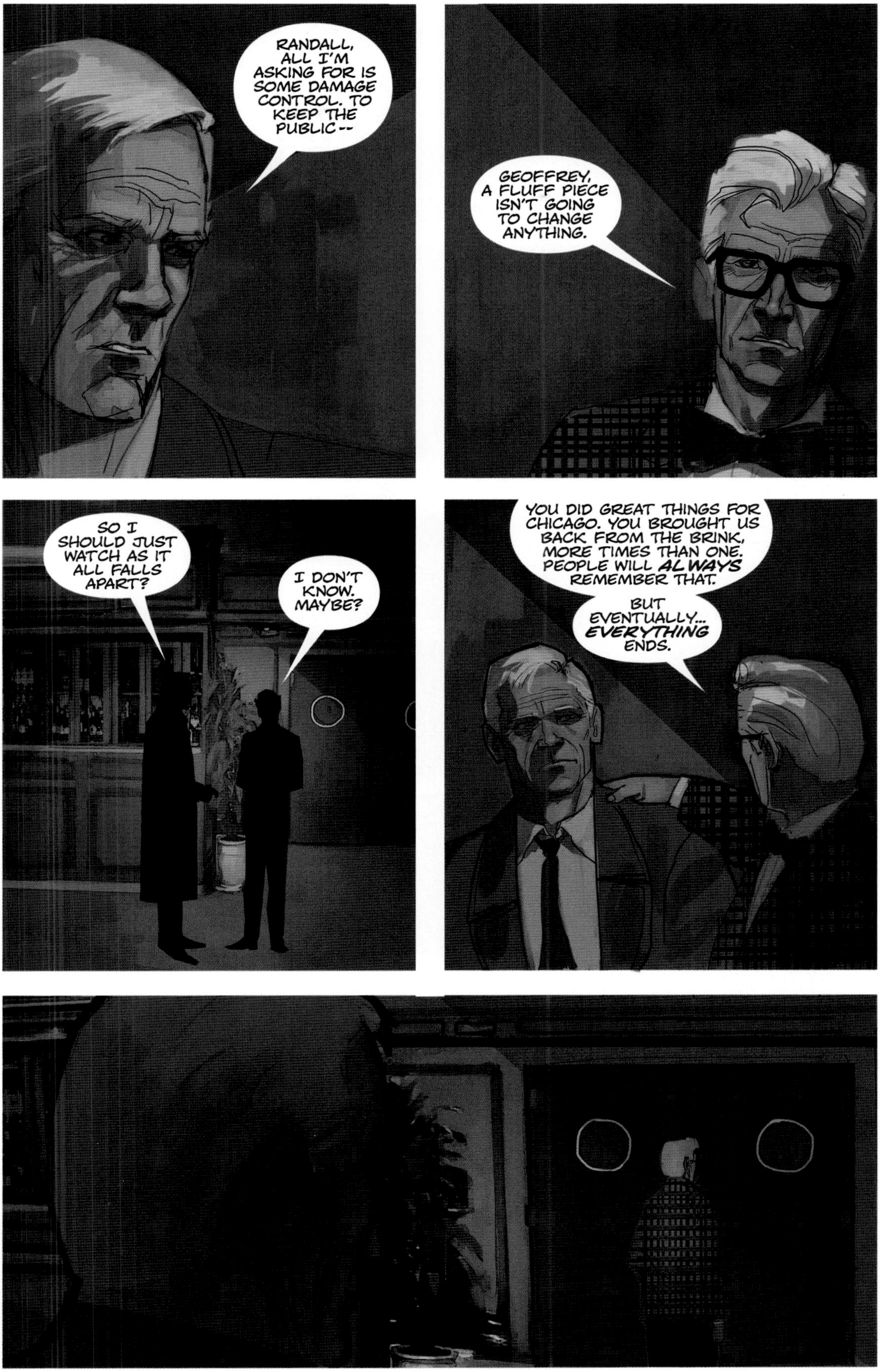
RANDALL, ALL I'M ASKING FOR IS SOME DAMAGE CONTROL. TO KEEP THE PUBLIC--
GEOFFREY, A FLUFF PIECE ISN'T GOING TO CHANGE ANYTHING.
SO I SHOULD JUST WATCH AS IT ALL FALLS APART?
I DON'T KNOW. MAYBE?
YOU DID GREAT THINGS FOR CHICAGO. YOU BROUGHT US BACK FROM THE BRINK, MORE TIMES THAN ONE. PEOPLE WILL ALWAYS REMEMBER THAT.
BUT EVENTUALLY... EVERYTHING ENDS.

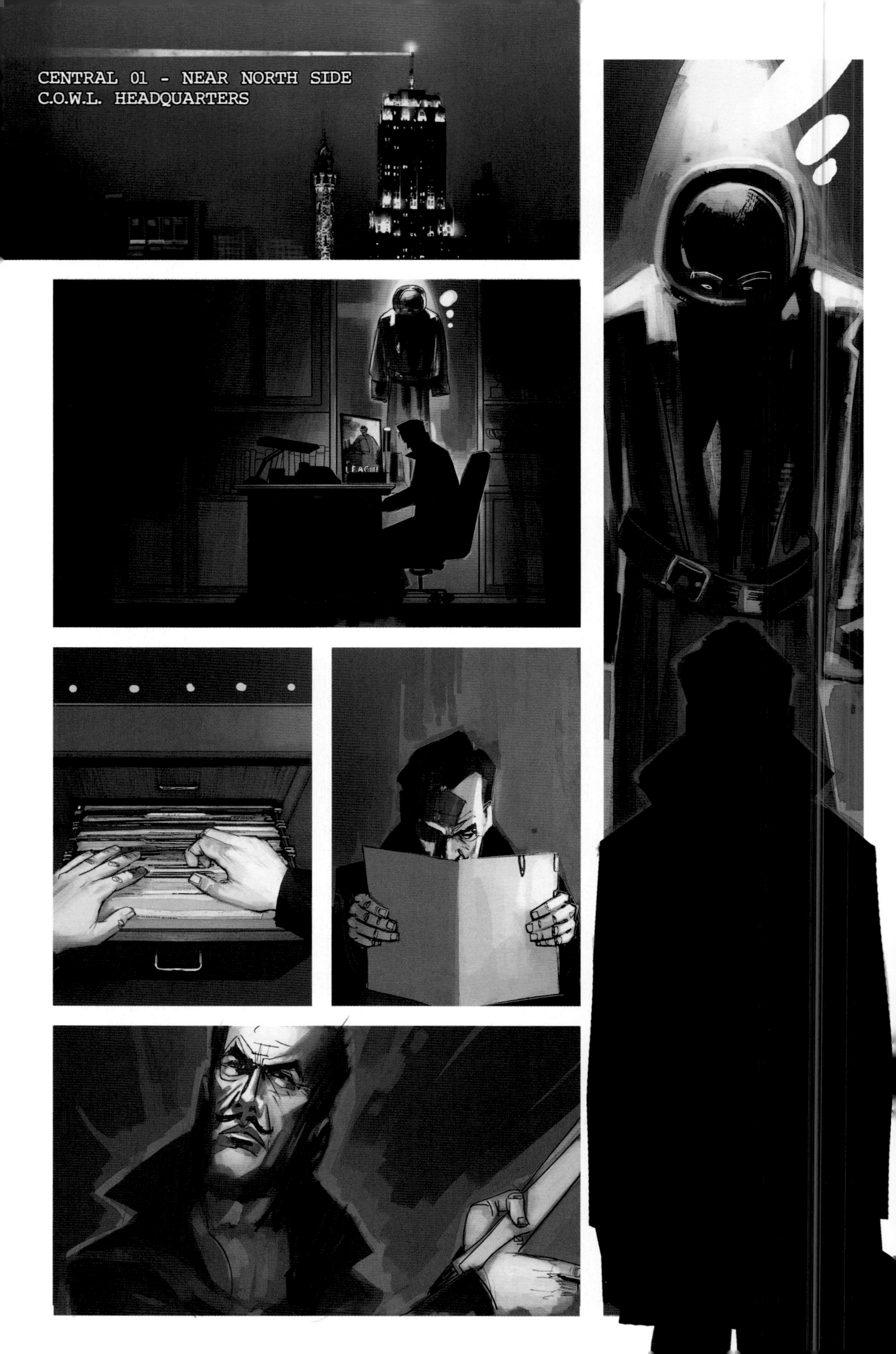
CENTRAL 01 - NEAR NORTH SIDE
C.O.W.L. HEADQUARTERS

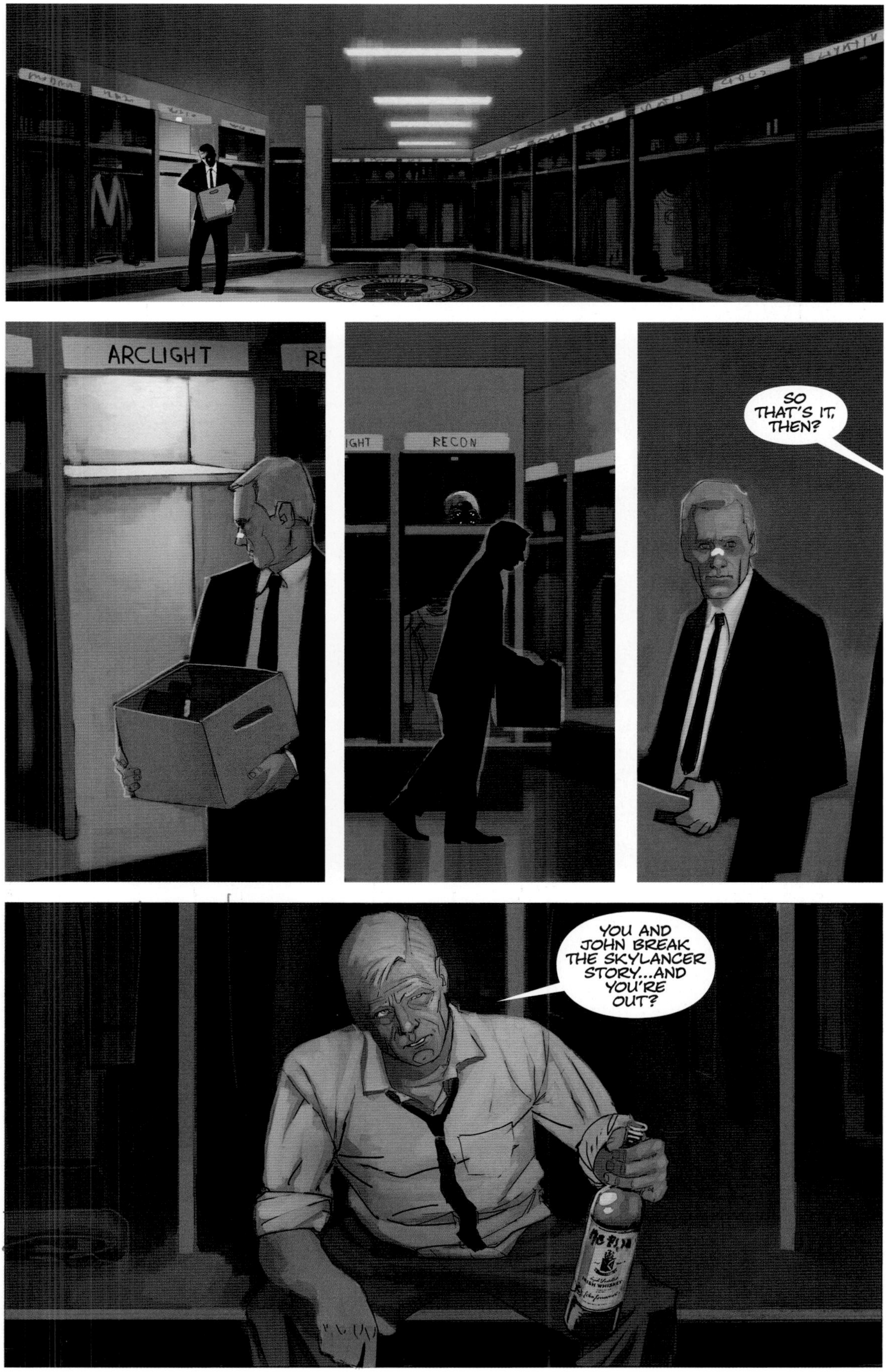
ARCLIGHT
RECON
SO THAT'S IT, THEN?
YOU AND JOHN BREAK THE SKYLANCER STORY...AND YOU'RE OUT?

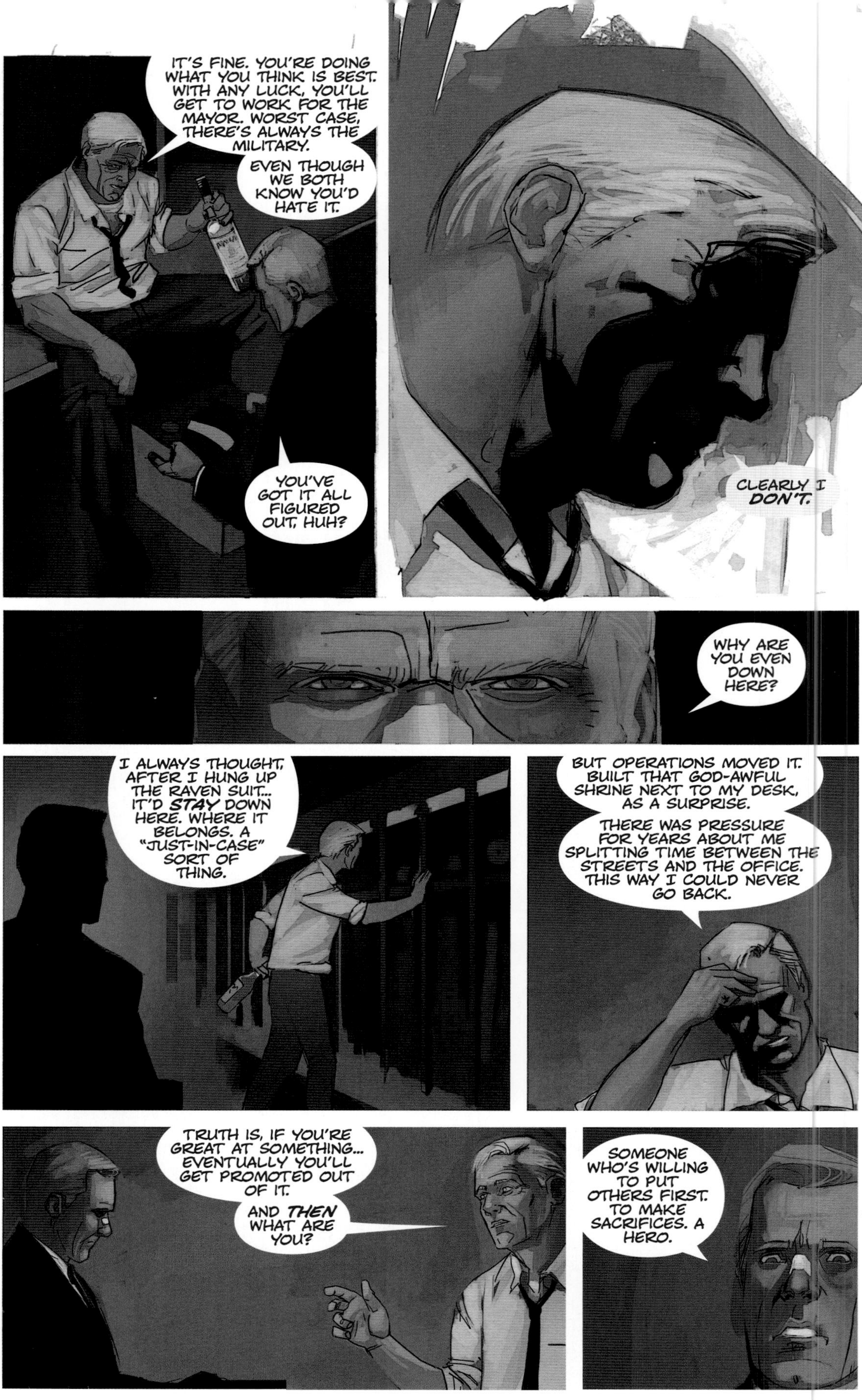

IT'S FINE. YOU'RE DOING WHAT YOU THINK IS BEST. WITH ANY LUCK, YOU'LL GET TO WORK FOR THE MAYOR. WORST CASE, THERE'S ALWAYS THE MILITARY.
EVEN THOUGH WE BOTH KNOW YOU'D HATE IT.
YOU'VE GOT IT ALL FIGURED OUT, HUH?
CLEARLY I *DON'T.*
WHY ARE YOU EVEN DOWN HERE?
I ALWAYS THOUGHT, AFTER I HUNG UP THE RAVEN SUIT... IT'D *STAY* DOWN HERE. WHERE IT BELONGS. A "JUST-IN-CASE" SORT OF THING.
BUT OPERATIONS MOVED IT. BUILT THAT GOD-AWFUL SHRINE NEXT TO MY DESK, AS A SURPRISE.
THERE WAS PRESSURE FOR YEARS ABOUT ME SPLITTING TIME BETWEEN THE STREETS AND THE OFFICE. THIS WAY I COULD NEVER GO BACK.
TRUTH IS, IF YOU'RE GREAT AT SOMETHING... EVENTUALLY YOU'LL GET PROMOTED OUT OF IT.
AND *THEN* WHAT ARE YOU?
SOMEONE WHO'S WILLING TO PUT OTHERS FIRST. TO MAKE SACRIFICES. A HERO.

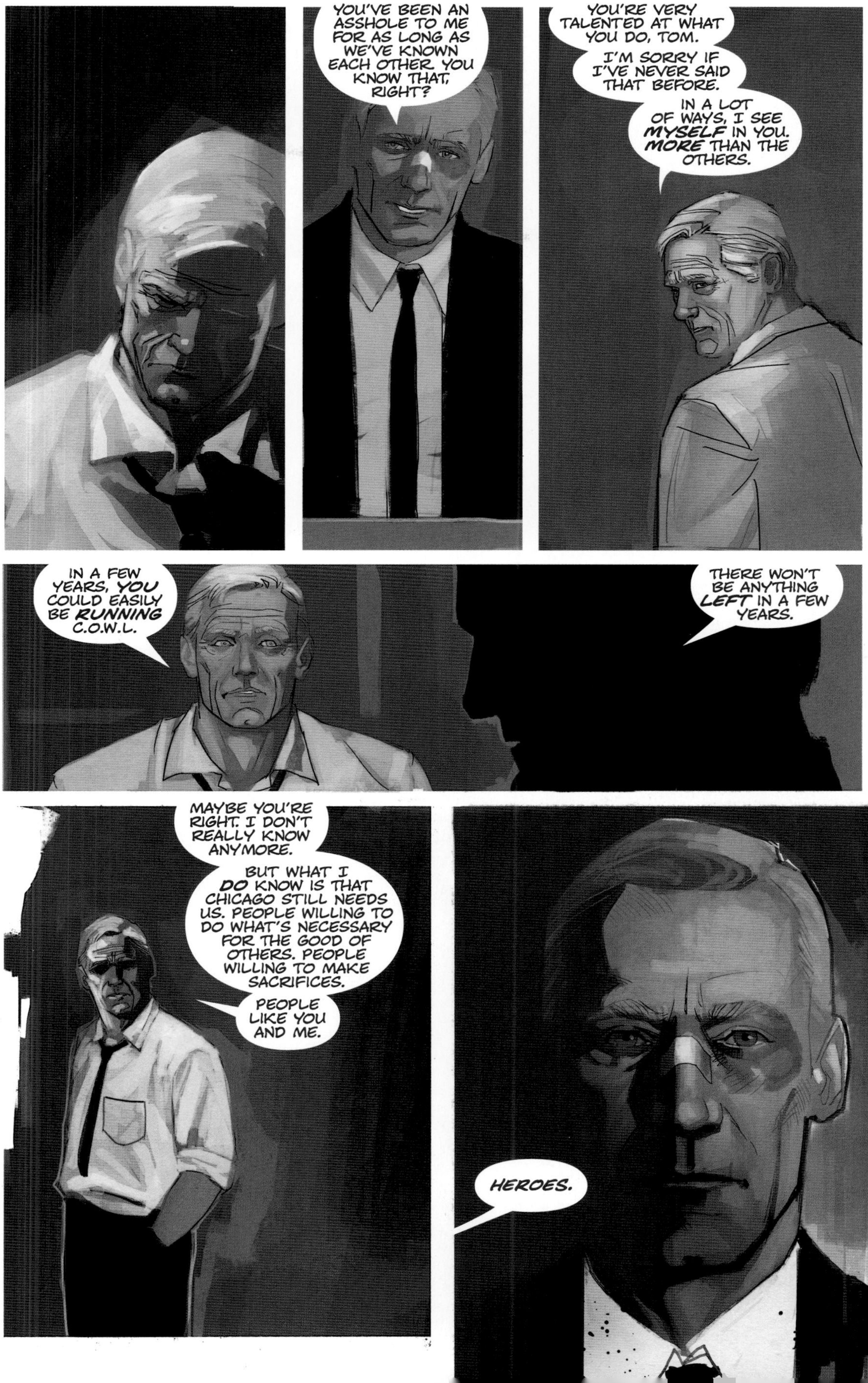
YOU'VE BEEN AN ASSHOLE TO ME FOR AS LONG AS WE'VE KNOWN EACH OTHER. YOU KNOW THAT, RIGHT?
YOU'RE VERY TALENTED AT WHAT YOU DO, TOM.
I'M SORRY IF I'VE NEVER SAID THAT BEFORE.
IN A LOT OF WAYS, I SEE MYSELF IN YOU. MORE THAN THE OTHERS.
IN A FEW YEARS, YOU COULD EASILY BE RUNNING C.O.W.L.
THERE WON'T BE ANYTHING LEFT IN A FEW YEARS.
MAYBE YOU'RE RIGHT. I DON'T REALLY KNOW ANYMORE.
BUT WHAT I DO KNOW IS THAT CHICAGO STILL NEEDS US. PEOPLE WILLING TO DO WHAT'S NECESSARY FOR THE GOOD OF OTHERS. PEOPLE WILLING TO MAKE SACRIFICES.
PEOPLE LIKE YOU AND ME.
HEROES.

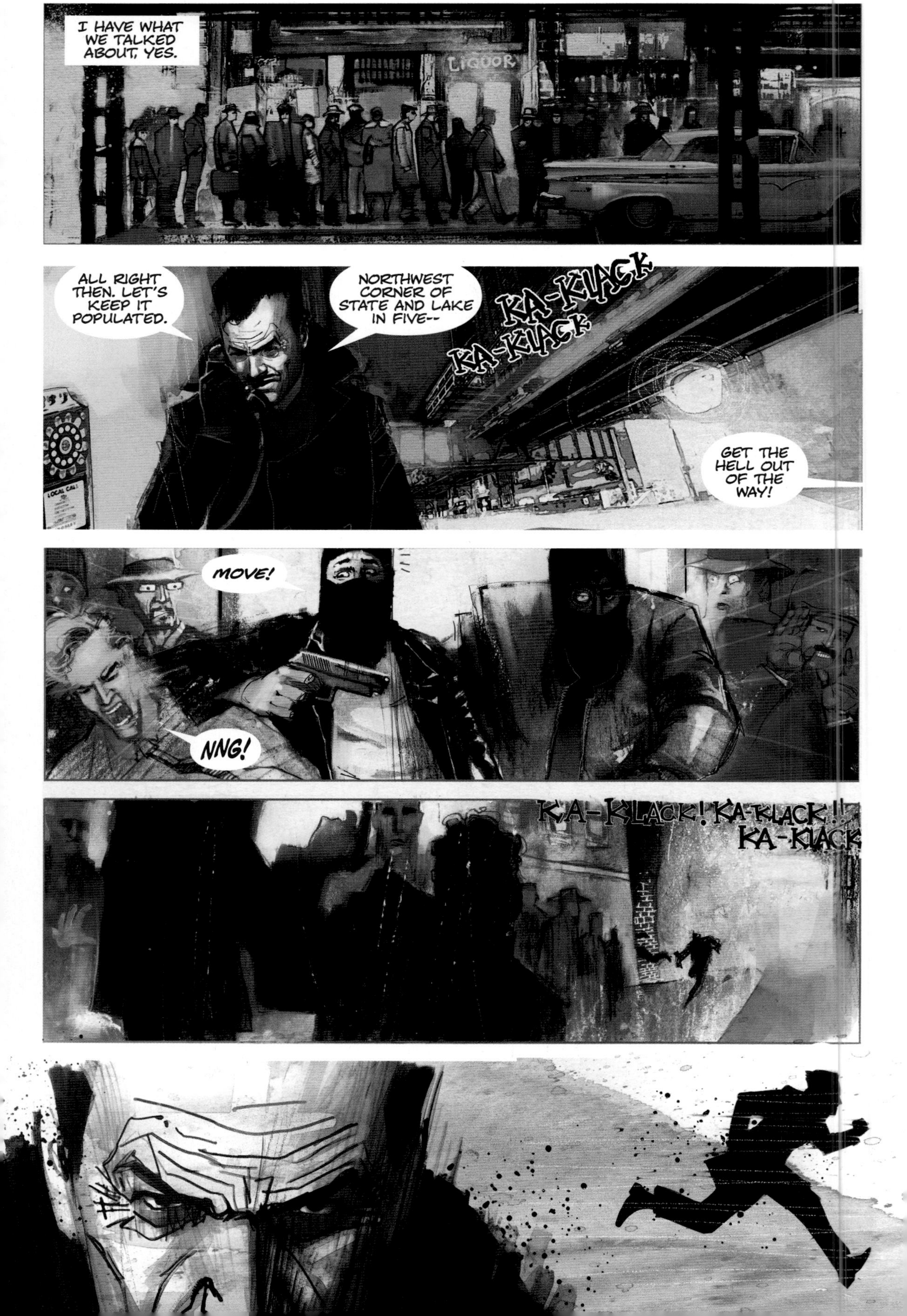
I HAVE WHAT WE TALKED ABOUT, YES.
LIQUOR
ALL RIGHT THEN. LET'S KEEP IT POPULATED.
NORTHWEST CORNER OF STATE AND LAKE IN FIVE--
KA-KLACK
KA-KLACK
GET THE HELL OUT OF THE WAY!
MOVE!
NNG!
KA-KLACK! KA-KLACK!!
KA-KLACK

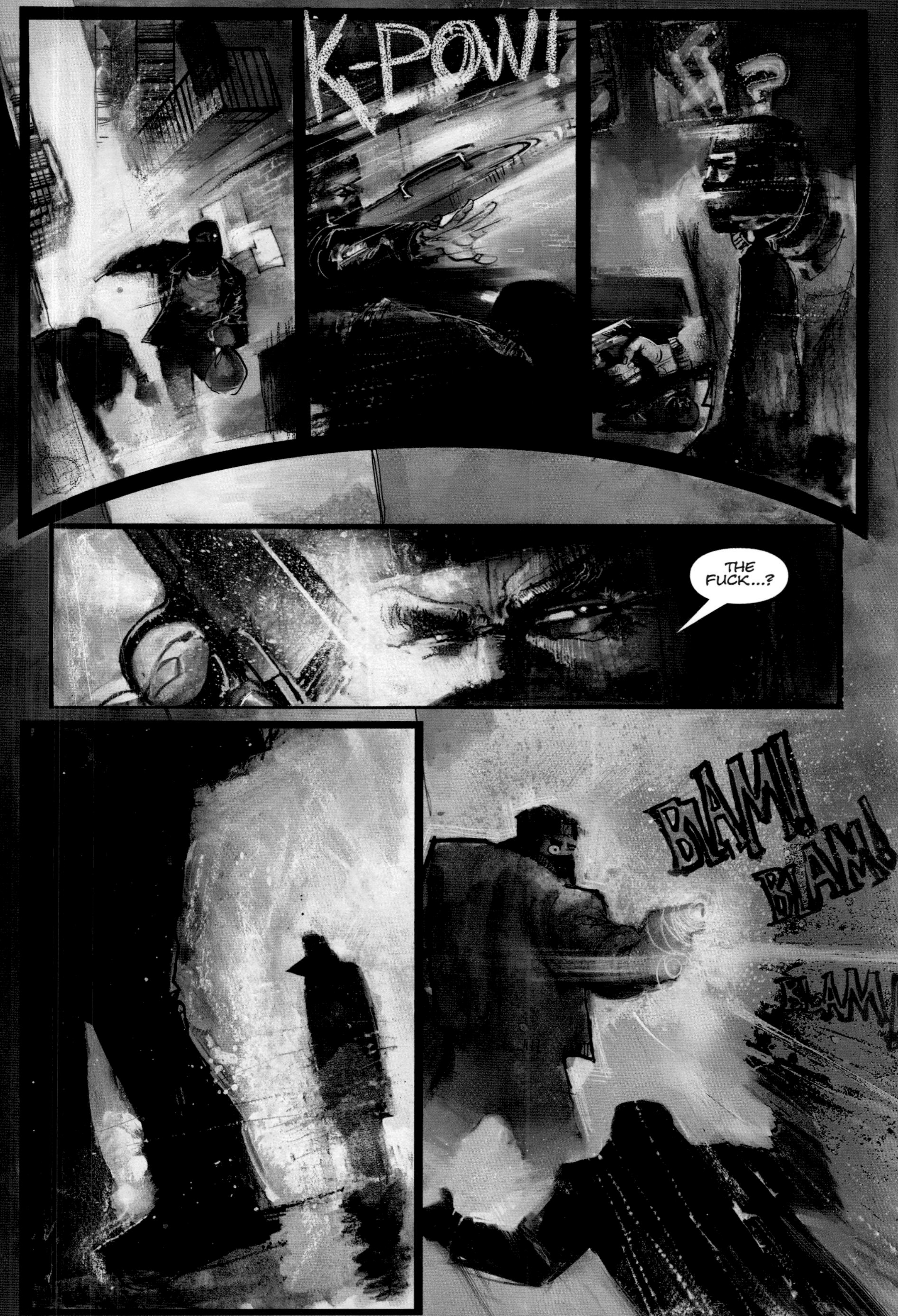
K-POW!
THE FUCK...?
BLAM!
BLAM!
BLAM!

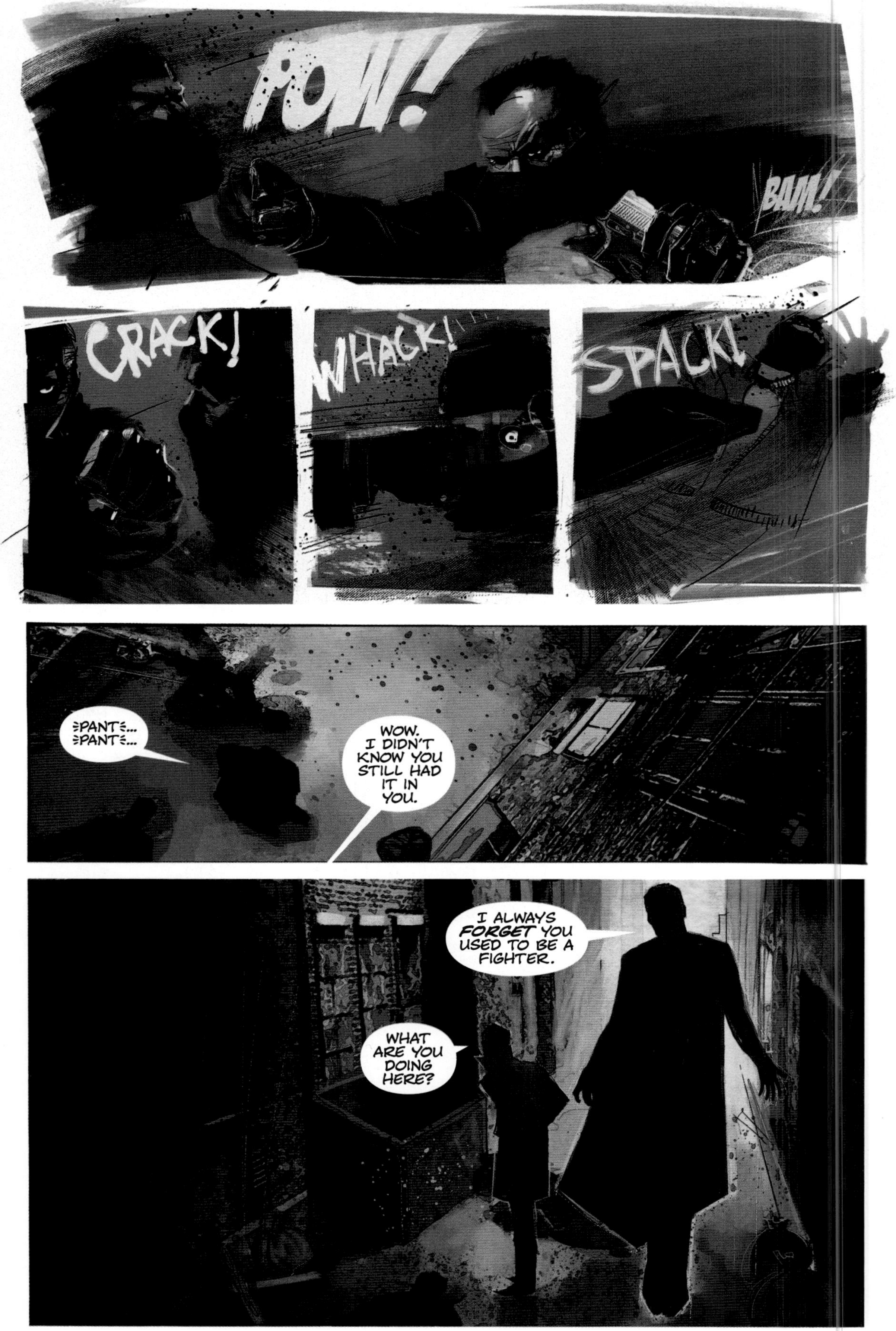
POW!
BAM!
CRACK!
WHACK!
SPACK!
PANT... PANT...
WOW. I DIDN'T KNOW YOU STILL HAD IT IN YOU.
I ALWAYS FORGET YOU USED TO BE A FIGHTER.
WHAT ARE YOU DOING HERE?

TRYING TO FIND YOU, ACTUALLY. BEFORE THE MEET. I HEARD THE SCREAMS... AND...

...YEAH...

THERE'S NO TALKING YOU OUT OF THIS, RIGHT?

YOU KNOW, THE ODDS OF THESE GUYS ROBBING THAT PLACE WHEN THEY DID, *WHERE* THEY DID, AND YOU JUMPING IN TO STOP THEM...

IF YOU *HADN'T*, YOU'D PROBABLY ALREADY BE WITH YOUR CONTACT.

THAT'S PRETTY WILD, WHEN YOU THINK ABOUT IT.

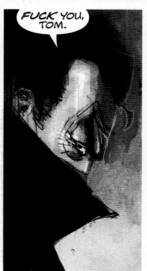

FUCK YOU, TOM.

...

I'M SORRY, JOHN.

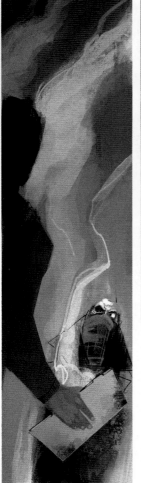

I ALWAYS THOUGHT I WOULD SEE THE END COMING.

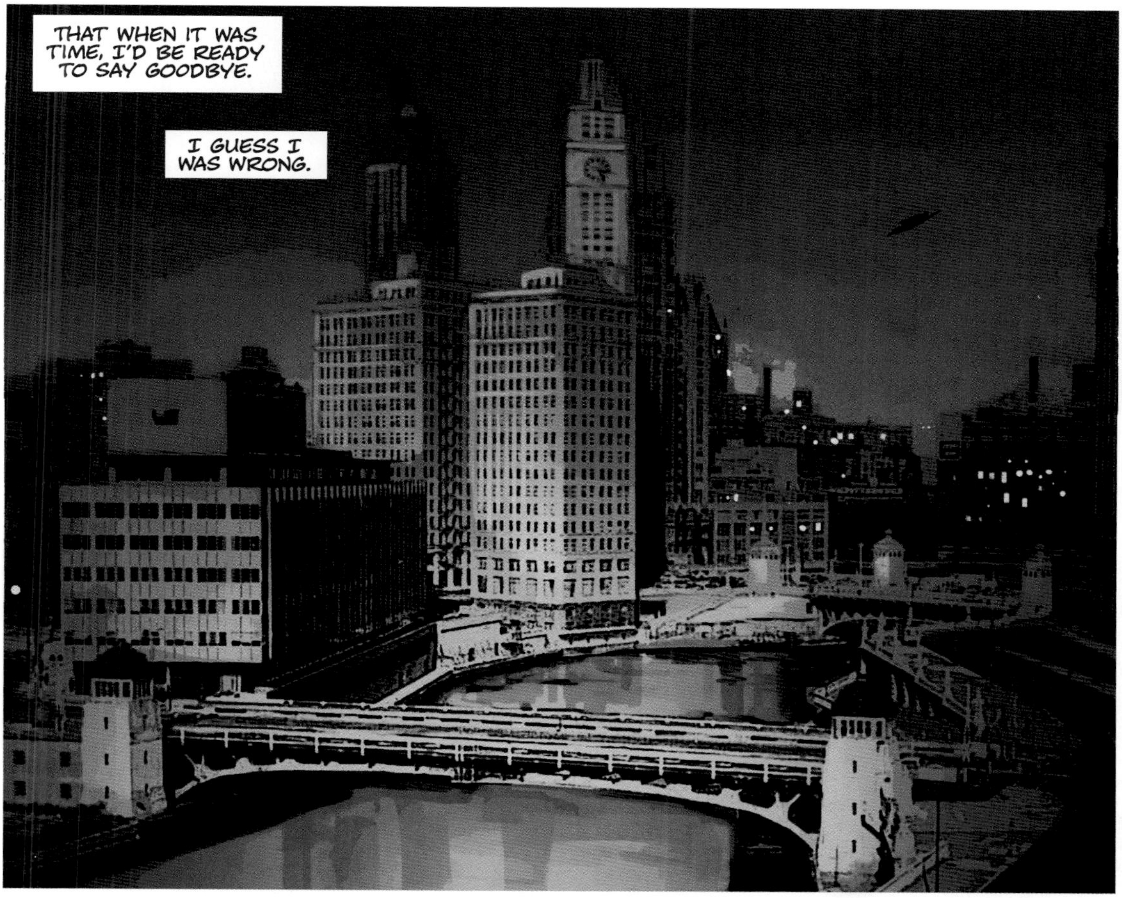
THAT WHEN IT WAS TIME, I'D BE READY TO SAY GOODBYE.
I GUESS I WAS WRONG.

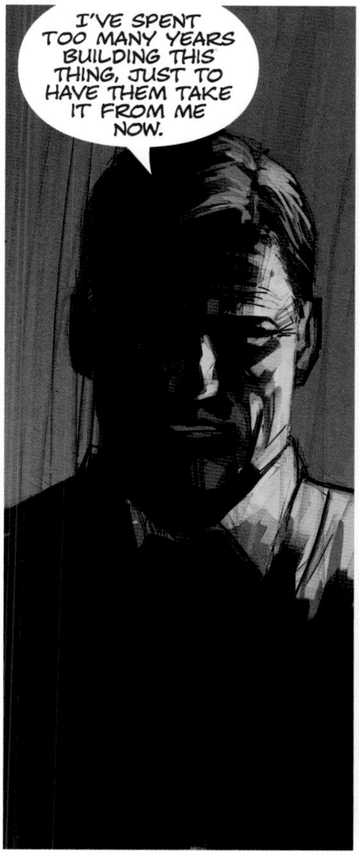
I'VE SPENT TOO MANY YEARS BUILDING THIS THING, JUST TO HAVE THEM TAKE IT FROM ME NOW.

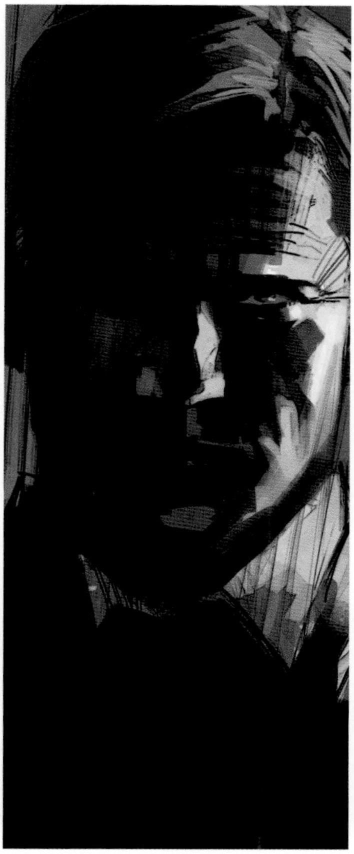

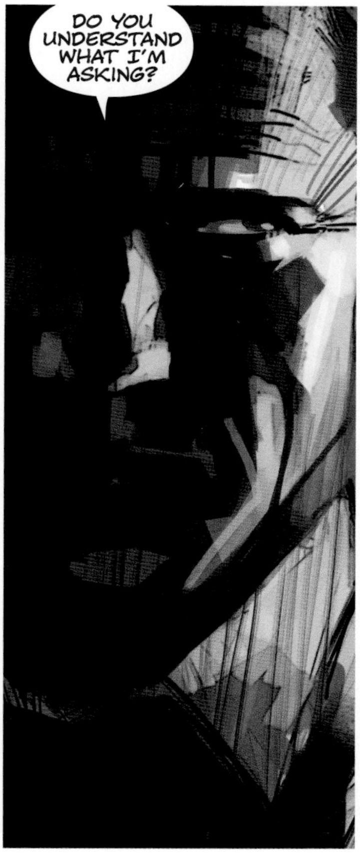
DO YOU UNDERSTAND WHAT I'M ASKING?

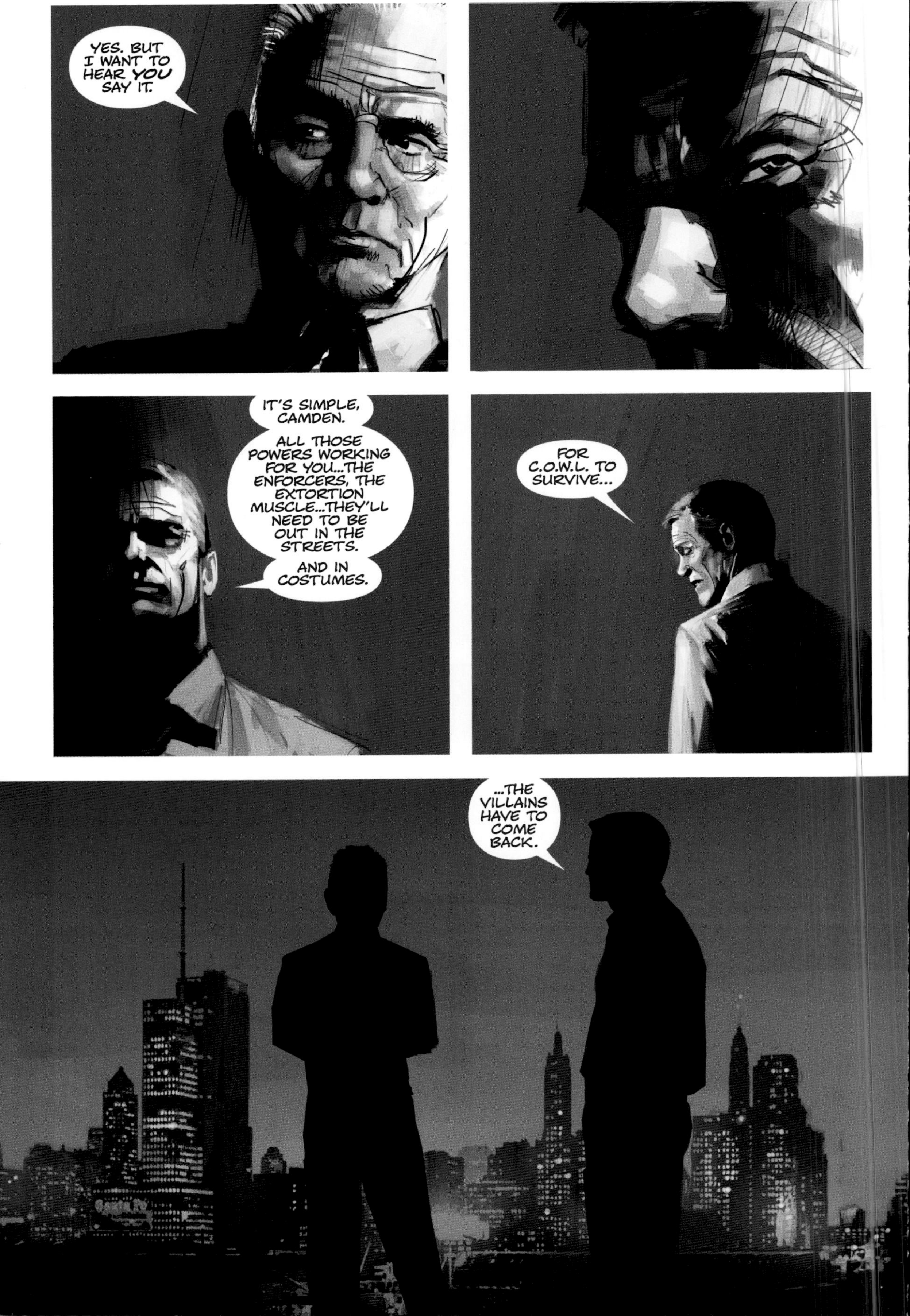
YES. BUT I WANT TO HEAR YOU SAY IT.
IT'S SIMPLE, CAMDEN.
ALL THOSE POWERS WORKING FOR YOU...THE ENFORCERS, THE EXTORTION MUSCLE...THEY'LL NEED TO BE OUT IN THE STREETS.
AND IN COSTUMES.
FOR C.O.W.L. TO SURVIVE...
...THE VILLAINS HAVE TO COME BACK.

FILE 001-67			
1.	SERIAL NO.	56-8754-7895	X
2.	REGISTRATION		RB: 78
3.	CLASSIFICATION	X-75-RD5	
4.			
COMMENTS:			
LOG NO.			
DEPT.			

RESTRICTED

C.O.W.L. DEPARTMENT USE ONLY

Name: Geoffrey Peter Warner
Date of Birth: 08/17/1907
Place of Birth:
Chicago, IL (Washington Park)
Height: 6'3"
Hair: Brown/Grey
Weight: 220lbs
Eyes: Blue

Alias: The Grey Raven (retired)

C.O.W.L. Position: Chief

Skills: Expert strategist, marksman, hand-to-hand combatant

Biography:
Warner grew up on the streets of Chicago's Southside. The son of a long-serving police officer, he applied to the police academy but never attended. For a time, Warner moved through the boxing circuit in the city, winning his fair share of fights and earning himself the nickname Warring Warner. In 1931, he hung up the boxing gloves and created his now-famous persona The Grey Raven, quickly making a name for himself protecting the helpless in the city's crime-filled, Depression-era streets.

When America entered World War II at the end of 1941, Warner added war hero to his list of accomplishments. As the leader of a covert ops unit called [redacted] Warner fought in Occupied France, Italy, [redacted] Germany.

Post-war, Warner returned to Chicago. Along with several other heroes-- notably his young sidekick, Sparrow, and fellow [redacted] Blaze-- Warner used his political contacts from the war to push for the formation of the Chicago Organized Workers League in 1949. Warner continued to fight as The Grey Raven until the mid-1950s, when he hung up his costume after [redacted] Now, retired from combat, he leads C.O.W.L. in an administrative and political capacity.

FILE 002-48			
1.	SERIAL NO.	28-1986-1010	X
2.	REGISTRATION	UNKNOWN	TM: 56
3.	CLASSIFICATION	B-445-TH8	
4.			

COMMENTS: NO ADDITIONAL INFORMATION PROVIDED

LOG NO.	5681125994
DEPT.	

C.O.W.L. CONFIDENTIAL DEPARTMENT USE ONLY

Name: Thomas Gregory Haydn
Date of Birth: 04/06/1932
Place of Birth:
Duluth, MN
Height: 6'0"
Hair: Blonde
Weight: 207lbs
Eyes: Brown

Alias: Arclight

C.O.W.L. Position: Tactical Division

Skills: Flight, focused energy bursts

Biography:
Haydn was born in Duluth, Minnesota, the son of a Great Lakes Captain. After the death of his mother, Haydn spent his formative years sailing with his father back and forth between Duluth and the other Great Lakes ports.

On his eighteenth birthday, Haydn joined the U.S. Army. He was assigned to "A" Company [redacted] and sent to fight in Korea. In late 1954, Haydn was recruited by [redacted]. He graduated at the top of his class and chose to join [redacted], a covert operation aimed at placing [redacted] operatives into key political positions throughout [redacted]

While on assignment in Europe in October 1956, Haydn was exposed to radiation near [redacted]. The incident left him with the ability to fly, as well as channel and discharge focused energy bursts.

In November, 1957, Haydn left the [redacted] and moved to Chicago where he joined the Chicago Organized Workers League. His powers quickly made him a standout, and he now works as part of the organization's elite Tactical Unit.

FILE 003-16			
1.	SERIAL NO.	56-9842-2356	X
2.	REGISTRATION	NONE	HG: 45
3.	CLASSIFICATION	A-258-PH7	
4.			

COMMENTS: NONE

LOG NO.	5685432586
DEPT.	TACTICAL

C.O.W.L.   RESTRICTED   DEPARTMENT USE ONLY

Name: Kathryn Beverly Mitchell
Date of Birth: 08/27/1933
Place of Birth:
Olympia, WA
Height: 5'7"
Hair: Blonde
Weight: 125lbs
Eyes: Blue

Alias: Radia

C.O.W.L. Position: Tactical Division

Skills: Telekinesis

Biography:
Mitchell was born in Olympia, Washington to a surgeon, Charles Mitchell, and his wife, Edith. Of Irish and German descent, she was raised
Catholic and attended St. Michael's Catholic School along with her
older brother, Raymond. Her mother was active in the city's artistic
community, and the family spent many weekends along the shores of Budd
Inlet socializing with other painters and photographers.

When Mitchell was seven-years-old she began to display telekinetic
abilities. Though Mitchell's parents initially thought it best to keep
her power a secret, they eventually sought help and brought their
daughter to doctors in Seattle. There, Mitchell learned to control her
powers.

Upon graduating high school, she attended Seattle University where she
studied Political Science. Post-college she moved between several
different jobs, none of which utilized her telekinetic abliity. In
1958, Mitchell decided that her abilities could be put to use helping
people and she left Seattle for Chicago, where she immediately applied
to join the Chicago Organized Workers League.

FILE 004-14			
1. SERIAL NO.	22-1992-0117	X
2. REGISTRATION	CLASSIFIED	TT: 56
3. CLASSIFICATION	Z-117-ZF1	
4.		

COMMENTS: CLASSIFIED

LOG NO.	8619753246
DEPT.	TACTICAL

CONFIDENTIAL

C.O.W.L.   DEPARTMENT USE ONLY

Name: Reginald Joseph Davis
Date of Birth: 11/15/1912
Place of Birth:
East Chicago, IN
Height: 6'0"
Hair: Black/Gray
Weight: 194lbs
Eyes: Brown

Alias: Blaze

C.O.W.L. Position: Deputy Chief, Head
of Tactical Division

Skills: Zero-point energy manipulation (technology-based)

Biography:
Davis was born in East Chicago, Indiana. His father was killed in Europe
during World War I, leaving his mother to raise him and his younger brother,
Elliot. But while Elliot manifested increased speed and reflexes (one of the
first known instances of super powers), Reginald did not. Reginald watched
as Elliot took to the streets in the mid-1930s as "The Dart," following in
the crimefighting footsteps of The Grey Raven.

When the U.S. entered World War II, Davis joined the U.S. Marines. He dis-
tinguished himself in combat and was hand-picked by The Grey Raven for an
elite commando unit, ███████████████████ On a covert mission in Germany,
Davis discovered a gauntlet implementing zero-point energy technology. With
it, he learned to manipulate energy and move objects with nothing more than
a gesture. Because of the cyan glow it created, soldiers dubbed him "The
Blue Blaze."

After the war, Davis returned to Chicago with Warner, perpetuating his Blaze
persona. He, along with Warner and Paul Braddock, started the Chicago Organized Workers League. Elliot, however, did not join.

During the 1950s, Elliot grew increasingly contemptuous of C.O.W.L., and
eventually became the de facto leader of the Chicago Six. In 1955, Elliot
brutally ██
██

Davis now serves as C.O.W.L.'s Deputy Chief as well as the head of its
Tactical Division.

CHICAGO ORGANIZED WORKERS LEAGUE

FILE 005-01			
1.	SERIAL NO.	04-2010-0626	-
2.	REGISTRATION	EXEMPT	XB: 14
3.	CLASSIFICATION	R-395-JK2	
4.			

COMMENTS: NONE

LOG NO.	5634822259
DEPT.	INVESTIGATIONS

CONFIDENTIAL

C.O.W.L. DEPARTMENT USE ONLY

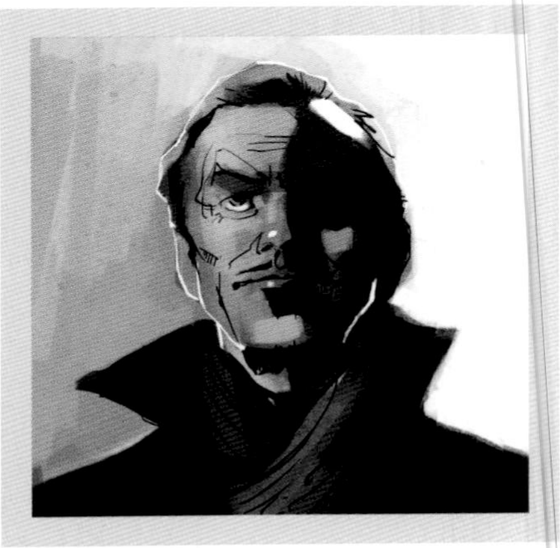

Name: Jonathan Christopher Pierce
Date of Birth: 10/12/1920
Place of Birth:
Sturgis, South Dakota
Height: 5'9"
Hair: Black
Weight: 175lbs
Eyes: Brown

Alias: None

C.O.W.L. Position: Detective

Skills: Covert operations, hand-to-hand combat

Biography:
Pierce was born in Sturgis, South Dakota. The son of an Army colonel, he spent his early years moving from military base to military base. Seeking to follow in his father's footsteps, Pierce enrolled at West Point in 1938 and was accepted with a nomination from Senator [redacted]

Upon graduating in 1942, Pierce became one of the first recruits of the Office of Strategic Services (OSS), the agency tasked with coordinating intelligence efforts against the Axis powers. He spent the war years conducting covert missions in Germany and aided in training resistance forces in Nazi-occupied France.

After the war, Pierce played a large role in Operation [redacted] and Operation [redacted] But when the OSS was splintered into pieces and became the Central Intelligence Agency, Pierce was sent to Chicago to infiltrate [redacted] members of which were suspected of being agents of the KGB.

Inspired by the work being done by the Chicago Organized Workers League, Pierce left the CIA in 1956, and joined the superhero organization's Investigations Division.

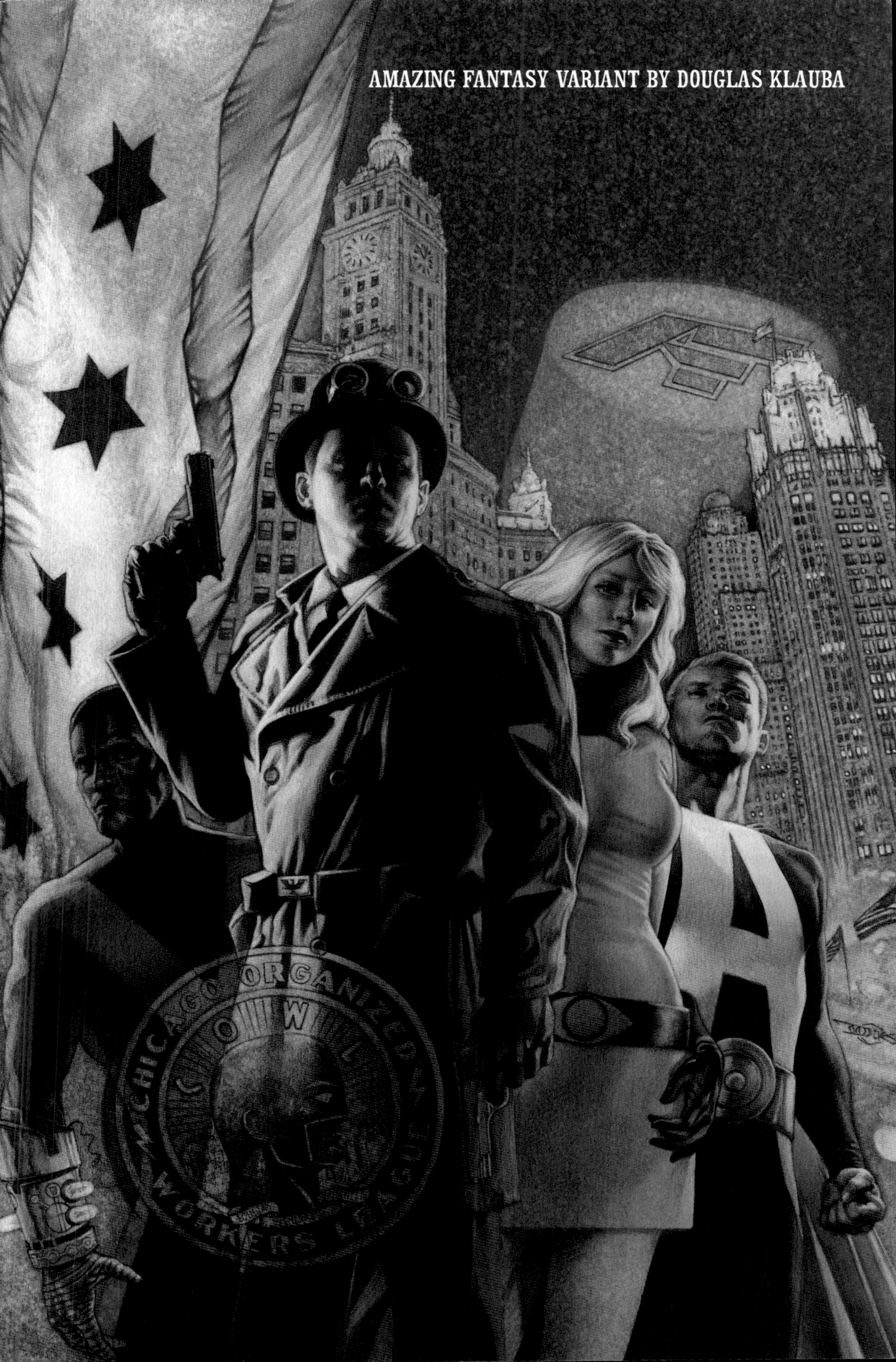
CHICAGO ORGANIZED
C O W L
WORKERS

AMAZING FANTASY VARIANT BY DOUGLAS KLAUBA

BEACH BALL/LAUGHING OGRE VARIANT BY ROD REIS

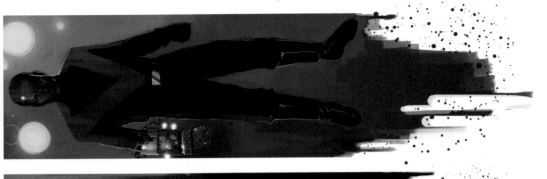

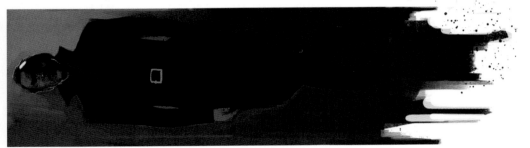

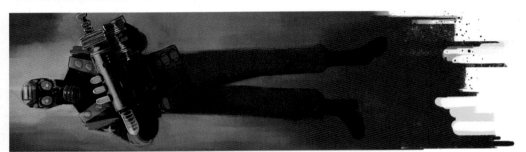

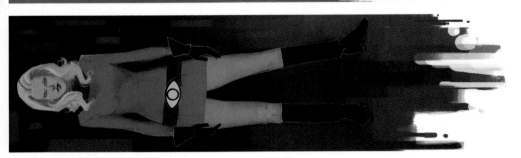

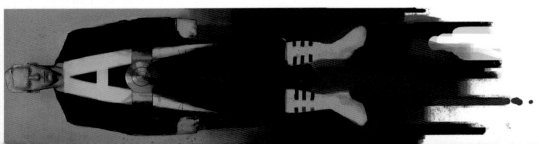